TRANSLATION AND PARATEXTS

As the 'thresholds' through which readers and viewers access texts, paratexts have already sparked important scholarship in literary theory, digital studies and media studies. *Translation and Paratexts* explores the relevance of paratexts for translation studies and provides a framework for further research.

Writing in three parts, Kathryn Batchelor first offers a critical overview of recent scholarship, and in the second part introduces three original case studies to demonstrate the importance of paratextual theory. Batchelor interrogates English versions of Nietzsche, Chinese editions of Western translation theory, and examples of subtitled drama in the UK, before concluding with a final part outlining a theory of paratextuality for translation research, addressing questions of terminology and methodology.

Translation and Paratexts is essential reading for students and researchers in translation studies, interpreting studies and literary translation.

Kathryn Batchelor is Associate Professor of Translation and Francophone Studies at the University of Nottingham, UK. She is the author of *Decolonizing Translation* (Routledge, 2009) and has co-edited four volumes of essays, including *Translating Frantz Fanon Across Continents and Languages* (Routledge, 2017) and *Intimate Enemies: Translation in Francophone Contexts* (Liverpool University Press, 2013).

Translation Theories Explored
Series Editor: Theo Hermans, UCL, UK

Translation Theories Explored is a series designed to engage with the range and diversity of contemporary translation studies. Translation itself is as vital and as charged as ever. If anything, it has become more plural, more varied and more complex in today's world. The study of translation has responded to these challenges with vigour. In recent decades the field has gained in depth, its scope continues to expand and it is increasingly interacting with other disciplines. The series sets out to reflect and foster these developments. It aims to keep track of theoretical developments, to explore new areas, approaches and issues, and generally to extend and enrich the intellectual horizon of translation studies. Special attention is paid to innovative ideas that may not as yet be widely known but deserve wider currency.

Individual volumes explain and assess particular approaches. Each volume combines an overview of the relevant approach with case studies and critical reflection, placing its subject in a broad intellectual and historical context, illustrating the key ideas with examples, summarising the main debates, accounting for specific methodologies, achievements and blind spots, and opening up new avenues for the future. Authors are selected not only on their close familiarity and personal affinity with a particular approach but also on their capacity for lucid exposition, critical assessment and imaginative thought. The series is aimed at researchers and graduate students who wish to learn about new approaches to translation in a comprehensive but accessible way.

Stylistic Approaches to Translation
Jean Boase Beier

Representing Others
Kate Sturge

Cosmopolitanism and Translation
Esperança Bielsa

Translating as a Purposeful Activity 2e
Christiane Nord

For more information about this series, please visit www.routledge.com/Translation-Theories-Explored/book-series/TTE

TRANSLATION AND PARATEXTS

Kathryn Batchelor

Routledge
Taylor & Francis Group

LONDON AND NEW YORK

First published 2018
by Routledge
2 Park Square, Milton Park, Abingdon, Oxon OX14 4RN

and by Routledge
711 Third Avenue, New York, NY 10017

Routledge is an imprint of the Taylor & Francis Group, an informa business

British Library Cataloguing-in-Publication Data
A catalogue record for this book is available from the British Library

Library of Congress Cataloging-in-Publication Data
Names: Batchelor, Kathryn, author.
Title: Translation and paratexts / Kathryn Batchelor.
Description: London : Routledge, [2018] | Series: Translation
    theories explored | Includes bibliographical references and
    index.
Identifiers: LCCN 2018001333 (print) | LCCN 2018020791
    (ebook) | ISBN 9781351110112 (Master) | ISBN
    9780815349228 (hardcover : alk. paper) | ISBN 9781138488977
    (softcover : alk. paper) | ISBN 9781351110112 (ebook)
Subjects: LCSH: Paratext. | Translating and interpreting.
Classification: LCC Z242.P37 (ebook) | LCC Z242.P37 B38 2018
    (print) | DDC 418/.02—dc23
LC record available at https://lccn.loc.gov/2018001333

ISBN: 978-0-8153-4922-8 (hbk)
ISBN: 978-1-138-48897-7 (pbk)
ISBN: 978-1-351-11011-2 (ebk)

Typeset in Bembo Std
by Swales & Willis Ltd, Exeter, Devon, UK

Printed and bound in Great Britain by
TJ International Ltd, Padstow, Cornwall

For Jon, Samuel and Alex

CONTENTS

FIGURES

ACKNOWLEDGEMENTS

In practical terms, this book could not have been written without the research leave semester granted by the School of Cultures, Languages and Area Studies, University of Nottingham, and the additional leave semester awarded through the PVC's Fund, Faculty of Arts, University of Nottingham. I am privileged to work for an institution that has the means to grant dedicated research time in this way, and am particularly grateful to colleagues who took on extra tasks in my absence.

On an intellectual level, I would like to thank Theo Hermans, Dorota Gołuch, and students at the Translation Research Summer School in 2013, where my interest in paratexts first evolved into a plan for a book. I am also grateful to Theo and the editors at Routledge for allowing me to extend the deadline several times in light of other projects and work pressures. Having a year 'off' to work on this book has allowed me to catch up with what has been happening in translation studies, beyond my own immediate research interests. I have been reminded time and again of the richness of our discipline, and of the collegiality of the international translation studies community.

In terms more specifically of content, I would like to thank Sarah Fang Tang for her considerable help with Chapter 5, and the School of Cultures, Languages and Area Studies Research Fund (University of Nottingham) for contributing towards her work. Sarah's contribution included identifying the corpus of Chinese translations and editions, providing summaries and translations of the paratextual material, and commenting on the ideas expressed in the chapter. For answering queries or giving feedback on chapter drafts, I would like to thank Cecilia Alvstad, Guyda Armstrong, Patricia Garcia, Paul Grainge, Martyn Gray, Theo Hermans, Victoria Wan Hu, Liu Jing, Catherine Johnson, Nancy Liu, Polly McMichael, Alex Mevel, Luis Pérez-González, Katherine Shingler and Chantal Wright. I apologise if I have forgotten to mention any others who helped along the way. I would also like to thank the Institute of Russian Literature (Pushkin House) for granting permission to use the cover image, and Global Series Network for allowing me to use the images included in Chapter 6.

On a personal level, I am extremely grateful for my family, who give me the kind of contentment that makes writing a book a relatively easy task. Having Michael Jackson on a loop in the background certainly added to the experience. Finally, it would not do to forget Charlie the cat, a most excellent research leave companion, despite his fondness for sitting on computers. If any typos remain, they can no doubt be attributed to him.

INTRODUCTION

Paratextuality . . . is first and foremost a treasure trove of questions without answers.

Gérard Genette, Palimpsests *(1997a, 4)*

A few months ago, I had the privilege of hearing the Hallé Orchestra perform Mussorgsky's *Pictures at an Exhibition*. Before lifting the baton, the conductor told the audience about Mussorgsky's close friendship with Viktor Hartmann, an architect and artist. Mussorgsky and Hartmann were roughly the same age, and both were struggling to achieve success in their careers. When Hartmann died, aged 39, his friends organised a posthumous exhibition of his work, and it was this that Mussorgsky turned into music, writing the piece as a memorial to Hartmann. The conductor explained that the works on display at the exhibition were not as we might imagine: most of them were small simple sketches or drawings rather than the more significant kinds of art works that – knowing Mussorgsky's lengthy and masterful music – most listeners assume. With this at the front of my mind, I heard the final movement in a completely new way: the majestic return of the promenade theme was no longer simply Mussorgsky striding through the exhibition, but an exhilarating celebration of his friend's life, however unsuccessful a life in other people's eyes; and the carillon bell of the Great Gate of Kiev that sounds alongside the promenade became the bell tolling Hartmann's death. The meaning of the movement, in other words, changed for me: it became about celebrating life in grief, and by extension about living life alongside the knowledge of our own deaths – a *memento mori* of sorts. How valid this interpretation of Mussorgsky's piece might be is not the point that I want to explore here; rather, I want simply to show that the threshold through which I entered the piece – the conductor's introduction – influenced how I interpreted it.

When thinking about the final form that this book might take, I was keen for the front cover to feature Hartmann's design for Kiev's Great Gate. My reasons for this were multiple: the image of the gate indicates something about the topic of the book, gesturing in particular to the key metaphor of the threshold; the fact that it is specifically Hartmann's gate rather than any other lends further texture to the story told in the previous paragraph; having an image-based cover rather than a blank or generic one makes the book more attractive (an aesthetic motivation) and appealing to readers (a commercial motivation). Like the conductor's introduction, I was aware that the cover of this book would serve as a threshold, and I wanted that threshold to serve its various purposes effectively.

If there has long been a basic awareness that we form opinions about texts based on surrounding or apparently superficial elements, it was not until the publication of Gérard Genette's book *Seuils* [*Thresholds*] in 1987 that scholars began to pay sustained attention to them. Genette labels such elements *paratexts* and, with great wit and erudition, analyses their importance to literary texts, anchoring his discussion in French publishing practices. Scholars have subsequently adapted Genette's term and theoretical framework to other kinds of texts, affirming the importance of the concept in allowing us to account more fully for the way in which texts are both produced and received.

While the notion of the paratext has gained some currency in translation studies, this book represents the first in-depth attempt to explore Genette's concept and its importance for translation studies research. The book is divided into three parts. Part I introduces Genette's theory, paying particular attention to the role accorded to translation within it (Chapter 1), and summarises existing research into paratexts in translation studies (Chapter 2) as well as in neighbouring disciplines (Chapter 3). The proliferation of research into paratexts in digital and media studies is particularly striking, and one of the goals of this book is to bring it to the attention of translation studies scholars in the hope of stimulating further interdisciplinary dialogue. Part II presents three case studies of paratexts in translation contexts, deliberately selecting genres that are relatively unexplored in existing translation studies research into paratexts. Chapter 4 thus interrogates connections between authorised translations and paratextual relevance and explores the strategies used to claim or contest authorisation in the paratexts of philosophical translations; Chapter 5 demonstrates the usefulness of paratexts for interrogating the discourses that surround the importation of scholarly works, combining this with a meta-reflection on the discipline of translation studies itself; and Chapter 6 investigates the shift in paratexts around subtitled films in the UK, drawing on concepts developed in media studies. The final part of the book draws together the insights gained in Parts I and II in order to propose a theory of paratextuality for translation studies, addressing questions of terminology and typologies (Chapter 7) and research topics and methodologies (Chapter 8).

Like all volumes in the Translation Theories Explored series, this book has been written with both graduate students and researchers in mind. The topic of paratexts cuts across a wide range of research domains, and many students and researchers may find themselves wanting to devote a relatively small part of their thesis or research work to a discussion of paratexts, rather than making paratexts the main focus of the enquiry. In such cases, it is unlikely that they will be able to spend a year researching and reflecting on relevant scholarship and developments, as I have had the privilege to do. I hope that the theory outlined in this book will offer such scholars a framework that is, in a basic sense, usable and useful. To this end I have proposed definitions and terminology that are underpinned by sustained critical reflection, and have addressed methodological issues that are relevant to a range of research topics. At the same time, the book is intended to serve as an invitation to further discussion, much like Genette's own work, which sees itself as 'an intro-duction, and exhortation, to the study of the paratext' (Genette 1997b, 404). In particular, I hope that scholars working in areas of translation studies touched upon only briefly in this book will take up Genette's exhortation, even if its promise and reach seem less obvious there. These include the domains of translation process research, news translation, and interpreting. As the framework continues to be debated and adapted in light of cultural differences and technological developments in these and other domains, it should continue to serve as a treasure trove of ques-tions, to the further benefit of our discipline.

References

Genette, Gérard. 1997a. *Palimpsests: Literature in the Second Degree.* Translated by Channa Newman and Claude Doubinsky. Lincoln and London: University of Nebraska Press.
——. 1997b. *Paratexts: Thresholds of Interpretation.* Translated by Jane E. Lewin. Cambridge: Cambridge University Press.

PART I

Genette's concept of the paratext and its development across disciplines

1

GENETTE'S PARATEXT

Seuils in context

A major figure in the French academic establishment since the 1960s, Gérard Genette has published almost twenty monographs or collections of essays over six decades and made key contributions to literary criticism and aesthetics. While it is difficult to summarise the achievements of such a long and productive career, it is perhaps helpful – as an introduction to this book, at least – to think of them as dividing into three broad domains, with three corresponding points of focus. The first point of focus is the literary text; the second (and the one with which we will be concerned) is the relation of the literary text to other texts around it; and the third is the relation between literature and the arts. The first corresponds roughly to Genette's first four major publications (*Figures I* (1966), *Figures II* (1969), *Figures III* (1972), *Mimologiques* (1976)),[1] in which Genette makes seminal contributions to poetics and narratology. The second corresponds to the three works that followed (*Introduction à l'architexte* (1979), *Palimpsestes* (1982), *Seuils* (1987)), in which Genette shifts the focus to transtextuality, or in other words to 'everything that brings [the text] into relation (manifest or hidden) with other texts' (Genette 1992, 81). The turn towards the third domain was anticipated to some extent in *Fiction et diction* (1991) but established more definitively in the two-volume *L'Oeuvre de l'art* (1994, 1997a); in these and subsequent works, notably *Figures IV* (1999) and *Figures V* (2000), Genette broadens out from literature to address questions on the nature of art and aesthetic response, drawing on a vast range of material that includes music, television, art and architecture.[2]

The work which is the focus of our concern, *Seuils* (1987), thus dates from the second phase of Genette's long career and is the third in a trilogy of works exploring a range of types of textual 'transcendance' (Macksey 1997, xviii). In *Palimpsestes*, Genette (1982) summarises the types of transcendence as intertextuality, paratextuality, metatextuality, hypertextuality and architextuality, stressing that these should not be viewed as 'separate and absolute categories without any reciprocal contact or overlapping' (Genette 1997b, 7). He defines paratextuality as the

> relationship that binds the text properly speaking . . . to what can be called
> its *paratext*: a title, a subtitle, intertitles; prefaces, postfaces, notices, fore-
> words, etc.; marginal, infrapaginal, terminal notes; epigraphs; illustrations;
> blurbs, book covers, dust jackets, and many other kinds of secondary signals,
> whether allographic [from a third party] or autographic [from the author].
>
> *Genette 1997b, 3*[3]

In *Seuils*, Genette (1997c) carries out an extensive study of the paratext, thus foregrounding an aspect of literary texts which, as he argues, had hitherto been 'disregarded
or misperceived' (14).[4] Some work on individual paratextual features did exist, as
Genette acknowledges: Claude Duchet, Leo Hoek, Charles Moncelet and others were
working in the domain of 'titrologie' (55n1), studying titles of literary works; Genette
also acknowledges Jacques Derrida's discussion of prefaces (196n1) and justifies the
brevity of the section on epitexts on the basis that 'critics and literary historians have
long made extensive use of the epitext in commenting on works' (346).[5] However, it
is true to say that, particularly since the emergence of New Criticism as the dominant
paradigm in the early twentieth century,[6] the focus of literary criticism was on close
reading of the text rather than consideration of external factors.[7]

   In *Seuils*, through the interrogation of myriad examples of texts and their paratexts, Genette shows that reading of a text never occurs in isolation from the paratext
around it, since a reader never comes to a text, but always to a book; and the book,
furthermore, circulates in a context which also affects its reception. Genette describes
Seuils as a 'synchronic and not a diachronic study' (13), in other words 'an attempt
at the general picture, not a history of the paratext' (13), and adopts a general, universalising terminology, speaking of 'the paratext', rather than specifying the focus
more precisely. However, his examples, which are drawn for the most part from the
French literary canon, together with his sketches of developments in uses of particular
paratextual elements, do edge his study towards an 'essay on the customs and institutions of the Republic of Letters' (14) at several points, a tendency which he himself
acknowledges. Aware of these limitations, Genette (14–15) himself cautions that
Seuils represents neither a universal theory of the paratext, nor even, as a survey of
French literary paratextual practices, an exhaustive study: 'what follows is only a wholly
inceptive exploration, at the very provisional service of what – thanks to others –
will perhaps come after'. As Chapter 3 in particular will make clear, Genette's hope that
his research might prompt further enquiry has been more than fulfilled, giving rise to
studies of paratextual elements in other national literary traditions as well as in relation
to other domains of cultural expression.

Genette's concept of the paratext

What is the paratext?

When getting to grips with any new theoretical framework, it is as well to start
with the simplest of questions. At first glance, the question 'what is the paratext?'

would appear to have a straightforward answer. In the opening paragraph of *Seuils*, Genette declares: 'the paratext is what enables a text to become a book and to be offered as such to its readers and, more generally, to the public' (1), something which 'ensure[s] the text's presence in the world' (1). Even in antiquity, when texts 'often circulated . . . in the form of manuscripts devoid of any formula of presentation' (3), Genette argues that the notion of paratext is still relevant, since 'the sole fact of transcription . . . brings to the ideality of the text some degree of materialization' (3). The paratext, then, is what turns a text – defined by Genette as 'a more or less long sequence of verbal statements that are more or less endowed with significance' (1) – into a physical, material thing, capable of being sold, distributed, read: it is the format of a book and its binding, as well as the various elements that are placed around the text proper in the process of turning the text into a book (title page, cover, blurbs etc.). This emphasis on the physical aspect of the paratext finds expression in the series of metaphors on which Genette draws to further explain the concept: the paratext is a 'threshold' (2), a 'vestibule' (2), an undefined 'zone' (2) between the inside and the outside, an 'edge' (2), a 'fringe' (2), a 'privileged place of a pragmatics and a strategy' (2). This physical definition is the one most commonly used by scholars in translation studies, as we will see in the next chapter.

However, at several points in the discussion, Genette evokes the possibility of the immateriality of the paratext. For example, when setting out his approach to the study of paratexts, Genette (4) states: 'A paratextual element, **at least if it consists of a message that has taken on material form**, necessarily has a *location*' (bold added; italics in original). In this scenario, Genette suggests that we can identify something as a paratextual element even if it is invisible, and indicates that the paratext is not a physical thing, but a 'message'. That we are to conceive of the paratext as a 'message' rather than a material element is given further support when Genette describes the proliferation of peripheral elements ('the jacket, the band, and the slipcase' (32)) not as an expansion of the paratext, but as 'an expansion – some will say an inflation – of at least the opportunities (that is, of the possible supports) for a paratext' (32). The difference between what Genette might have said and what he does say here is significant, for with this wording he asserts that the paratext is *not* the peripheral element itself; such material elements simply provide opportunities for a paratext – a paratext being, by implication, something else. With this statement, then, Genette appears to complicate his earlier assertion that the paratext is 'what enables a text to become a book' (1), for in a hypothetical situation in which the material elements surrounding a text carried no paratextual message (a situation which Genette's description of peripheral elements as mere opportunities for paratexts would appear to allow), there would be no paratext. It is not clear what the logical conclusion of this position would be. (Would the text fail to become a book? What should we call the material thing that we hold between our hands as we read?) In actual fact, Genette's careful analysis of the various messages conveyed through peripheral or ephemeral elements – however minor or innocuous those elements first appear – means that a hypothetical situation of this kind could never become a reality. As Genette confidently asserts, 'a text without a paratext does not exist and never has existed' (3). Still, the question of what exactly a paratext *is* remains.

To explore this further, let us consider Genette's reflections on the substantial status of the paratext. Genette notes that almost all of the paratexts that he considers are 'of a textual . . . kind' (7), but stresses that 'paratextual value . . . may be vested in other types of manifestation' (7), including the 'purely factual' (7) such as the age or sex of the author, the era in which the text was written, or the genre to which it belongs. Genette (7) explains: 'By *factual* I mean the paratext that consists not of an explicit message . . . but of a fact whose existence alone, if known to the public, provides some commentary on the text and influences how the text is received.' In relation to what he terms 'contextual affiliation' (8), Genette suggests that 'in principle, every context serves as a paratext' (8), whether or not it is 'brought to the public's attention by a mention that, itself, belongs to the textual paratext' (8). These remarks on the factual paratext indicate that the definition of a paratext depends not on materiality but on function: anything that 'provides some commentary on the text and influences how the text is received' (7) is part of the paratext.

The importance of this function-based criterion emerges at several other points in Genette's discussion, notably when he is discussing the dividing line between paratext and text on the one hand, and paratext and external context on the other. With regard to the first of these divisions, Genette discusses the case of notes added to the text by the author and clarifies that if the note is connected to a text 'that is itself discursive and with which it has a relation of continuity and formal homogeneity' (328), then the note 'belongs more to the text, which the note extends, ramifies, modulates *rather than comments on*' (328, my emphasis). The criterion used here for deciding whether notes of this kind belong to the text or the paratext has nothing to do with their material realisation or physical location; rather, the criterion is functional, or in other words based on what the note *does*. In simple terms, if the note comments on the text, then it is part of the paratext.

Genette uses the same criterion for the second type of dividing line, i.e. that between paratext and external context. In his preliminary observations on the epitext, defined as 'the distanced elements . . . located outside the book' (5) and contrasting with the 'peritext', which is physically attached to the text, Genette states that 'the epitext – in contrast to the peritext – consists of a group of discourses whose function is not always basically paratextual (*that is, to present and comment on the text*)' (345, my emphasis). When considering such discourses (which include, for example, interviews or correspondence with the author), Genette speaks of them as potentially containing paratextual information, as the following citations make clear, but not as paratexts in and of themselves: 'we must look on these various exercises [authors' conversations, correspondence, journals] as occasions capable of furnishing us with paratextual scraps' (346); 'the . . . mass of collected conversations constitutes a mine of paratextual evidence (364); 'recordings . . . are a mine of paratextual information' (370); 'let us not conclude . . . that the journal in general is paratextually destitute' (392). The common point that emerges is that the paratext is not the element itself (the interview, correspondence, recording, journal, etc.), but only that small part of the element which serves to present or comment on the text in question.

If the answer to the question of what a paratext is, then, is functional rather than material, why does Genette prioritise spatial metaphors and open his book with a description of the paratext that encourages readers to conceptualise it in terms of its physical qualities? Furthermore, why does he structure his book along the same lines, constructing a typology that is based on the various verbal manifestations of paratext (author attribution, title, dedication, preface, etc.) rather than in terms of function or message? To attempt to answer these questions, let us return to Genette's observations on the epitext, cited above. In his contrast of epitext and peritext, Genette slips in a crucial point, namely that, whereas the epitext's function 'is not always basically paratextual' (345), the peritext's *is*. He brings this point into explicit focus in the second half of the sentence, as the following citation, now given in full, demonstrates:

> the epitext – in contrast to the peritext – consists of a group of discourses whose function is not always basically paratextual (that is, to present and comment on the text), whereas the more or less unchanging regime of the peritext is constitutively and exclusively inseparable from its paratextual function.

> *345–6*

The peritext, then, or in other words those elements which 'enable a text to become a book' (1) and that 'ensure the text's presence in the world' (1), is always paratextual: it always serves to 'present and comment on the text' (345). Peritext *is* paratext (but paratext is not just peritext). The inseparability of the peritext from its paratextual function goes a long way to explaining not only Genette's emphasis on the various material manifestations of the paratext but also the apparent inconsistency in the meaning of the term 'paratextual' as employed in the course of his argument. This adjective collocates with no fewer than forty-eight different nouns, ranging from 'element' (the most frequent collocation) to one-off collocations including 'drudgery' (409), 'game' (284) and 'jumble' (64). While many of these collocations fit a function-based understanding of paratext, others require a material-based definition. When Genette explains, for example, that his analysis of what he terms the 'publisher's peritext' (16) will not encroach on the discipline of '*bibliology*' (16, italics in original), but will concern itself only with the 'strictly paratextual value' (16) of the relevant elements, it is clear that by 'paratextual value' he is referring to the ability of those elements to carry out a particular set of functions. On the other hand, when Genette describes the 'paratextual evolution' (63) of Marcel Proust's *A la recherche du temps perdu*, outlining the changes in number of volumes and the prominence given to the overarching title relative to the individual volume titles, he is speaking primarily of an evolution in the peritexts, or in other words in the physical properties and presentation of the text. Of course, such an evolution would also have an influence on the way in which Proust's text is read – this is the point of the inseparability of peritext and paratextual function – but that is not the primary meaning of the adjective 'paratextual' in this context.

In summary, then, and in answer to the question posed at the start of this section, we can define Genette's *paratext* as follows:

> The paratext consists of any element which conveys comment on the text, or presents the text to readers, or influences how the text is received. Paratextual elements may or may not be manifested materially; where they are, that manifestation may be physically attached to the text (peritext) or may be separate from it (epitext). Any material physically attached to the text by definition conveys comment on the text, or presents the text to readers, or influences how a text is received. A peritext is therefore by definition paratextual. Other elements constitute part of a text's paratext only insofar as they achieve one of the functions listed above, i.e. convey comment on the text, present the text to readers, or influence how a text is received.

The paratext and authorial intention

Of course, with such a function-based definition, our question is still only partially answered; in order to fully understand what Genette means by *paratext*, we now need to address who is doing the presenting, commenting or influencing. This question is one that Genette includes in the list of features that a researcher needs to consider when 'defin[ing] the status of a paratextual message':

> Defining a paratextual element consists of determining its location . . .; the date of its appearance and, if need be, its disappearance . . .; its mode of existence . . .; the characteristics of its situation of communication – its sender and addressee *(from whom? to whom?)*; and the functions that its message aims to fulfil.
>
> *4, italics in original*

While Genette's phrasing here would seem to suggest a relatively open answer to the question of who is doing the commenting, influencing or presenting of a text, he in fact limits the senders of the paratext to the author or those closely connected to the author, and even goes so far as to make a connection with authorial intention one of the defining aspects of the paratext itself. Genette states, for example, that the paratext is 'always the conveyor of a commentary that is authorial or more or less legitimated by the author' (2), and when he argues that the paratext is a zone of influence on the public, he states that that influence is 'at the service of a better reception for the text and a more pertinent reading of it (more pertinent, of course, in the eyes of the author and his allies)' (2).[8] He goes on to declare: 'to say that we will speak again of this influence [of the author and his allies on the public] is an understatement: all the rest of this book is about nothing except its means, methods, and effects' (2). According to this statement, studying the paratext is not about studying material elements around a text; rather, it is the study of the way in which authors (and their allies) look to shape the reception of their work.

Genette's insistence on a connection between paratext and authorial intention can be found throughout the book, and occasionally comes into play as the deciding factor for determining whether a particular element is to be considered part of the paratext. The following selection of quotations shows how crucial the connection with authorial intention is for Genette's discussion:

> many future readers become acquainted with a book thanks to, for example, an interview with the author (if not a magazine review or a recommendation by word of mouth, *neither of which, according to our conventions, generally belongs to the paratext, which is characterized by an authorial intention and assumption of responsibility*).
>
> *3, my emphasis*

> the peritext of scholarly editions . . . sometimes contains elements that do not belong to the paratext in the sense in which I define it. Examples of such elements would be extracts from allographic reviews.
>
> *5n8*

> By definition, something is not a paratext unless the author or one of his associates accepts responsibility for it, although the degree of responsibility may vary.
>
> *9*

> The friendly inscription . . . always calls . . . for . . . a specification . . . For example, from Zola to Flaubert for *L'Assomoir*: 'To my great friend Gustave Flaubert, in hatred of good taste.' Obviously and necessarily, these specifications by motivation . . . *include an (authorial) comment on the work and thereby enter*, by right and on an equal footing, *the field of the paratext*.
>
> *140, my emphasis*

> I will not dwell on the publisher's epitext: its basically marketing and 'promotional' function *does not always involve the responsibility of the author in a very meaningful way.*
>
> *347, my emphasis*

> The most essential of the paratext's properties . . . is functionality. Whatever aesthetic intention may come into play as well, the main issue for the paratext is not to 'look nice' around the text but rather *to ensure for the text a destiny consistent with the author's purpose.*
>
> *407, my emphasis*

In the final pages of his book, Genette presents a brief defence of his insistence on authorial purpose, arguing that this aspect of his theory is in fact imposed by the subject matter at hand:

> The relevance I accord to the author's purpose, and therefore to his 'point of view,' may seem excessive and methodologically naïve. That relevance is, strictly speaking, imposed by my subject, whose entire functioning is based – even if this is sometimes denied – on the simple postulate that the author 'knows best' what we should think about his work.
>
> *408*

Genette argues that 'the correctness of the authorial (and secondarily, of the publisher's) point of view is the implicit creed and ideology of the paratext' (408), one which has been 'held almost unconditionally for centuries' (408). Writing in the mid-1980s, Genette acknowledges that the primacy of the author's viewpoint is under attack from a number of angles, but argues: 'valid or not, the author's viewpoint is part of the paratextual performance, sustains it, inspires it, anchors it' (408).

Contradictions and blurry edges

Genette's insistence on authorial intention as a defining feature of the paratext gives rise to certain contradictions within the concept of the paratext itself. First, the insistence on a connection between authorial responsibility and paratext conflicts with Genette's reader-focused statement that any contextual or factual information may serve as paratext: it is hard to see how such information could come under the control of the author and his allies or how the author could assume responsibility for it in any meaningful way. Second, there is an incompatibility between the criterion of authorial responsibility and Genette's statement that all peritexts are paratextual, since it can easily be shown that there are some peritexts that are not sanctioned by the author or which even go directly against his wishes, as Genette himself acknowledges. While these contradictions might be considered relatively minor in the context in which Genette's typology was originally elaborated, they are magnified as soon as we try to adapt Genette's theory to translated texts. We will begin to explore these difficulties in the following chapter and return to them in Part III.

For now, let us remain with Genette's theory and examine two questions to which his statements on authorial intention give rise; namely, who the author's allies are, and how loose the connection with authorial responsibility or purpose can be before the element is no longer considered paratextual. While Genette does occasionally decline to dwell on a particular feature on the basis that the sender is not authorial (as, for example, in the case of the publisher's epitexts cited above), he generally adopts an inclusive approach towards paratextual elements where the link to authorial intention is only tentative, and appears to take a relatively broad view of who might be considered the author's allies. In general terms, for example, and running slightly counter to the justification of superficial treatment of the publisher's epitext noted above, Genette takes the publisher to be an authorial ally. Thus, in his introduction to the chapter on the publisher's peritext, Genette considers elements such as the book's material construction, cover page and title page to be paratextual elements, stating that they are 'executed by the typesetter and printer but decided on by the publisher, *possibly in consultation with the author*' (16, my emphasis). In a similar vein, Genette takes the editors of posthumous works to be the author's allies, suggesting:

> Being immutable, the text in itself is incapable of adapting to changes in its public in space and over time. The paratext – more flexible, more versatile, always transitory because transitive – is, as it were, an instrument of adaptation. Hence the continual modifications in the 'presentation' of the text . . ., modifications that the author himself attends to during his lifetime and that after his death become the responsibility (discharged well or poorly) of his posthumous editors.
>
> *408*

The possibility of disagreement between editor and author is evoked here through the idea that the editor's responsibilities might be discharged 'well or poorly', and this potential for disagreement is something that Genette addresses at various other points in his discussion. Even where the disagreement is significant and the material at hand is therefore connected with the publisher's intention, rather than the author's, however, Genette does not exclude the material from the text's paratext. For example, in the case of books that are presented as part of a particular series or genre, Genette states:

> With these sometimes very emphatic forays into the area of generic or intellectual choices, the paratext that most typically derives from and depends on primarily the publisher obviously encroaches on the prerogative of an author, who thought himself an essayist but ends up a sociologist, linguist, or literary theorist.
>
> *23*

Similarly, Genette evokes the possibility for disagreement between author and publisher with regard to title: 'responsibility for the title is always shared by the author and the publisher. It is shared in actual fact, of course, save when there has been a complete and forceful takeover' (74). Changes in authorial intention over time are treated in a parallel manner: in the case of Marcel Proust's *A la recherche du temps perdu*, for example, Genette states that Proust initially had to resign himself to having the work published in separate volumes rather than as a single thick volume as per his original preference. Later on, Proust himself came to envisage a work 'much more distinctly segmented, and supplied with an abundant titular apparatus' (305). Genette argues that the paratextual evolutions undergone by the work over time 'obviously, even if fortuitously, conformed to Proust's original intentions but perhaps not to his final intentions' (63), and concludes:

> In any case, the fact remains that since 1913 two or three generations of readers will have had different perceptions of Proust's work and accordingly will doubtless have read it differently, depending on whether they were receiving it as a set of autonomous works or as a unitary whole, with a single title, in three volumes.
>
> 63

In this citation, and in many other places in Genette's discussion, emphasis is placed on the influence exerted by the paratext on the reader, rather than on the connection between the paratextual element and the sender of the paratext. Crucially, with none of these examples does Genette take these observations to their logical conclusion as implied by the definitions of paratext that he provides; namely, that in the case of such disagreements, the affected peritextual elements would not be considered part of the paratext.

Instead, Genette introduces a number of nuances into his descriptions of paratextual material, distinguishing, for example, between the 'official and the unofficial (or semiofficial)' (9–10) paratext. While the official paratext is one for which 'the author or publisher cannot evade responsibility' (10), responsibility for the unofficial or semiofficial paratext 'can always more or less [be] disclaim[ed]' (10) by the author. Although Genette does not make much of this distinction throughout the book – preferring, instead, to take a broad approach to the identity of the author's allies, as outlined above – it is nevertheless useful in allowing him to still consider as part of the paratext those messages for which the author claims no responsibility. Thus, in the case of allographic peritextual material that straddles the line between paratext (e.g. preface) and metatext (e.g. critical essay) and is often found in posthumous editions, he explains: 'the fact that the author has long been dead frees the preface from any sort of semiofficial status' (270). In other words, while an allographic preface written during the author's lifetime would be (at very least) semiofficial, having some connection, however ambiguous, to the author's responsibility, with the author dead the preface becomes unofficial, and the preface writer thus unbound by any sense of obligation to the author.

Another way in which Genette nuances the connections between authorial intent and the paratext is by distinguishing between paratextual function, value and effect. In his discussion of book titles, for example, Genette states that the connotative function of titles is 'attached (whether or not by authorial intent) to the descriptive function' (93) but reflects: 'perhaps we go too far in calling a sometimes unintended effect a function, and it would no doubt be better to speak here of connotative *value*' (93, italics in original). Elsewhere Genette introduces the notion of paratextual effect, once again with the aim of distinguishing between deliberate authorial commentary, and that which is less controlled or potentially ambiguous. For example, when discussing the 'paratextual scraps' (346) that may be offered by authors' journals and suchlike, Genette explains that 'they must often be sought with a magnifying glass or caught with rod and line: here once again, we are dealing with paratextual *effect* (rather than function)' (346, italics in original).[9]

If readers are frustrated by the lengthy and at times contradictory answer to the simple question of what a paratext is, it might be as well to stress that the complexity of the response is in some senses a necessary part of the paratext's very definition. To try to define the paratext is always to negotiate around its blurry borders, both inward-facing (towards the text) and outward-facing (towards the broader context). While some elements can be relatively clearly and unambiguously identified as part of the paratext, others sit less comfortably within its parameters. Genette himself stresses this point on numerous occasions,[10] but also cautions against allowing the indeterminacy of the boundaries to lead to an expansion of the paratext's domain:

> One of the methodological hazards attendant on a subject as multiform and tentacular as the paratext, it seems to me, is the imperialist temptation to annex to this subject everything that comes within its reach . . . Inasmuch as the para-text is a transitional zone between text and beyond-text, one must resist the temptation to enlarge this zone by whittling away in both directions.
>
> *407*

The key to resisting this temptation, for Genette, is to insist on the function of the paratext as being 'to ensure for the text a destiny consistent with the author's purpose' (407). While it is possible to appreciate Genette's reasons for wishing to contain the paratext, his insistence on a link to authorial intention creates significant contradictions at the heart of the notion of the paratext, as I have argued above. An alternative way of demarcating the paratext, more compatible with translation contexts, will be proposed in Part III. In the remainder of this chapter, I provide a brief overview of the essentials of Genette's typology and, in a final section, outline the place that he envisages for translation within his framework.

Genette's typology

In the section on paratext and authorial intention above, I cited the list of questions that Genette states the researcher needs to ask in order to 'define the status of a paratextual message' (4). These questions provide the variables for Genette's paratextual typology, allowing paratextual elements to be classed according to their spatial, temporal, substantial, pragmatic and functional qualities. A very brief summary of these variables and the main descriptors developed by Genette is offered below; I will return to them and explore how they might be supplemented or altered for translation studies research contexts in Part III.

Spatial variables

To determine the spatial variables, the researcher must determine the location of the paratext, relative to the text; as we saw above, this leads Genette (4–5) to identify two contrasting variables, *peritext* (within the same volume as the text) and *epitext* (separate from it).

Temporal variables

Temporal variables allow us to class the paratext according to the date of its appearance or disappearance relative to the appearance of the text itself: Genette (5–6) suggests that paratexts might thus be classed as *prior* (appearing before the text), *original* (appearing at the same time as the text), *later* (appearing after the text – for example, on the occasion of a second edition) and *delayed* (appearing long after the text). Genette also proposes a set of variables that allow us to categorise the temporal aspect of paratexts relative to the author's life (*posthumous* vs *anthumous*) (6).

Substantial variables

Within Genette's framework, which deals with printed literature, paratexts are 'almost all' (7) *textual*, and Genette pays limited attention to substantial variables as a result. As we saw above, however, Genette does envisage paratexts that do not take on material form, referring to these as *factual* paratexts (7).

Pragmatic variables

As discussed above, Genette limits the senders of paratextual messages to the author and his allies, referring to material emanating from the latter as '*allographic* paratext' (9, italics in original). When discussing the prefatorial situation of communication, Genette adds another category, *actorial*, to denote situations in which 'the alleged author of a preface may be one of the characters in the action' (179). To account for further complexities and ambiguities, Genette also introduces a set of variables which he calls 'regime' (181), and which allow for variations in the fictionality or authenticity of the preface sender. Genette is careful to stress that, when identifying the sender of a paratext, it is not a question of identifying its '*de facto* producer' (8), but rather the one to whom the paratext is attributed and who accepts responsibility for it. With regard to addressees, Genette distinguishes between 'the public in general' (9) and the narrower category of 'readers of the text' (9), both of whom are addressees of the *public* paratext. He contrasts this with the *private* paratext, paratextual messages which are not intended for a public readership, and which, in their most extreme form as messages from the author to himself, are designated the *intimate* paratext (9).

Functional variables

Drawing on a concept developed in speech act theory, Genette argues that the 'illocutionary force' (10) of a paratextual message can encompass informing, making known an intention or interpretation, conveying a decision, expressing a commitment, giving advice, issuing commands, or even operating as performatives (performing the action described). Beyond this broad sketch, however, Genette suggests that the functions of paratexts need to be 'brought into focus inductively'

(13), since functional choices, unlike other variables, 'can have several purposes at once, selected – without exclusion of all the others – from the (more or less open) repertory appropriate to each type of element' (12). As he considers each para-textual element (title, preface, epigraph, etc.), Genette outlines those repertories, thereby sketching out lists of the most common functions, if not a full typology for the reason given above. The most extensive repertory is that provided for prefaces; here, Genette outlines the themes most commonly addressed in authorial and allo-graphic prefaces and groups them under headings corresponding to the two key functions of prefaces: the 'themes of the why' (198) connect with the function of 'get[ting] the book read' (197), while the 'themes of the how' (209) link to the function of 'get[ting] the book read properly' (197). Genette suggests that both sets of themes represent 'a repertory that is much more stable than one would believe *a priori*, and in particular much more stable than authors themselves believe' (163), thus indicating that outlining a taxonomy of functions (if not a typology) may in fact be more possible than originally anticipated.

Translation in Genette's framework

Translation as paratext

The only place in which Genette directly addresses the question of how transla-tion might fit into his typology is in the conclusion to his 400-page study. Here, Genette outlines three practices that he has omitted from the discussion, yet whose 'paratextual relevance seems . . . undeniable' (405): translation, serial publication, and illustration. Genette sketches out the paratextual relevance of translation in the following terms:

> The first of the three practices is *translation*, particularly when it is more or less revised or checked by the author, as Groethuysen's German version of *Les Nourritures terrestres* was by Gide; and all the more so when the entire task is undertaken by the author alone, in keeping with the established practice of a bilingual writer such as Beckett, each of whose translations must, in one way or another, serve as commentary on the original text.
>
> *405*

Genette is arguing here for an approach that would view a translated version of a text as part of the paratext of the original text, by virtue of the fact that the way the translation is done conveys some kind of commentary on the original or, in other words, offers an elucidation of how the text itself (that is, the original) is to be understood. If we reprise Genette's description of the nature of the paratext, then this view of translation would see translation as 'a discourse that is fundamentally heteronomous, auxiliary, and dedicated to the service of something other than itself that constitutes its raison d'être . . . the paratext is always subordinate to "its" text, and this functionality determines the essence of its appeal and its existence' (12). In this line of thinking, the translation is at the service of the original; it is a text that points not to itself, but to the original from which it derived. For readers to benefit from the translation's ability to serve as commentary on the original text, they would, of course, have to be aware of the distance and differences between the original text and its translation, or in other words would have to read them in a comparative mode. They would also need some awareness of the potential alternative renderings not chosen by the translator – for a translation can only act as commentary insofar as it reveals decision-making processes.

Genette builds a number of caveats into his sketch of translation's paratextual relevance: first, the translator would need to work closely with the author, or, better still, be the author; second, if the translator is the author, then the commentary is to be 'used with care, for the right to be unfaithful is an authorial privilege' (405n2). The first caution derives from Genette's insistence on the connection between paratext and authorial intention, discussed above; the second suggests that the author-translator may use his creative freedom to introduce aspects into the translation that are not there in the original, or ignore those that are. While each of these cautions is no doubt valid in some respects, Genette argues himself here into something of a corner. If the author has the right to be unfaithful to his own text, but the translator pure and servile by implication does not, then in this sense translations produced without the author would be more reliable commentaries on the text. Yet these translations are only loosely linked to authorial intention, and their ability to serve as paratexts is accordingly limited. In Genette's reasoning, then, and despite his assertion of their 'undeniable' (405) value, interpreting translations as paratexts is a process that is fraught with difficulty and perhaps even fundamentally flawed. We will return to this issue at several points in later chapters.

Translation as text, with its own paratext

Although Genette does not acknowledge it directly, there is another way in which he envisages translated texts within his typology. By drawing on examples from translated texts at various points in his study, he implies (though never states directly) that the translated version can be considered a text in its own right, with its own paratexts. In his discussion of cover design, for example, Genette first highlights the case of yellow covers in France at the beginning of the twentieth century, explaining that they were synonymous with licentiousness; he then offers a 'more subtl[e] and specific' (25) example of the paratextual significance of cover design, explaining that 'not too long ago the cover of the French translation of Thomas Mann's *Doctor Faustus* . . . showed a sheet of paper very faintly imprinted with a musical score' (25). In Genette's discussion, the cover of the translated text is not treated any differently to the cover of non-translated texts; both are considered to be part of the paratext, conveying certain messages about the content of the book.

Other examples provided by Genette suggest that the possibility for viewing translations as texts with their own paratexts is predicated not on a view of translations as independent of their originals, but on a view of translations as synonymous with originals. In other words, the translated text is considered to be the original text; considering its paratext is no different from considering the paratext of a new edition of an original work. This view emerges very clearly in Genette's discussion of epigraphs. Having established that epigraphs normally appear at the same time as the first publication of the text in question, Genette evokes the possibility of variation in subsequent editions:

> it would no doubt be easy to find . . . cases of epigraphs delayed or deleted by an author's decision or a publisher's oversight (not to mention changes from one edition to another). I have a pocket edition of *For Whom the Bell Tolls* in French translation (*Pour qui sonne le glas*), and the epigraph from Donne, despite its fundamental importance, is missing.
>
> *150*

In this citation, Genette provides the example of the French translation of *For Whom the Bell Tolls* as an example of a later edition of John Donne's text; the fact that it is a French version rather than an English one is not accorded any relevance. Similarly, in a discussion of prefaces that belong to the 'later' category, Genette explains:

> Its canonical occasion is the second edition, which may come on the heels of the original edition but which often presents a very specific pragmatic opportunity . . . Or the occasion may be a translation – for example, the preface to the French edition (1948) of *Under the Volcano* [*Au-dessous du volcan*] (1947), or the preface to the 1982 American edition of Kundera's *The Joke* (1967).
>
> *174*

Categorising prefaces that are provided for translations as *later* rather than *original* unequivocally establishes translations as later versions of an original text, rather than as new texts. Furthermore, according to this model, the author of the translated text is the author of the original text; the translator does not assume any kind of authorship. Genette makes this point explicitly when he categorises prefaces and notes written by translators to their translation as 'allographic' (263, 322), or in other words as 'written by [a] third party and accepted by the author' (9).

There are, however, a couple of places in *Seuils* where Genette evokes the possibility of some level of creative intervention by the translator. For example, to his discussion of allographic prefaces written by translators, discussed above, he appends the following note:

> In the case of a translation, the preface may be signed by the translator, as we have just seen. The translator-preface-writer may possibly comment on, among other things, his own translation; on this point and in this sense, his preface then ceases to be allographic.
>
> *264n22*

Genette's statement that the translator's preface ceases be allographic when the translator is commenting on his own translation is intriguing: although Genette does not state as much explicitly, he is presumably implying here that the preface becomes authorial in such places. This note thus suggests that the translator is to be considered author of the translation process, but not of the final product; the work of the translator, and the responsibility for it, is to some extent embedded in the translated version, yet the text itself still belongs fully to the author.

Another exception to Genette's overall assumption that the translator is an authorial ally rather than assuming any kind of authorship of his own is found in Genette's discussion of the way in which authors have historically appended 'all kinds of nobiliary ranks and all kinds of functions and distinctions, honorific or real' (54) to their names. One of the examples that Genette provides is that of Paul-Louis Courier, who 'gives himself the title "Winegrower, member of the Legion of Honor, formerly a mounted gunner"' (54) when 'reediting and revising the translation of Longus by "Monsieur Jacques Amyot, during his lifetime bishop of Auxerre and master chaplain of the court of the kings of France"' (54). Courier is thus included here as one in a line of authors who give themselves status-enhancing titles; yet unlike the others, Courier is not an author, but a translator. The book to which Genette is presumably referring here is the ancient Greek romance *Daphnis and Chloe*, by 'Longus' (probably not his real name); Jacques Amyot provided the first translation into French in 1559; and the book under discussion by Genette in this example is the revised version of 1813, produced by Paul-Louis Courier. Courier is thus not even the first translator, but the second – but the crucial point here is that Genette presents the case of Courier's self-given title as an example of a 'possible appendage to *the author's name*' (54, my emphasis). The elements of the paratext which derive from Courier are thus treated as a part of the paratext, even though there is clearly no connection between the second-century Longus and the nineteenth-century Courier. The reasons for Genette's shift in conceptualisation of authorship and translation here are not clear and do not appear to have anything to do with the ancient nature of the text in question; indeed, the other mention of the sixteenth-century translator Amyot (263) describes him as an 'allographic' preface writer, or in other words reverts to the view of the translator as third party rather than as author.

In summary, then, the role played by translation in Genette's typology is premised on a view of translation that does not completely ignore the possibilities for meaning-laden decision-making that translation processes offer, but which nevertheless adopts a conservative view of the changes wrought through translation, viewing translations as synonymous with later editions of an original text and involving no change to authorship. Needless to say, such a view runs counter to the understanding of translation that currently holds sway in the discipline of translation studies whereby translation is seen as a creative process of rewriting. As we shall see in the following chapter, this has not prevented the concept of the paratext from being widely taken up in translation studies, but it has led to a certain glossing over of certain aspects of Genette's definition and approach.

Notes

1 To these could also be added *Nouveau Discours du récit* (1983), which reprises the discussions in *Figures III* and submits them to further scrutiny, as well as *Métalepse* (2004), which interrogates the relevance of the rhetorical figure of the metalepsis to narratology.
2 Between 2006 and 2016, Genette also published the five-volume Bardadrac suite, a series of diverse reflections that Genette (2014) describes as 'un romanesque plus ou moins fictionnalisé dans mon existence' [a novelistic that has been more or less fictionalised into my existence].
3 It should be noted that when Genette (1979, 87) first coins the term *paratextualité* in *Introduction à l'architexte*, he uses it to denote relations between the original text and texts of imitation and transformation such as pastiche and parody.
4 From this point on, all references to *Seuils* are by page number only. The page numbers refer to the English version, *Paratexts: Thresholds of Interpretation* (1997c).
5 See Lane (1992, 13–15) for an overview of the terms used by literary theorists prior to Genette to designate what Genette would term *paratextual elements*.
6 See Habib (2008, 621–6) for a summary of New Criticism and its influence.
7 Research which has some aspects in common with Genette's concerns in *Seuils* was also being carried out in other disciplines: in 1978, for example, Derrida (1978) published a long essay on Kant's *Critiques* interrogating the concepts of the *ergon* (work of art) and the *parergon* (that which frames it) in the contexts of painting and philosophy; book history, which is concerned with the book as material object, was emerging as a field in the 1980s (see Finkelstein and McCleery, 2006); and scholars researching mass communications and media in the 1970s and 1980s were already drawing on the idea of frames, exploring their 'tremendous power . . . to shape the manner in which we interpret certain issues and situations' (Kuypers 2009, 181). Genette does not refer to any of these developments, perhaps because the motivation for his innovations lay within his own discipline and the shortcomings that he perceived within it.
8 The use of the masculine pronoun here and in all subsequent quotations from Genette (1997c) reflects the approach taken in that volume, which is explained by the translator as follows: 'Possessive adjectives and personal pronouns that refer to authors in general, or to publishers, editors, readers, and critics in general, are in the masculine' (Lewin 1997, xxv).
9 See also Genette's discussion of authors' letters (1987, 373).
10 See, for example, Genette (1997b, 346).

References

Derrida, Jacques. 1978. *La Vérité en peinture*. Paris: Flammarion.
Finkelstein, David, and Alistair McCleery, eds. 2006. *The Book History Reader*. New York and London: Routledge.
Genette, Gérard. 1966. *Figures I*. Paris: Editions du Seuil.
——. 1969. *Figures II*. Paris: Editions du Seuil.
——. 1972. *Figures III*. Paris: Editions du Seuil.
——. 1976. *Mimologiques: voyage en Cratylie*. Paris: Editions du Seuil.
——. 1979. *Introduction à l'architexte*. Paris: Editions du Seuil.
——. 1982. *Palimpsestes*. Paris: Editions du Seuil.
——. 1983. *Nouveau Discours du récit*. Paris: Editions du Seuil.
——. 1987. *Seuils*. Paris: Editions du Seuil.
——. 1991. *Fiction et diction*. Paris: Editions du Seuil.
——. 1992. *The Architext: An Introduction*. Translated by Jane E. Lewin. Berkeley: University of California Press.
——. 1994. *L'Oeuvre de l'art: immanence et transcendance*. Paris: Editions du Seuil.
——. 1997a. *L'Oeuvre de l'art: la relation esthétique*. Paris: Editions du Seuil.

——. 1997b. *Palimpsests: Literature in the Second Degree*. Translated by Channa Newman and Claude Doubinsky. Lincoln and London: University of Nebraska Press.

——. 1997c. *Paratexts: Thresholds of Interpretation*. Translated by Jane E. Lewin. Cambridge: Cambridge University Press.

——. 1999. *Figures IV*. Paris: Editions du Seuil.

——. 2000. *Figures V*. Paris: Editions du Seuil.

——. 2004. *Métalepse*. Paris: Editions du Seuil.

Genette, Gérard, interview by Caroline Broué. 2014. "Théorie littéraire: dernier volet de la suite Bardadrac". *La Grande Table (2ème partie)*. France Culture, 21 February. Accessed 22 November 2017 from www.franceculture.fr/emissions/la-grande-table-2eme-partie/theorie-litteraire-dernier-volet-de-la-suite-bardadrac.

Habib, M.A.R. 2008. *A History of Literary Criticism and Theory*. Oxford: Blackwell.

Kuypers, Jim A. 2009. "Framing Analysis". In *Rhetorical Criticism*, edited by Jim A. Kuypers, 181–204. Plymouth, UK: Lexington Books.

Lane, Philippe. 1992. *La Périphérie du texte*. Paris: Editions Nathan.

Lewin, Jane E. 1997. Translator's Note. In *Paratexts: Thresholds of Interpretation*, by Gérard Genette. Translated by Jane E. Lewin, xxv. Cambridge: Cambridge University Press.

Macksey, Richard. 1997. "Foreword". In *Paratexts: Thresholds of Interpretation*, by Gérard Genette, xi–xxii. Cambridge: Cambridge University Press.

2

PARATEXTS IN TRANSLATION STUDIES

The first significant engagement with Genette's notion of the paratext in Western Anglophone translation studies can be found in two essays that appeared in the journal *Target* in 1996, one by Theo Hermans (1996) and the other by Urpo Kovala (1996). The English version of Genette's book would appear the following year, boosting interest in the paratext and its potential importance for research into translation. The two *Target* essays both consider paratexts *of* translations, rather than viewing translations *as* paratexts to original texts, or in other words focus on the second way in which translations fit into Genette's typology outlined in the previous chapter. As might be expected, these translation studies scholars do not adopt Genette's conservative view of translation as transparent reproduction of an original, but pay attention to paratexts as sites of translator intervention or adaptation of the text to its new environment. Although these studies were the first to draw explicitly on the term *paratext*, interest in paratextual elements goes back to the earliest days of translation studies as a separate discipline. Translators' prefaces, in particular, have been included in anthologies of reflections on translation in the context of efforts to establish translation studies as a discipline (see, for example, Lefevere (1977) or Schulte and Biguenet (1992)). Early efforts to outline a consistent, systematic scheme for describing translations also appealed to paratextual elements: José Lambert and Hendrik van Gorp (2014 [1985]), for example, suggest that the first stage of analysis should involve the gathering of information about the 'general macro-structural features' (48) of the translation: 'Is the translation identified as such (as a "translation", or as an "adaptation" or "imitation")? . . . Is the translator's name mentioned anywhere? . . .; Does the translator or the editor provide any meta-textual comment (preface, footnotes)?' (48). Answering these questions clearly requires the researcher to interrogate the paratexts of the translation rather than the translated text itself.

Since the publication of Hermans' and Kovala's essays, over 100 articles making explicit appeal to the concept of the paratext have been published in English alone, and two edited volumes devoted to the topic have appeared in recent years (see Gil-Bardají, Orero and Rovira-Esteva (2012b) and Pellatt (2013a)). In addition, scholars such as Mona Baker (2006), Theo Hermans (2007), Gaby Thomson-Wohlgemuth (2009), Sharon Deane-Cox (2014) and Sameh Hanna (2016) have incorporated the study of paratexts into their research monographs. The bulk of the research is into literary fiction, in line with Genette's own focus, but there is a limited amount of research into other domains, including audiovisual translation (Matamala 2011; Bucaria 2014; Bernabo 2017), news translation (Zhang 2012), music (García Jiménez 2012; Taviano 2013), comics (Brienza 2009), interpreting (Jiang 2013), and various non-fiction genres such as philosophy (Castro Ramírez 2012; Batchelor 2016), political texts (Delistathi 2011; Batchelor and Harding 2017), travel writing (Dybiec-Gajer 2013), ethnographic literature (Batchelor 2018 in press) and religious texts (Hassen 2012; Kloppenburg 2013).

The most widely studied type of paratext is the translator's preface, as Şehnaz Tahir-Gürçağlar (2013, 91) also observes. This is perhaps fitting given that Genette himself devotes more than a quarter of his book to exploring prefatorial material, encompassing within that category material which either precedes or follows the text. Other popular areas of concern are translators' notes (see, for example, Sardin 2007; Lopes 2012; Xu 2012; Valdeón 2014); book covers (e.g. Harvey 2003;[1] O'Sullivan 2005; Frank 2007; Delistathi 2011; Gerber 2012; Kung 2013; Nergaard 2013); book titles (e.g. Cachin 2006; Poldsaar 2010; Farø 2013); and factual information about the translations, such as which language the book was translated from (e.g. Coldiron 2010; Agirrezabalaga 2012) and who it was translated by (e.g. Simon 2000; Alvstad 2003; Hanna 2016). Many studies treat several types of paratextual material together rather than focusing on one type alone. Although there are some studies on epitextual material such as translators' memoirs (Kellman (2010)) and author–translator dialogue (Jansen (2013)), it is fair to say that interest to this point has primarily been in analysing peritextual material of translated texts, often in comparison with the peritexts of the original. A number of scholars, notably Danielle Risterucci-Roudnicky (2004), José Yuste Frías (2010) and Valerie Pellatt (2013c), focus on the translation of the original paratextual material, the latter two both drawing on the term *paratranslation* for this activity, as I shall explain below.

Much of the research into paratexts combines analysis of paratexts with analysis of translations themselves, presumably because there is widespread agreement with Tahir-Gürçağlar's (2011, 115) caution that paratextual analysis reveals 'the mediating features of the paratexts and show[s] how translations are presented but not how they *are*. Examination of paratexts . . . cannot be a substitute for textual translation analysis' (italics in original). A similar point is made by Alexandra Lopes (2012) in regard specifically to prefaces when she argues that, 'regardless of what the translator *actually* did, prefaces and preface-like material are constrained by the accepted discursive practices applicable to the format' (129, italics in original), and are thus a 'rather poor indicator of the strategies employed by translators' (130).

Definitions of *paratext* in translation studies and engagements with Genette's theory

Approximately half of the existing studies which make explicit appeal to the paratext offer a definition of the term, while others use the term or its adjectival variant, *paratextual*, without defining it or linking it to Genette. Those which do provide a definition almost all describe the paratext in material terms, often limiting the paratext effectively to Genette's peritext. Thus Cecilia Alvstad's (2003, 274n1) definition of the paratext as 'what presents the literary text and makes it a book, e.g. title, name of the author, preface, illustrations' is typical (for further examples, see Koş 2008, 60; Borgeaud 2011, 32; and Bilodeau 2013, 1). A number of studies stress the mediatory aspect of the functional definition provided by Genette, quoting Genette's (1997, 2, italics in original) portrayal of the paratext as 'a zone not only of transition but also of *transaction*: a privileged place of pragmatics and strategy' (see, for example, Zhang 2012, 1; Deane-Cox 2014, 26). In the two edited collections mentioned above, the editors extend the material aspect of the definition to include epitexts, combining this with a functional definition. Thus Pellatt (2013b, 1) states:

> In this volume we regard paratexts as any material additional to, appended to or external to the core text which has functions of explaining, defining, instructing, or supporting, adding background information, or the relevant opinions and attitudes of scholars, translators and reviewers.

In a similar vein, Gil-Bardají, Orero and Rovira-Esteva (2012a, 7) argue that the term *paratext* is associated with an 'area of thinking' in which

> the text [is] conceived of as a continuum and as an extension of itself which goes beyond the novel, the essay or poetry anthology to include not only front and back covers, introductions, prologues, indices or illustrations (or what Genette termed *peritexts*) but also reviews, interviews with the author, literary criticism, etc. (or what Genette termed *epitexts*).

They explain that external elements are considered to be paratexts when they 'surround and extend' (7) the text, citing in French Genette's (1997, 1) words in relation to this function: 'precisely in order to *present* it in the usual sense of this verb but also in the strongest sense: to *make present*' (italics in original).

To my knowledge, none of the studies draw on the aspects of Genette's definition of the paratext that stress its connection with authorial intention, as discussed in Chapter 1. Indeed, the way in which Genette's functional definition is typically quoted by translation studies scholars is emblematic of scholars' deliberate elision of this aspect of Genette's paratext. The full quotation from Genette on the function of the paratext runs as follows:

> Indeed, this fringe, **always the conveyor of a commentary that is authorial or more or less legitimated by the author**, constitutes a zone between text and off-text, a zone not only of transition but also of *transaction*: a privileged place of a pragmatics and a strategy, of an influence on the public, an influence that – whether well or poorly understood and achieved – is at the service of a better reception for the text and a more pertinent reading of it **(more pertinent, of course, in the eyes of the author and his allies)**.
>
> *Genette 1997, 2, italics in original, bold emphasis mine*

Scholars in translation studies routinely abbreviate this passage, omitting the two sections in bold and thus avoiding the need for a discussion of the extent to which a definition based on authorial intention renders the concept problematic for the study of translations. The use of Genette's theoretical framework in translation studies might thus be termed pragmatic: scholars tend to take those aspects of his framework which can be readily adapted to the discipline without any significant theoretical manoeuvring and move ahead with analysis of paratextual elements in accordance with the key concerns of their research.

There are, however, a handful of scholars who do engage with Genette's theoretical framework in a more sustained manner. One of the key articles that addresses the theoretical issues around the concept of the paratext is Tahir-Gürçağlar's (2002) 'What Texts Don't Tell: The Uses of Paratexts in Translation Research'. This has been widely cited by translation studies scholars and often forms the foundation for their use of the concept of the paratext. Tahir-Gürçağlar discusses Genette's suggestion that translations might be viewed as paratexts and argues that it will 'serve translation research little' (46), primarily on the basis that it presupposes a subservient relationship between translation and original. Citing Genette's (1997, 12) description of the paratextual element as 'always subordinate to "its" text', Tahir-Gürçağlar (2002, 46) states:

> the implications of this statement for translation research are clear. They mean that translation, when regarded as paratext, will serve only its original and nothing else – not the target readership who enjoys it, not the target literary system that may be so influenced by it as to trigger a series of translations of similar texts, not the translator who may enjoy a reputation for having translated that specific text, not the publisher who may make considerable money out of that specific title, and not the source text itself whose 'afterlife' (Benjamin, 1968) is ensured by translation.

By listing these key areas of translation research, Tahir-Gürçağlar indicates that to view translations as paratexts is to close off productive avenues of research and to turn back on advances made in the discipline over recent decades. Furthermore, she argues that Genette's conceptualisation of translation as paratext 'runs counter to a perspective that regards translation as initiated in the target culture' (46), cannot be reconciled with the claims of postcolonial studies, fails to consider how translations may alter original texts, and allows no room for consideration of pseudo-translations. In summary, she strongly dismisses Genette's suggestion that viewing translations as paratexts represents a fruitful domain of enquiry, and suggests that the usefulness of paratexts to translation research comes from viewing translations as texts in their own right and conceiving of paratexts as 'presentational materials accompanying translated texts and text-specific metadiscourses formed directly around them' (44). In so doing, and without addressing the issue directly, she decouples the notion of paratext from authorial intention, rendering it much more straightforward for use by translation studies scholars.

While Tahir-Gürçağlar's proposed definition of the paratext undoubtedly increases the productivity of the concept with regard to translation-related research, her dismissal of Genette's suggestion that translations might be viewed as paratexts is based to a certain extent on an overextrapolation of his outline of the subservience of the paratext, and also disregards certain aspects of Genette's discussion. While Tahir-Gürçağlar is correct to argue that viewing translations as paratexts is to be interested in what they tell us about the source text, rather than what they may say about the target culture, her claim that viewing translations in this way is to assume that they 'will serve only [their] original and nothing else' (2002, 46) seems exaggerated. Nowhere does Genette indicate in his study that any given element that has paratextual value cannot also convey other things; on the contrary, as we saw in Chapter 1, he stresses that the epitext – into which category translations-as-paratexts would fall – 'consists of a group of discourses whose function is not always basically paratextual' (Genette 1997, 345) and which should be looked on as 'occasions capable of furnishing us with paratextual scraps (sometimes of prime interest), though they must often be sought with a magnifying glass or caught with rod and line' (Genette 1997, 346). To consider translations as paratexts, then, is not to disregard the many other ways in which they may be of interest to a researcher; rather, it is about scrutinising them for the ways in which they may comment on or (make) present the original text.

Another aspect of Genette's argument that Tahir-Gürçağlar overlooks is his emphasis on the flexibility of the paratext and the way in which it serves to adapt the text itself to new environments and concerns. As we saw in Chapter 1, Genette (1997, 408) contrasts the immutability of the text with the mutability of the paratext, suggesting that 'the paratext – more flexible, more versatile, always transitory because transitive – is, as it were, an instrument of adaptation'. If we extrapolate from this description of the paratext to a description of translation, following Tahir-Gürçağlar's approach, then far from presenting a view of translation that is unable to account for the ways in which translations may manipulate a text or adapt it to a new environment, it allows for and even encourages a view of translation as an 'instrument of adaptation', flexible (transitory) and inevitably moulded to a particular target audience (transitive).

Admittedly, Genette's continued insistence on the connection between paratext and authorial intention places potential constraints on the extent to which the paratext's versatility can be played out, and in this sense the notion of translation-as-paratext undoubtedly remains problematic for translation studies researchers. Nevertheless, this brief discussion shows that Genette's view of the paratext's relation to the text is more nuanced and the idea of viewing translation as paratext potentially more productive than Tahir-Gürçağlar's analysis would suggest.

An alternative angle from which to critique Tahir-Gürçağlar's criticism of Genette is presented by Deane-Cox (2014). Arguing that Tahir-Gürçağlar overlooks the conditions placed by Genette on viewing translations as paratext – specifically, the involvement of the author in the translation process, as discussed above – Deane-Cox (28) argues that Tahir-Gürçağlar is wrong to assume that Genette 'posits a widespread and subservient analogy of translation as paratext', suggesting instead that the parallel between paratext and translation collapses completely 'once any process of rewriting occurs beyond authorized or self-translation'.[2] In Deane-Cox's view, then, considering translations as paratexts has limited scope not because of Genette's view of the paratext as subservient to the text, but because of the need to maintain a close connection between the translator and the author. Like Tahir-Gürçağlar, Deane-Cox's overall approach is to move away from the notion of the translation as paratext and instead to consider translations as texts, with their own paratexts. Deane-Cox carves out a specific place for the translator within Genette's typology alongside the other non-authorial contributors to the paratext identified explicitly by Genette (such as the publisher or third party preface writers). She does this by positing the additional category of the 'translatorial paratext' (29), which denotes material authored by the translator as opposed to the author, editor, or other third party. This echoes the solution put forward by Tahir-Gürçağlar (2013, 93) in an article on prefaces to translated works, in which she argues that translators' prefaces are neither authorial nor allographic but need to be 'handled separately in a category of their own'.

Two Francophone critics who engage with Genette's suggestion that translations can be viewed as paratexts are Maïca Sanconie (2007) and Evelyn Dueck (2014). Sanconie examines Vladimir Nabokov's self-translation of his 1932 novel *Otchaïnié*, into English in 1966, asking whether the translation has to be accompanied by prefatorial material for its commentating paratextual function to be fully realised: 'si la traduction sécrète du commentaire, il est légitime de se demander s'il faut le canaliser dans la préface pour lui donner sa valeur "énarrative" maximale' [if translation secretes commentary, it is reasonable to ask whether that commentary has to be channelled through the preface to achieve its full exegetical potential] (Sanconie 2007, 178). Although Sanconie does not propose any kind of general response to this question, her study suggests that the paratextual messages or values that a translation conveys are far less easy to identify than they are for many other kinds of paratextual elements. We will return to this point in Chapter 8.

Dueck (2014) similarly picks up on the idea that a translation might be considered paratextual in the sense that it conveys commentary on the source text, but highlights different objections to this logic:

> il y a au moins deux points qui mettent en question la définition de la traduction comme paratexte: d'une part, le fait que la traduction est elle-même

un texte littéraire (et non pas uniquement para-textuelle) et de l'autre, le fait
qu'elle est signée aussi bien par l'auteur que par le traducteur.
[There are at least two possible objections to defining translation as paratext: first,
the fact that the translation itself is a literary text (and not uniquely para-textual)
and second, the fact that it is signed by the author as well as by the translator.]

214

With the first objection, Dueck is distinguishing between the type of writing that characterises text and paratext in Genette's model: while the former
is literary (a poem, a novel), the latter is pragmatic and commercial (Dueck
2014, 215), destined above all to ensure a good reception of the literary text.
Designating a translated text as a paratext is from this perspective problematic,
since it clashes with the usually literary nature of the translated text. With the
second objection, Dueck points to complexities around questions of authorship
of translations, already evoked above. Ultimately rejecting Genette's idea of
translation-as-paratext, the bulk of Dueck's study is devoted instead to studying the paratexts of translated texts, specifically those of the French translations
of Paul Celan's work. Like Deane-Cox, Dueck argues in favour of creating
additional categories in order to study the paratexts of translated texts – though
rather than one additional category, Dueck creates four. These are the *péritexte traductif* [translatorial peritext], *the péritexte traduit* [translated peritext], *the
épitext traductif* [translatorial epitext] *and the épitexte traduit* [translated epitexts]
(see Dueck (2014, 213)). The distinction between 'traductif' [translatorial] and
'traduit' [translated] is made on the basis that the former encompasses peritextual
elements signed by the translator or publisher, while the latter refers to translated source text paratexts (see Dueck 2014, 213).

Key themes in paratext-related translation research

In this section, I identify the research themes with which analysis of paratextual material most frequently intersects, with the aim of giving readers a sense of the variety and
richness of current research in this area. Separating key themes out from each other in
this way does not imply any clear divisions between them; on the contrary, many of
them overlap, and many of the studies could be treated under more than one heading.

Paratexts as documentary sources for historical research

As noted above, unconnected with Genette's elaboration of the importance of the
paratext, a significant part of the efforts to establish and consolidate translation studies as a discipline and translation theory as a field of research lay in constructing a
historical tradition. This was achieved in part by producing anthologies of translation
theory that reached as far back into the past as possible, drawing a significant amount
of their material from translators' prefaces and other paratextual material – for, as
Astradur Eysteinsson and Daniel Weissbort (2006, 6) observe, 'the primary writers on

translation, historically, have been the translators themselves'. Some of these anthologies seek to construct regional traditions ('Western', 'Asian'), while others focus on national traditions ('German', 'Chinese'). While such tradition-building uses of paratexts are extremely significant, we should note that collections of prefatorial material are also sometimes made with other goals in mind. Annie Cointre and Annie Rivara's (2006) collection of translators' prefaces to French translations of English novels, for example, aims primarily to explore the phenomenon of Anglomania in France in the eighteenth and early nineteenth century.

Paratexts have also been shown to offer extremely useful clues for literary historiographers, allowing them to reconstruct the publishing histories of particular authors or formulate clearer pictures of the flow of literary works across borders. Anne Coldiron (2010, 339), for example, draws on a combination of quantitative data, corpus content analysis and paratextual data to challenge 'central critical narratives about English Renaissance poetry', while Guyda Armstrong (2013, 197–211) shows that paratextual features such as print types and decorative elements can prove crucial for reconstructing the transmission histories of particular works, particularly when historical records on individuals named explicitly in paratextual sites are non-existent and their identity therefore obscure.

Paratexts as places of potential translation or translator visibility

In one of the first essays to adopt the term *paratext* in relation to translated texts, noted above, Hermans (1996) connects common paratextual practices with the prevailing cultural ideology of translation, arguing that the tendency for readers to erase the translator's intervention is premised largely on 'the hierarchy implied by the order (and, more often than not, the size) of the names on the title page' (26). Despite the dominance of this ideology, Hermans argues that the translator is always discursively present in the translated text, exploring in subsequent publications the ways in which that presence may become manifest in both textual and paratextual material. In *The Conference of the Tongues* (2007), for example, Hermans shows that paratexts are one of the elements which can 'puncture the illusion' (24) of originality in 'covert translations' (23), or in other words those which 'work hard to look like originals' (24). More generally, when paratexts are used to discuss translation choices, they become places where the inherent self-referentiality of translation is 'raised to self-reflexivity' (51). Paratexts are also places where translators can 'signal their agenda' (33) or their ideological sympathy or antipathy towards the author or text (53ff.). Hermans suggests that this latter process can be viewed as a way of putting the author's words 'as if between quotation marks' (56), setting up a critical distance between translator and text and thus providing a frame within which the text itself is to be read. Hermans gives an example of a particularly crude framing in the first English translation of the Qur'an: the translator's preface presents the text 'as belonging to a hostile camp' (58), and has the effect of casting 'every word of the translation' (59) 'under the cloud of the translator's disdain for the original' (59).

While Hermans' primary concern in his research on paratexts is to show that the translator is always discursively present, rather than to argue overtly for an increase in visibility or a disruption of existing hierarchies through changes to paratextual practices,[3] other theorists take a more combative stance. In this, they are echoing Venuti's (1995) call for greater visibility for translators. Yuste Frías (2012, 132), for example, explaining the merits of the concept of 'paratranslation' (an issue to which I return in Chapter 7), argues: 'Thanks to the concept of paratranslation, translators can vindicate, once and for all, their visible figure within the books' physical and material space.' From a different theoretical perspective, but nevertheless in the same vein, Siri Nergaard (2013) takes issue with the 'marginalized position' (203) of translators in the publishing process and argues in favour of translators having more input, combined with 'a politics of visibility of translations and translators' (204). A similarly prescriptive approach is taken by Ellen McRae (2012), who recalls Peter Newmark's declaration made in 1983 that 'a translated novel without a translator's preface ought to be a thing of the past' (17), arguing that 'translators are in a unique position to act as ambassadors between cultures . . . their prefaces are an excellent locus for disseminating their understanding to readers' (2012, 80). An important cross-cultural perspective on these debates, and a reminder that low translator visibility in paratexts is not a universal phenomenon, is offered by Isabelle Bilodeau (2013). In her study of *yakusha atogaki* (translator afterwords) in literary translations, she notes the contrast between Western publishing conventions and those in Japan, where there is 'multiple naming of the translator in the peritext (particularly the cover)' (2) and where publishers typically 'reserv[e] space for translators to write in the first person between the covers' (2), concluding that 'the production of commentary is an integral part of these [Japanese] translators' occupation' (17).

A significant variation on the broad theme of paratexts and visibility is provided by a cluster of studies which focus on issues that arise when a particular translator *is* particularly visible within the target culture. Michelle Woods (2012), for example, discusses the paratexts produced by Adolf Hoffmeister, Czech translator of James Joyce, arguing that Hoffmeister's 'verbal and visual paratexts are all experimental texts in themselves' (2). She thus connects the issue of visibility with questions of the boundaries between paratext and text and the multiple simultaneous functions served by paratexts in the new context. While Hoffmeister's visibility serves to aid Joyce's entry into the target culture, in the case of the translator discussed by Mary Louise Wardle (2012), visibility has a negative effect. Aldo Busi, translator of Lewis Carroll's *Alice in Wonderland*, is a controversial figure in contemporary Italian society, his views on paedophilia causing a scandal some eight years after the publication of his *Alice* translation. Wardle (40) suggests that

> some of the scandal attached to Busi 'rubs off', as it were, on Carroll. This effect is achieved not only because of the obtrusive translation strategies adopted but also simply by virtue of the fact that it is Busi's name – and all that it stands for – that appears on the cover alongside Lewis Carroll's.

This case raises questions around the power of translations to affect an author's image in the receiving culture, an issue that will be discussed further below.

In some studies, the visibility of translators is linked with reflections on intercultural power dynamics. Sherry Simon (2000), for example, examines Gayatri Spivak's translation of short stories by Mahasweta Devi, *Imaginary Maps*, noting the considerable paratextual apparatus that Spivak provides for the work, which includes the prominent display of her own name on the front cover in the same size font as the author's. Simon (242) suggests that Spivak is using her name 'pour faire entrer cet auteur indien, bengali, dans les salons et bureaux des féministes de l'Occident' [to introduce this Indian, Bengali author to the salons and offices of Western feminists]. Simon shows that while aspects of this exploitation of the translator's reputation can be interpreted positively, it is also open to more negative readings:

> La traduction des textes indiens vers l'anglais participe . . . d'un lourd héritage . . . Peut-il être question d'appropriation, lorsque la médiatrice se réclame d'un espace interstitiel d'appartenance . . .? . . . Quel genre de porte la traduction ouvre-t-elle? A qui profite le passage?
> [The translation of Indian texts into English is part . . . of a difficult legacy . . . When the mediator claims to represent an interstitial space of belonging, might it be a case of appropriation . . .? . . . What sort of gate does the translation open? Who benefits from going through it?]
>
> *244*

While Simon's reflections are prompted by the respective positions occupied by Spivak and Devi in global power relations, Rim Hassen's (2012) study of women translators of the Qur'an addresses the visibility–invisibility dichotomy on the basis of gender. Hassen contrasts two translations by women living in Muslim countries with two translations by women based in the United States, finding that the translations by the former conceal the gender of the translator, while the latter foreground it. Hassen suggests that translations which conceal the translator's feminine identity 'consolidate the power and authority of the dominant conservative discourse' (73), while those that stress the translator's feminine identity use that fact to 'negotiate between conservative Muslim conceptions of femininity on the one hand, and Western perceptions of gender on the other' (75). In a move that has undoubted parallels to Simon's exploration of cultural appropriation, Hassen suggests that the visibility of the feminine identity in the translations by the translators based in the US 'could have the effect of "exoticizing" their positions' (75), creating cultural products which conform to Orientalist stereotypes. In both of these studies, visibility thus becomes linked with questions of power dynamics in intercultural relations.

Paratexts and socio-cultural contexts (and consequences) of translation

Context-oriented research accounts for a large part of the existing studies on translation paratexts. In this sense, research into paratexts cannot be separated from the various so-called 'turns' of translation studies, most notably the cultural and sociological turns.[4] These turns have been associated with a variety of theoretical frameworks including postcolonial theory, Bourdieusian sociology, Gramscian theories of hegemony, and narrative theory, all of which have been drawn on by scholars in the context of research into translation paratexts. While the range of studies in this category is very broad and does not lend itself to easy summaries, one way of categorising the research is in terms of the interrelation between ideology and society. Thus it is possible to distinguish between research into societies within which there is a dominant ideology, forcefully imposed by the group in power, on the one hand, and research into societies in which multiple ideologies openly compete, on the other.

Research in the first category is concerned to explore the ways in which the dominant ideology is asserted within paratextual material, and intersects with the broader theme of translation and censorship. Gaby Thomson-Wohlgemuth's (2009) book-length study of translation in the GDR, for example, dedicates a large part of the study to paratextual analysis, notably of epitexts in the form of print permit files submitted by publishers to the censors and of afterwords to published translated children's literature. The overall aim of the study is to assess the degree of ideological influence of the GDR system on literary output, or in other words to use the paratextual material as documentary evidence enabling a deeper understanding of the functioning of GDR society. Another example of research in this category is Hou Pingping's (2013) study of the paratexts of the official English translations of the *Selected Works of Mao Tse-tung*. As translations which were 'organized by China's Central Publicity Department under the Central Committee of the CPC' (37), the paratexts reinforced Maoist ideology at every level. This included red covers, enthusiastic dust cover endorsements, title pages prominently featuring Mao's name together with visual portraits, introductory notes containing 'ideologically significant judgements' (38), and publication notes warning against unreliable alternative (non-official) translations.

Examples of studies which fall into the second category include Deane-Cox's (2014) work on retranslation, which incorporates paratextual analysis in its effort to understand how retranslations are 'shaped by their socio-cultural conditions of production' (18) as well as whether – and how – they position themselves relative to each other. Like Deane-Cox, Sameh Hanna (2016) draws on a Bourdieusian framework, examining a wealth of peritextual and epitextual material in order to understand the dynamics governing the 'production, dissemination and consumption of the Arabic translations of Shakespeare's tragedies' (10). The idea that translators use paratexts to position themselves ideologically is also explored by Mona Baker (2006), who draws on narrative theory. Baker shows how narrative viewpoints are accentuated or suppressed through spatial or temporal reframing in paratexts, demonstrating the potential for close analysis of paratextual material to be incorporated into wider research on the construction of narratives in and through translations. The concerns of research that focuses on individual translations overlaps with those that are seen in these broader studies. Examples include Christina Delistathi's (2011) analysis of the 1933 Greek translation of *The Communist*

Manifesto, Martha Cheung's (2010) discussion of the paratexts by Yan Fu in his 1898 translation of Thomas Huxley's *Evolution and Ethics* and Roberto Valdeón's (2014) study of Nigel Griffin's 1992 translation of the 1552 work, *Brevísima relación de la destrucción de las Indias*, to name just three. Valdeón's study is of note for the way in which it evokes the possibility for different paratextual elements to convey different ideological messages: the efforts of Griffin 'to resist . . . the ideological position of earlier English editions' are to some extent undermined, in Valdeón's view, by the retention of an ideologically loaded engraving by Theodor de Bry on the front cover. This study thus highlights the importance of analysing verbal and visual paratexts together.

Paratexts and gender

As part of the fertile intersection between paratextual analysis and research connecting translation and socio-cultural and ideological contexts, recent years have also seen the publication of a number of articles connecting paratexts with questions of gender. Such studies fall broadly into two groups. Those in the first group explore the ways in which female translators use paratexts to create a space for their voice or assert their own identity (often in historical or cultural contexts which would suppress or exclude women's voices), while those in the second show how paratexts have often been used to assert dominant (misogynistic) views and to contain women's writing within boundaries considered acceptable.

An example of the first type of study is an article by Jessica Malay (2006) that focuses on the paratexts produced by the sixteenth-century scholar and courtier Elizabeth Cooke Hoby Russell for her translations. As 'acceptable avenues for female textual production' (164), translation paratexts represented a space in which Russell could construct an identity for herself, and Malay shows that she exploited them to the full, even going so far as to ennoble herself (162). While Russell featured her individual identity prominently, the female translator whose paratextual contributions are analysed by Alison E. Martin (2011) combined a much more 'self-effacing' approach (16) with one that nevertheless allowed her to 'construct an identity for herself as a competent translator and amateur botanist' (17). Martin shows that Reid made particular use of footnotes, through which she 'supplement[ed] and correct[ed] information' (17) with a level of mathematical precision which 'implied that her annotations were well-researched and accurate' (17). Both of these historical studies of female translators thus show that paratexts offered a means through which female and translatorial subservience could be challenged in ways which on the surface posed little challenge to the established hierarchies, but which were nevertheless powerful.

An example of the second type of study is found in Valerie Henitiuk's (2011) analysis of the prefaces, introductions and notes to translations of *The Pillow Book* by Japanese author Sei Shônagon. Henitiuk critiques the 'regressive gender attitudes' (247) espoused by the translator of the canonical English version, amongst others, arguing that 'such paratextual materials provide evidence of the central role gender continues to play in the framing of a woman writer by her (predominantly male) translators' (240). Henitiuk points out that the canonical version, together with its 'undeniably misogynist response' (247) to Sei Shônagon, was until 2006 the only complete translation into English and was also used as the source text for versions into other languages. It thus had far-reaching implications for the world-wide reception of the Japanese writer.

Paratexts and image-formation

The shaping of Sei Shônagon's authorial image through translation paratexts ties in with another area of research with which paratextual studies frequently intercon-nects; namely, explorations of the influence of paratexts on target culture images of a particular source culture author or of the source culture more generally. Research on the former includes Stella Linn's (2003) study of the images of Federico García Lorca in a range of target cultures, which shows that there are significant 'national differences in . . . image building: Lorca's heroic role as a "martyr for freedom" is emphasised much more in the French paratextual discourse than in the English and Dutch part of the translation corpus' (2003, 60). Caroline Summers' (2017) study of East German writer Christa Wolf similarly explores the contribution of transla-tors, publishers and reviewers to the construction of authorial identity through a range of translation paratexts. While Linn and Summers are concerned with the image and reception of a literary author, Şebnem Susam-Sarajeva's (2006) *Theories on the Move* explores the ways in which paratextual material of translations of work by Roland Barthes and Hélène Cixous contributed to the images that the receiving cultures came to hold of these French theorists and their associated theories.[5] The shifts in authorial image evidenced through such studies raise important questions in relation to Genette's insistence on the connections between paratext and autho-rial intention, an issue to which I shall return in Part III.

Studies that engage with the related but distinct topic of how paratexts influ-ence target culture images of source cultures span a range of language and cultural pairings and are linked to analyses of cultural stereotyping in translation. Szu-Wen Kung (2013), for example, finds that American cover designs of Taiwanese lit-erature aim to 'trigger the readers' initial interest towards the translation through the stereotypical representation of foreignness or even Orientalism' (62). Phrae Chittiphalangsri's (2010) study of nineteenth-century English and French transla-tions of the Sanskrit drama *Śakuntalā* similarly shows that paratexts were key sites for the development of the Orientalist narrative, and suggests that translators used them as places in which they could advertise their own legitimacy as scholars able to represent the Orient to the English public (see also Chittiphalangsri (2014) for further examination of this issue). The possibility that such representations are not necessarily always imposed by the receiving culture is evoked in Pellatt's (2013c) comparison of the twin volumes of Chinese Premier Zhao Ziyang's memoirs edited by Bao Pu, one produced for a Chinese-speaking audience and the other for an English-speaking audience. In contrast with the Orientalism identified by

Kung and Chittiphalangsri, the Orientalism that Pellatt identifies in the English-language version of Ziyang's memoirs is an auto-Orientalism, or in other words, 'a new kind of Orientalist discourse which is created by none other than the Chinese themselves' (102).

Richard Watts' (2005) analysis of Caribbean and North African literature in US translations presents an interesting variation on the way in which publishers appeal to stereotypes of foreign cultures through paratexts. Watts shows that, while publishers do invoke the 'timeless context of Caribbean colonialism' (162), there is also a strong tendency to situate the texts within the broader stereotypical category of 'World Literature, one in which otherness is always in play but often remains vague' (168). In her study of African, Asian and Latin American literature in Swedish translation, Cecilia Alvstad (2012, 82) draws similar conclusions, stating: 'these literatures are generally translated by the same publishers and presented paratextually as belonging together as part of a larger whole. In other words, there is a strong paratextual construction of sameness'. As part of this construction of sameness, many publishers adopt exoticising as well as universalising discourses, emphasising that foreign texts give access to unfamiliar worlds whilst simultaneously stressing their potential to offer universal insights. In a cogent discussion that draws on the work of David Damrosch, Alvstad (2012, 90) argues that it is possible to see exotic and universalist elements as 'two sides of the same coin'. While Alvstad explores this dual strategy with regard to publishers' paratexts, it is also possible to see it at work in the combination of translation approach and paratextual adaptation. The study by Kung (2013, 62), for example, mentioned above, observes that in the case of the Taiwanese fiction translated for the US market, the strategy pursued in the paratext apparently clashes with the strategy pursued in the translation, the latter 'reduc[ing] the foreignness of the source culture items to a great extent'. While Kung presents this as a contradictory strategy, Watts' and Alvstad's discussions, as well as other research in the domain of postcolonial translation studies, suggest that such an approach may in fact be typical and consistent within itself: the foreignness of the text is made manageable for the target reader through a simultaneous process of reduction of foreignness (through domestication) and intensification of those aspects of foreignness with which the target audience is already familiar (through exoticisation).[6]

Furthermore, studies of translation between Western cultures indicate that very similar strategies can be observed here too, at least with regard to cultural stereotyping through paratexts. Carol O'Sullivan's (2005) study of paratexts of Italian fiction in English, for example, notes the 'startling' (71) convergence in cover design of both translations and pseudo-translations from Italian, observing that the covers 'show, as a rule, photographic images of conspicuously Italian buildings and cityscapes' (65). Studies of Australian children's fiction in French and German translation similarly conclude that the source culture is represented by a limited number of tropes that correspond to longstanding cultural stereotypes (see Frank (2007) and Gerber (2012), respectively). Reading these case studies alongside each other allows us to hypothesise that the use of cultural stereotyping through paratexts is a common – perhaps even default – strategy in the marketing of foreign texts, rather than being something that is reserved for distant (exotic) cultures.

Paratexts and agency

As the discussion of book covers suggests, research into paratexts pushes to the fore questions around the agents involved in producing translated products. Tahir-Gürçağlar's (2013) study of allographic preface writers, for example, demonstrates the importance of paying attention to the relative prominence and power of those who contribute to translation paratexts if we are to understand how those paratexts function. Writing from a Bourdieusian perspective, Tahir-Gürçağlar argues that preface writers often 'have a more established literary position than the translators' (98) and are able to use that discursive and symbolic power to '"consecrate" the translator and create some literary capital for him or her' (98–9).

While this kind of paratextual contribution relies on the identity of the contributor being made explicit, other studies focus on the work of hidden contributors, notably editors. Nathalie Mälzer (2013), for example, draws on her own experiences of working as a literary translator to sketch out in very striking terms the extent of editorial interventions in both text and paratext. In the case of Gaëlle Guernalec-Levy's *L'Amant inachevé*, for example, the editor took a number of measures to turn the book into a more explicitly erotic novel, replacing the rather neutral cover image with one showing the naked legs of a prostrate woman, and even extensively rewriting sex scenes in the text itself (see Mälzer (2013, 159–64)). In her conclusion, Mälzer (170) suggests that translation research would benefit from 'shifting the focus from the study of cultural adaptation in literary translations carried out by translators to the adaptations made by the various agents of the publishing industry to bring these books to the market'. That translators are often marginalised with regard to paratextual publishing decisions is confirmed by other accounts by practising translators, such as those by Nergaard (2013), Yuste Frías (2012) and, with regard to dubbing, Anna Matamala (2011).[7] While Nergaard and Yuste Frías argue for a change to publishing practices that would allow translators greater input, Matamala echoes Mälzer's recommendation, emphasising the importance of industry-based awareness in audiovisual translation research.

Concluding remarks: roads not yet (well-)travelled

As this summary of existing research shows, the concept of the paratext has opened up rich seams of enquiry and offered original perspectives in product-oriented and context-oriented research.[8] It has also proved important to translation history and to discussions of agency in translation. In light of these developments, few would dispute the importance of Genette's concept of the paratext for translation studies. Yet there is still much more to be done, both in terms of scope and on a theoretical level. Most of the research to date has been into literary translation, with few excursions into other genres; hardly any scholars have taken up

Genette's invitation to explore the notion of translation as paratext, and discussions of Genette's theory have been relatively brief. As the next chapter will show, scholars in neighbouring disciplines have engaged more closely and arguably more productively with Genette's framework itself, proposing expansions and alterations in light of technological developments and in relation to different types of text, notably filmic, televisual, digital and internet-based ones. Many of these developments hold particular relevance for scholars in translation studies, and are likely to offer an important stimulus for research. Further reflections on Genette's theoretical framework and on other potentially productive directions for translation studies research involving paratexts will be presented in Part III.

Notes

1 Note that Harvey (2003) uses the term *bindings* rather than *paratexts* to refer to titles, cover photos and back cover blurbs.
2 As I will show in Chapter 4, the idea that authorised translations have any specific claim on paratextual relevance is deeply problematic.
3 It is fair to say, however, that Hermans's overall stance is in favour of greater visibility. This emerges, for example, when he argues: 'This hierarchy . . . is nothing new. Historically it has been construed in a number of ways, mostly around oppositions such as those between creative versus derivative work, primary versus secondary, art versus craft, authority versus obedience, freedom versus constraint, speaking in one's own name versus speaking for someone else . . . And in case we think these are after all natural and necessary hierarchies, it may be useful to remind ourselves of the fact that in our culture the male/female distinction, too, has been construed in terms of very similar oppositions' (Hermans 1996, 44).
4 For discussion of these turns, see, for example, Snell-Hornby (2006) and Wolf (2014).
5 We should note, however, that Susam-Sarajeva (2006, 15 *passim*) uses the term *extratextual material* to denote such elements.
6 See Batchelor (2009, 206 *passim*) for a discussion of this issue in the context of postcolonial translation studies.
7 It is arguably also the case that authors are frequently side-lined in similar ways, at least in some sectors of the publishing industry. See, for example, Davis (2012), or blogs by writers such as Thomsen (2017) or Eulberg (2014).
8 These terms are taken from Saldanha and O'Brien (2014).

References

Agirrezabalaga, Elizabete Manterola. 2012. "What Kind of Translation is it? Paratextual Analysis of the Work by Bernardo Atxaga". In *Translation Peripheries: Paratextual Elements in Translation*, edited by Anna Gil-Bardají, Pilar Orero and Sara Rovira-Esteva, 83–100. Bern: Peter Lang.

Alvstad, Cecilia. 2003. "Publishing Strategies of Translated Children's Literature in Argentina: A Combined Approach". *Meta: journal des traducteurs / Meta: Translators' Journal* 48 (1–2): 266–75.

———. 2012. "The Strategic Moves of Paratexts: World Literature through Swedish Eyes". *Translation Studies* 5 (1): 78–94.

Armstrong, Guyda. 2013. *The English Boccaccio: A History in Books*. Toronto: University of Toronto Press.

Baker, Mona. 2006. *Translation and Conflict: A Narrative Account*. London and New York: Routledge.

Batchelor, Kathryn. 2009. *Decolonizing Translation*. Manchester: St Jerome Publishing.

———. 2016. "Translation Paratexts and the Pushing Hands Approach to Translation History". In *The Pushing-Hands of Translation and its Theory: In Memoriam Martha Cheung, 1953–2013*, edited by Douglas Robinson, 137–49. London and New York: Routledge.

———. 2018 in press. "Sunjata in English: Paratexts, Authorship, and the Postcolonial Exotic". In *The Palgrave Handbook of Literary Translation*, edited by Jean Boase-Beier, Lina Fisher and Hiroko Furukawa. Basingstoke: Palgrave Macmillan.

Batchelor, Kathryn, and Sue-Ann Harding, eds. 2017. *Translating Frantz Fanon across Continents and Languages*. London and New York: Routledge.

Bernabo, Laurena E. 2017. "*Glee*-talia: Adapting *Glee* for an Italian Audience". *Critical Studies in Media Communication* 34 (2): 168–76.

Bilodeau, Isabelle. 2013. "Discursive Visibility: Quantifying the Practice of Translation Commentary in Contemporary Japanese Publishing". In *Emerging Research in Translation Studies: Selected Papers of the CETRA Research Summer School 2012*, edited by Gabriel González Núñez, Yasmine Khaled and Tanya Voinova. Antwerp: CETRA, University of Leuven. Accessed 4 July 2017, from www.arts.kuleuven.be/cetra/papers.

Borgeaud, Emily. 2011. "The Agency of the Printed Page: Re-contextualizing the Translated Text". In *Translation Research Projects 3*, edited by Anthony Pym, 31–41. Tarragona: Universitat Rovira i Virgili.

Brienza, Casey. 2009. "Paratexts in Translation: Reinterpreting 'Manga' for the United States". *International Journal of the Book* 6 (2): 13–20.

Bucaria, Chiara. 2014. "Trailers and Promos and Teasers, Oh My! Adapting Television Paratexts across Cultures". In *Media and Translation: An Interdisciplinary Approach*, edited by Dror Abend-David, 293–313. New York, London, New Delhi and Sydney: Bloomsbury Academic Publishing.

Cachin, Marie-Françoise. 2006. "A la recherche du titre perdu". *Palimpsestes* (Presses Sorbonne Nouvelle) Special Issue: 285–296.

Castro Ramírez, Nayelli. 2012. "La representación de la 'tradición filosófica alemana' en sus traducciones al español: una mirada paratextual". *Mutatis Mutandis* 5 (1): 3–16.

Cheung, Martha. 2010. "Rethinking Activism: The Power and Dynamics of Translation in China during the Late Qing Period (1840–1911)". In *Text and Context: Essays on Translation and Interpreting in Honour of Ian Mason*, edited by Mona Baker, María Calzada Pérez and Maeve Olohan, 237–58. Manchester: St Jerome Publishing.

Chittiphalangsri, Phrae. 2010. "Paratext as a Site of the Struggle for Distinction: Nineteenth-Century Orientalist Translations of Śakuntalā". *Second International Conference on Literature and Comparative Literature*. Chulalongkorn University. Accessed 18 September 2017 from www.phd-lit.arts.chula.ac.th/proceedings_2nd/02.pdf.

———. 2014. "On the Virtuality of Translation in Orientalism". *Translation Studies* 7 (1): 50–65.

Cointre, Annie, and Annie Rivara, eds. 2006. *Recueil de préfaces de traducteurs de romans anglais 1721–1828*. Saint-Etienne: Publications de l'Université de Saint-Etienne.

Coldiron, A.E.B. 2010. "Translation's Challenge to Critical Categories: Verses from French in the Early English Renaissance". In *Critical Readings in Translation Studies*, edited by Mona Baker, 337–58. London and New York: Routledge.

Davis, Caroline. 2012. "Publishing Wole Soyinka: Oxford University Press and the Creation of 'Africa's own William Shakespeare'". *Journal of Postcolonial Writing* 48 (4): 344–58.

Deane-Cox, Sharon. 2014. *Retranslation: Translation, Literature and Reinterpretation*. London: Bloomsbury.

Delistathi, Christina. 2011. "Translation as a Means of Ideological Struggle". In *Translation and Opposition*, edited by Dimitris Asimakoulas and Margaret Rogers, 204–22. Clevedon: Multilingual Matters.

Dueck, Evelyn. 2014. *L'Etranger intime: les traductions françaises de l'oeuvre de Paul Celan (1971–2000)*. Berlin/Boston: De Gruyter.

Dybiec-Gajer, Joanna. 2013. "Paratextual Transitions of Travel Texts. The Case of Jan Potocki's Voyage en Turquie et en Egypte (1789) and its Polish Translation". *inTRAlinea*. Accessed 18 September 2017 from www.intralinea.org/specials/article/paratextual_transitions_of_travel_texts.

Eulberg, Elizabeth. 2014. "What authors have NO control over". *Elizabeth Eulberg Blog*, 30 July. Accessed 4 December 2017 from www.elizabetheulberg.com/what-authors-have-no-control-over/.

Eysteinsson, Astradur, and Daniel Weissbort. 2006. "General Introduction". In *Translation – Theory and Practice. A Historical Reader*, edited by Daniel Weissbort and Astradur Eysteinsson, 1–7. Oxford: Oxford University Press.

Farø, Ken. 2013. "Dänische Delikatessen. Linguistic Changes within the Translation of Titles". In *Authorial and Editorial Voices in Translation 2: Editorial and Publishing Practices*, edited by Hanne Jansen and Anna Wegener, 109–28. Quebec: Editions québecoises de l'oeuvre.

Frank, Helen T. 2007. *Cultural Encounters in Translated Children's Literature*. Manchester: St Jerome Publishing.

García Jiménez, Rocío. 2012. "Translation and Paratext: Two Italian Songs in 1960s Spain". In *Translation Peripheries: Paratextual Elements in Translation*, edited by Anna Gil-Bardají, Pilar Orero and Sara Rovira-Esteva, 135–47. Bern: Peter Lang.

Genette, Gérard. 1997. *Paratexts: Thresholds of Interpretation*. Translated by Jane E. Lewin. Cambridge: Cambridge University Press.

Gerber, Leah. 2012. "Marking the Text: Paratextual Features in German Translations of Australian Children's Fiction". In *Translation Peripheries: Paratextual Elements in Translation*, edited by Anna Gil-Bardají, Pilar Orero and Sara Rovira-Esteva, 43–61. Bern: Peter Lang.

Gil-Bardají, Anna, Pilar Orero and Sara Rovira-Esteva. 2012a. "Introduction: Translation Peripheries. The Paratextual Elements in Translation". In *Translation Peripheries: Paratextual Elements in Translation*, edited by Anna Gil-Bardají, Pilar Orero and Sara Rovira-Esteva, 7–12. Bern: Peter Lang.

Gil-Bardají, Anna, Pilar Orero and Sara Rovira-Esteva, eds. 2012b. *Translation Peripheries: Paratextual Elements in Translation*. Bern: Peter Lang.

Hanna, Sameh. 2016. *Bourdieu in Translation Studies: The Socio-cultural Dynamics of Shakespeare Translation in Egypt*. London and New York: Routledge.

Harvey, Keith. 2003. "'Events' and 'Horizons' – Reading Ideology in the 'Bindings' of Translations". In *Apropos of Ideology*, edited by María Calzada Pérez, 43–69. Manchester: St Jerome Publishing.

Hassen, Rim. 2012. "Online Paratexts and the Challenges of Translators' Visibility: A Case of Women Translators of the Quran". *New Voices in Translation Studies* 8: 66–81.

Henitiuk, Valerie. 2011. "Prefacing Gender: Framing Sei Shônagon for a Western Audience, 1875–2006". In *Translating Women*, edited by Luise von Flotow, 239–61. Ottawa: University of Ottawa Press.

Hermans, Theo. 1996. "The Translator's Voice in Translated Narrative". *Target* 8 (1): 23–48.

———. 2007. *The Conference of the Tongues*. Manchester: St Jerome Publishing.

Jansen, Hanne. 2013. "The Author Strikes Back. The Author–Translator Dialogue as a Special Kind of Paratext". In *Tracks and Treks in Translation Studies*, edited by Sonia Vandepitte, Catherine Way and Reine Meylaerts, 247–66. Amsterdam: John Benjamins.

Jiang, Hong. 2013. "The Ethical Positioning of the Interpreter". *Babel* 59 (2): 209–23.

Kellman, Steven G. 2010. "Alien Autographs: How Translators Make their Marks". *Neohelicon* 37: 7–19.

Kloppenburg, Geerhard. 2013. *Paratext in Bible Translations with Special Reference to Selected Bible Translations into Beninese Languages*. SIL e-Books: SIL International.

Koş, Ayşenaz. 2008. "Analysis of the Paratexts of Simone de Beauvoir's Works in Turkish". In *Translation Research Projects 1: Tarragona: Intercultural Studies Group*, edited by Anthony Pym and Alexander Perekrestenko, 59–68. Tarragona: Universitat Rovira i Virgili.

Kovala, Urpo. 1996. "Translations, Paratextual Mediation, and Ideological Closure". *Target* 8 (1): 119–47.

Kung, Szu-Wen. 2013. "Paratext, an Alternative in Boundary Crossing: A Complementary Approach to Translation Analysis". In *Text, Extratext, Metatext and Paratext in Translation*, edited by Valerie Pellatt, 49–68. Newcastle upon Tyne: Cambridge Scholars Publishing.

Lambert, José, and Hendrik van Gorp. 2014 [1985]. "On Describing Translations". In *The Manipulation of Literature: Studies in Literary Translation*, edited by Theo Hermans, 42–53. Abingdon and New York: Routledge.

Lefevere, André. 1977. *translating literature: the german tradition: from luther to rosenzweig*. Van Gorcum: Assen/Amsterdam.

Linn, Stella. 2003. "Translation and the Authorial Image: The Case of Federico García Lorca's *Romancero gitano*". *TTR: traduction, terminologie, rédaction* 16 (1): 55–91.

Lopes, Alexandra. 2012. "Under the Sign of Janus: Reflections on Authorship as Liminality in Translated Literature". *Revista Anglo Saxonica* 3: 129–55.

McRae, Ellen. 2012. "The Role of Translators' Prefaces to Contemporary Literary Translations into English: An Empirical Study". In *Translation Peripheries: Paratextual Elements in Translation*, edited by Anna Gil-Bardají, Pilar Orero and Sara Rovira-Esteva, 63–82. Bern: Peter Lang.

Malay, Jessica L. 2006. "Elizabeth Russell's Textual Performances of Self". *Comitatus* 37: 146–68.

Mälzer, Nathalie. 2013. "Head or Legs? Shifts in Texts and Paratexts brought about by Agents of the Publishing Industry". In *Authorial and Editorial Voices in Translation 2: Editorial and Publishing Practices*, edited by Hanne Jansen and Anna Wegener, 153–76. Quebec: Editions québécoises de l'oeuvre.

Martin, Alison E. 2011. "The Voice of Nature: British Women Translating Botany in the Early Nineteenth Century". In *Translating Women*, edited by Luise von Flotow, 11–35. Ottawa: University of Ottawa Press.

Matamala, Anna. 2011. "Dealing with Paratextual Elements in Dubbing: A Pioneering Perspective from Catalonia". *Meta* 56 (4): 915–27.

Nergaard, Siri. 2013. "The (In)Visible Publisher in Translations. The Publisher's Multiple Translational Voices". In *Authorial and Editorial Translation 2: Editorial and Publishing Practices*, edited by Hanne Jansen and Anna Wegener, 177–208. Quebec: Éditions québécoises de l'oeuvre.

O'Sullivan, Carol. 2005. "Translation, Pseudotranslation and Paratext: The Presentation of Contemporary Crime Fiction Set in Italy". *EnterText* 4 (3): 62–76.

Pellatt, Valerie. ed. 2013a. *Text, Extratext, Metatext and Paratext in Translation*. Newcastle upon Tyne: Cambridge Scholars Publishing.

——. 2013b. "Introduction". In *Text, Extratext, Metatext and Paratext in Translation*, edited by Valerie Pellatt, 1–6. Newcastle upon Tyne: Cambridge Scholars Publishing.

——. 2013c. "Packaging the Product: A Case Study of Verbal and Non-verbal Paratext in Chinese–English Translation". *Journal of Specialised Translation* 20: 86–106.

Pingping, Hou. 2013. "Paratexts in the English Translation of the *Selected Works of Mao Tse-tung*". In *Text, Extratext, Metatext and Paratext in Translation*, edited by Valerie Pellatt, 33–47. Newcastle upon Tyne: Cambridge Scholars Publishing.

Poldsaar, Raili. 2010. "Foucault Framing Foucault: The Role of Paratexts in the English Translation of The Order of Things". *Neohelicon* 37: 263–73.

Risterucci-Roudnicky, Danielle. 2004. "'Doubles-Seuils' ou le péritexte à l'épreuve de l'étranger". *Textuel* 46: 51–9.

Saldanha, Gabriela, and Sharon O'Brien. 2014. *Research Methodologies in Translation Studies*. Abingdon and New York: Routledge.

Sanconie, Maïca. 2007. "Préface, postface, ou deux états du commentaire par des traducteurs". *Palimpsestes* 20: 177–200.

Sardin, Pascale. 2007. "De la note du traducteur comme commentaire : entre texte, paratexte et prétexte". *Palimpsestes* 20: 121–36.

Schulte, Rainer, and John Biguenet, eds. 1992. *Theories of Translation: An Anthology of Essays from Dryden to Derrida*. Chicago: University of Chicago Press.

Simon, Sherry. 2000. "Quand la traductrice force la note: Gayatri Spivak traductrice de Mahasweta Devi". In *Paratextes: Etudes aux bords du texte*, edited by Mireille Calle-Gruber and Elisabeth Zawisza, 239–51. Paris: L'Harmattan.

Snell-Hornby, Mary. 2006. *The Turns of Translation Studies: New Paradigms or Shifting Viewpoints?* Amsterdam: John Benjamins.

Summers, Caroline. 2017. *Examining Text and Authorship in Translation. What Remains of Christa Wolf?* Cham, Switzerland: Palgrave Macmillan.

Susam-Sarajeva, Şebnem. 2006. *Theories on the Move: Translation's Role in the Travels of Literary Theories*. Amsterdam and New York: Rodopi.

Tahir-Gürçağlar, Şehnaz. 2002. "What Texts Don't Tell: The Uses of Paratexts in Translation Research". In *Crosscultural Transgressions. Research Models in Translation Studies 2: Historical and Ideological Issues*, edited by Theo Hermans, 44–60. Manchester: St Jerome Publishing.

——. 2011. "Paratexts". In *Handbook of Translation Studies Volume 2*, edited by Yves Gambier and Luc van Doorslaer, 113–16. John Benjamins.

——. 2013. "Agency in Allographic Prefaces to Translated Works: An Initial Exploration of the Turkish Context". In *Authorial and Editorial Voices in Translation 2: Editorial and Publishing Practices*, by Hanne Jansen and Anna Wegener, 89–108. Quebec: Editions québécoises de l'oeuvre.

Taviano, Stefania. 2013. "Global Hip Hop: A Translation and Multimodal Perspective". *Textus: English Studies in Italy* 26: 97–112.

Thomsen, Kyra. 2017. "Writers on the reality of book covers". *Writer's Edit*. Accessed 4 December 2017 from https://writersedit.com/fiction-writing/writers-reality-book-covers/.

Thomson-Wohlgemuth, Gaby. 2009. *Translation Under State Control: Books for Young People in the German Democratic Republic*. New York and London: Routledge.

Valdeón, Roberto A. 2014. "The 1992 English Retranslation of *Brevísima relación de la destrucción de las Indias*". *Translation Studies* 7 (1): 1–16.

Venuti, Lawrence. 1995. *The Translator's Invisibility: A History of Translation*. New York: Routledge.

Wardle, Mary Louise. 2012. "Alice in Busi-Land: The Reciprocal Relation between Text and Paratext". In *Translation Peripheries: Paratextual Elements in Translation*, edited by Anna Gil-Bardají, Pilar Orero and Sara Rovira-Esteva, 27–42. Bern: Peter Lang.

Watts, Richard. 2005. *Packaging Post/Coloniality: The Manufacture of Literary Identity in the Francophone World*. Lanham, Boulder, New York, Toronto and Oxford: Lexington Books.

Wolf, Michaela. 2014. "The Sociology of Translation and its 'Activist Turn'". In *The Sociological Turn in Translation and Interpreting Studies*, edited by Claudia V. Angelelli, 7–22. Amsterdam and Philadelphia: John Benjamins.

Woods, Michelle. 2012. "Framing Translation. Adolf Hoffmeister's Comic Strips, Travelogues, and Interviews as Introductions to Modernist Translations". *Translation and Interpreting Studies* 7 (1): 1–18.

Xu, Minhui. 2012. "On Scholar Translators in Literary Translation. A Case Study of Kinkley's Translation of 'Biancheng'". *Perspectives* 20 (2): 151–63.

Yuste Frías José. 2010. "Au seuil de la traduction: la paratraduction". In *Event or Incident/ Evénement ou incident: On the Role of Translation in the Dynamics of Cultural Exchange/Du Rôle des traductions dans les processus d'échanges culturels*, 287–316. Bern: Peter Lang.

———. 2012. "Paratextual Elements in Translation: Paratranslating Titles in Children's Literature". In *Translation Peripheries: Paratextual Elements in Translation*, edited by Anna Gil-Bardají, Pilar Orero and Sara Rovira-Esteva, 117–34. Bern: Peter Lang.

Zhang, Meifang. 2012. "Stance and Mediation in Transediting News Headlines as Paratexts". *Perspectives: Studies in Translatology* 21 (3): 1–16.

3
PARATEXTS IN DIGITAL, MEDIA AND COMMUNICATION STUDIES

As we saw in Chapter 1, Genette developed the concept of the paratext in relation to literary texts, in an era in which print culture was dominant. Over the past decades, the paratext has had what Dorothee Birke and Birte Christ (2013, 65) term a 'tremendously successful career in literary studies', a point which is supported by Frederik Aström's (2014) bibliometric survey of citations of Genette as well as by Birke and Christ's (2013, 65) own observation that 'the distinction between text and paratext is now one of the basic analytical tools taught in textbook introductions to the study of narrative and explicated in handbooks on literary analysis'. Although Genette's approach to key theoretical notions such as author and meaning does not sit well with a number of influential literary theoretical paradigms, notably poststructuralist ones,[1] its value and appeal remain strong. This is perhaps in no small part due to the openness that Genette builds into his framework, describing it as a 'wholly inceptive exploration' (Genette 1997, 14), as noted in Chapter 1. This openness has allowed scholars to adapt Genette's framework to the digital era as well as to other kinds of texts, notably film, television and videogames, and, to a lesser extent, news. Genette (1997, 407) himself anticipates the expansion of his framework beyond literature in the conclusion to *Seuils*, suggesting:

> if we are willing to extend the term [paratext] to areas where the work does not consist of a text, it is obvious that some, if not all, of the other arts have an equivalent of our paratext: examples are the title in music and in the plastic arts, the signature in painting, the credits or the trailer in film, and all the opportunities for authorial commentary presented by catalogues of exhibitions, prefaces of musical scores . . ., record jackets, and other peritextual or epitextual supports. All of them could be subjects for investigations paralleling this one.

This invitation is, admittedly, accompanied by a caution against allowing the concept of the paratext to expand too far, as noted in Chapter 1; nevertheless, numerous scholars have taken up Genette's invitation to build on his work, often extending the definition of the paratext in ways that directly counter Genette's (1997, 407) insistence on 'the most essential of the paratext's properties', namely its function of 'ensur[ing] for the text a destiny consistent with the author's purpose'. In this chapter, I outline the most significant developments of Genette's framework in the two disciplines that can be argued to have developed the concept of the paratext most intensely, namely digital studies and media studies. As these are disciplines with which translation studies often intersects, they offer important avenues for thinking about the ways in which a paratextual framework for translation may be elaborated. The concept of the paratext has also been applied in a more limited manner to the analysis of print and online newspapers, and I provide a brief overview of these developments at the end of the chapter.

Paratexts of digitised and born-digital literature

Although the capability to digitise literary texts has existed for a couple of decades, it is only since the arrival of e-readers in the early 2000s, coupled with the expansion of the internet, that digital channels have become a mainstream way of accessing literature.[2] At the same time, 'born-digital' (Desrochers and Apollon 2014b, xxx) texts have grown rapidly in number and variety, as part of what scholars have termed a 'digital turn, shift, age or era (not to mention revolution)' (Desrochers and Apollon 2014b, xxx). The range of digitised and born-digital literature currently extends from e-books which largely 'mimic the format and appearance of print books' (McCracken 2013, 105) to 'enhanced e-books' which retain the basic premise of a single verbal text but supplement it with videos, photographs, games and other interactive elements. Moving still further along the spectrum away from the format of traditional printed text, digital literature also encompasses transmedia storytelling, where stories 'unfold across multiple media platforms, with each medium making distinctive contributions to our understanding of the [story] world' (Jenkins 2008, 293). The texts in this mode of storytelling might include videogames, novelisations, websites, online videos, and alternate reality games, with no one text typically being considered central.

Scholars investigating the relevance of paratexts to this domain highlight the fast-developing nature of the field and the academic reflections that accompany it: Birke and Christ (2013, 79), for example, stress that scholarship on digitised and digital texts is 'still far from having developed a coherent conceptual vocabulary to talk about digital narrative phenomena and its different forms and genres'. While any attempts to elaborate typologies of paratexts pertaining to digital and digitised literature must therefore remain provisional and incomplete,[3] scholars share a strong sense of the value of interrogating the paratextual productions that accompany these new modes of reading. Patrick Smyth (2014, 331) posits, for example, that 'Genette's *Paratexts* remains a necessary model for the reception, contextualization, and interpretation of texts – whether analog or digital', while Birke and Christ (2013, 66) argue that the paratext 'can be a highly productive tool for the analysis of medial difference and medial change'.

While affirming the ongoing value of Genette's seminal work, scholars nevertheless show that it is not only the typology of paratextual elements that needs to be reviewed in light of the digital turn, but also the very concept of the paratext itself. For the shift to the digital, particularly at the more innovative end of the spectrum outlined above, calls into question the underlying concepts on which the concept of the paratext rests, forcing interrogations of the notions of text, author and reader before the paratext itself can be reconceptualised.

To take the first of these underlying concepts, e-books that mimic print storytelling would appear at first sight to be able to rely on the same conceptualisation of text used by Genette, i.e. to refer to a literary work expressed in verbal form, generally clearly distinguishable from whatever may surround it, and generally fixed.[4] In other words, Genette's view of the text aligns with the generally accepted conceptualisation of the text on which print culture is classically based, namely 'static and authored content' (Pressman 2014, 334). While e-books appear to replicate the 'text' as associated with print culture, the text that they make manifest is in fact far from static, as Smyth (2014, 322–3) explains:

> Ebooks, unlike their print predecessors, tend to provide no substantive, consistent record of their iterations. This is often spun for the positive: . . . small corrections, additions, and updates can be slipped into ebooks quietly, allowing authors to keep up with the curve in real time. However, these practices become problematic when ebook authors use this capability to remove criticized segments from their work or correct errors or mistakes that have been commented on in writing . . . Earlier editions are typically not recoverable without extraordinary efforts at preservation, comparison, and collation. Thus, individuals or organizations who attempt to archive an ebook may be left with a variance of texts, all bearing the same title and with identical metadata.

The transience of e-book texts is made more acute by the digital rights management (DRM) software through which they are made available: designed to protect the e-book industry by preventing copying, the software also makes it impossible to archive particular iterations of e-books, at least for institutions and individuals who are not able or willing to enter the legal grey area of removing DRM software (see Smyth (2014, 322) for further discussion). Furthermore, in physical terms, there is also a difference between the text of print culture and the text of digital culture: whereas texts in print culture can be saved (and, in this sense, exist) only in combination with the material object through which the verbal or pictorial utterances of which they consist are expressed, the text of digital culture exists in binary code independently of whatever material object is subsequently used to make it readable by a human being. In digital culture, in other words, we have moved from *text* to *content*, from 'utterances fixed by writing' (Ricoeur 1991, 135) to 'information divorced from form and physicality' (Smyth 2014, 329), 'rendered in code and stored as electrons' (Pressman 2014, 342). The implications of this shift for theories of paratextuality will be outlined below.

While e-books still present the illusion of a text that is on a par with the text associated with print culture, other types of digital literature move more boldly away from traditional formats, with consequences for conceptualisations of reader and author, as well as text. In transmedia storytelling, for example, where different parts of the story are told through different platforms, and readers play a key role in constructing the resulting narrative through active engagement with the various components, traditional definitions of *text* and *reader* become unworkable: the story consists of multiple interconnected texts rather than a single text; the story that results is not linear (there is no order in which readers must access the various texts); and the reader plays a crucial role in putting together the story, often engaging with interactive components (games, problem-solving) along the way. There is no single author of the overall story; different groups and individuals create different components and, in some cases, further components which also contribute towards the building of the story are produced by readers (for further discussion, see Nottingham-Martin (2014) and Strehovec (2014)).

In order to make Genette's concept of the paratext workable for the digital milieu, scholars tend to take a fairly loose definition of the paratext as their starting point, generally seeing it as 'framing elements' which 'shape the reading experience' (McCracken 2013, 106), and as the 'specific form' (Birke and Christ 2013, 66) in which a text is presented or how it is 'transform[ed] . . . into a material, marketable object' (Benzon 2013, 92).[5] Their analyses then proceed inductively, examining elements which can be seen to have a paratextual function, and proposing further developments of Genette's theory so that those elements can be adequately described and their functions explored. In the sections that follow, I shall describe the paratextual elements thus identified and outline the new terminology and metaphors that are proposed.

Elements

In some respects, the paratext that surrounds e-books is not radically different from the paratext surrounding print books: readers are not confronted by an alien experience, unlike anything previously encountered, but rather access the texts in a way which at least feels similar – even if this similarity is only an illusion. As Ellen McCracken (2013, 118) observes, 'many of the peritexts of e-books strive to create simulacra of print texts and are primarily word-based'. Corey Pressman (2014, 342) describes this illusion in further detail: 'E-reading platform apps and e-reading devices provide an explicitly skeuomorphic reading experience, including skeuomorphs like page curl, animated flipping pages, simulated dog-earing, and pen-mimicking colored highlighting.' Nevertheless, even at this end of the spectrum, there are significant subtle differences, all of which have an impact on the way in which the text is experienced. On the one hand, there are some para-textual elements that fall away or become less prominent, such that Birke and Christ (2013, 76) talk of a 'scarcity of paratext'; on the other, there is a proliferation of new and radically different ones. The further one moves along the spectrum from e-books which mimic printed books to transmedia projects, the greater these differences. Some scholars, notably Pressman (2014, 347), see these shifts as part of a positive linear development, marking a journey 'into secondary orality' which ultimately enriches and represents an 'opportunity of great enormity' (342);[6] oth-ers, such as McCracken (2013), view the changes negatively, describing paratextual alterations as distortions, mutilations or sabotage. In an effort to understand the divergence between Pressman's position and McCracken's, I shall survey the range of paratextual elements that have emerged in the digital milieu, structuring my discussion around the five key functions that they serve,[7] while acknowledging that many elements serve more than one function simultaneously.

Functions

Making the text present in the world

One of the most basic functions of the paratext that is identified by Genette (1997, 1) is to 'make present' the text, turning it into something that can be bought or bor-rowed and ultimately read. The paratextual elements which achieve this function are broadly termed the 'publisher's peritext' (16) and encompass such aspects as the format of the book (paperback or hardcover), the font, the front cover design, and so on. As noted above, the process of making present a text is fundamentally different in the digital context: binary code is made present to the reader by being converted into words or images through an algorithm and made accessible via an e-reading device or computer interface. Without these elements – source code, metadata, algorithms and some kind of e-reading device – digital texts cannot be present in the world, and for this reason scholars such as Marcello Vitali-Rosati (2014, 113) have argued that they can legitimately be viewed as a 'dynamic paratext' (see also Strehovec 2014). Others, such as Yra van Dijk (2014) and Barbara Bordalejo (2014), are more hesitant, observing that a feature such as the source code is not generally visible to the reader and therefore cannot serve as a 'vestibule' (van Dijk 2014, 34) in Genette's sense, even if the text 'could not exist without it' (Bordalejo 2014, 130). If scholars are divided over whether underlying features such as code should be viewed as paratexts, there is general consensus that e-reading devices themselves can be considered to be 'peritexts', and several of the more sustained reflections on the topic offer valuable interrogations of the way in which the design and functionalities of these peritexts affect modes of reading and interpretation and require reworkings of the concept of the paratext. These will be explored in further detail in the next section.

Remaining with the materialisation of the text for a moment longer, let us con-sider the process by which a reader comes to borrow or purchase a book. Whereas in print culture in the era in which Genette was writing (i.e. preceding the internet), a reader would have gone into a library or bookshop, perhaps after reading a review of a book or perhaps with the aim of browsing and selecting on the spot, in today's digital era consumers of digital literature are most likely to purchase or borrow a book through a website such as Amazon or by using a search engine such as Google. For this reason, scholars have argued that search engines, websites and online archives such as the Electronic Literature Organization (ELO) can also be seen as paratexts (see, in particular, van Dijk (2014) and Pressman (2014)). This suggestion is further supported by the fact that these internet-linked features also provide information which shapes how texts are received: in the case of the anthologised work *Lexia to Perplexia*, for example, van Dijk (2014, 27) shows how the Google hits for the work frame it 'ineluctably . . . as "literature," or at least as part of a canon of some sort' and suggests that even if the reader doesn't click on the hits, 'the knowledge that there is an academic discourse about the work greatly enhances its symbolic value'. In this sense, the search engine results serve the same function as the various paratextual elements in printed literature that affirm the work's or the author's status, such as dedications or series affiliations. The key difference, as van Dijk (2014, 26) acknowledges, is that search engine results are not influenced directly by the author or his associates; we will return to the question of authorisation in the context of digital paratexts below.

Commercial

Genette pays relatively little attention to what he terms the 'publisher's epitext' (1997, 347) on the basis that 'its basically marketing and "promotional" function does not always involve the responsibility of the author in a very meaningful way' (347). In the context of digital literature, however, the more open interpretation of authorship and authorisation leads critics to include features that serve a primarily commercial function in their analyses of the paratext. Indeed, Bhaskar (2011, 27) argues that, 'in the contemporary landscape of publishing . . ., marketing is a fundamental aspect of the book publishing process' and that Genette's framework needs to be adapted for 'a digital-saturated and market-oriented age of content dissemination'.

To illustrate the extent to which marketing permeates almost all aspects of the paratext in digital contexts, we can observe that it is not only the more obvious paratextual elements such as webpages and websites that serve a commercial purpose,[8] but that e-reading devices and even texts themselves also fulfil commercial paratextual functions. In the case of e-reading devices, Smyth (2014, 317) shows that content providers are able to 'log individualized reading behaviours' and that this information can be used by publishers and sellers for targeted marketing of other books. In other words, the paratextual device that serves to make present one text thus also becomes part of the commercial paratext for other texts. Other facets of the design of e-readers also serve a commercial function: whereas readers accessing a printed book would see the original cover every time they pick it up, readers accessing books via one of the 'special offers' Kindles would instead, in McCracken's

(2013, 111) formulation, see a 'screensaver that advertises credit cards, anti-aging cream, and luxury cars'. In this case, the paratextual device that makes present the text serves as part of the commercial paratext for other, non-literary products. With regard to the text itself, e-reading devices allow readers to download free samples of e-books, typically comprising an excerpt from the beginning of the text. These are intended to encourage readers to purchase the full e-book, and the text extracts thus become part of their own commercial paratext.[9] Another growing phenomenon allows for entire texts to serve as commercial paratexts to an author's other work, in addition to being texts in their own right: publishers, notably Amazon, are promoting the publication of shorter-length works which serve in part to encourage readers to purchase longer works by the same author (see McCracken 2013, 111; Smyth 2014, 327–8). In light of the growing importance of content that functions both as content and as marketing, Bhaskar (2011, 26) proposes replacing Genette's term *paratext* with the term *paracontent*, arguing that the new notion is more adequately suited to the 'specificities and demands of contemporary content industries'. While Bhaskar builds a cogent case for the new term, this and other attempts towards new semantic labels have had limited take-up; as Nadine Desrochers and Daniel Apollon (2014b, xxxv) note, scholars prefer instead to 'refer back and with deference to Genette'.

Navigational

In e-books, the key navigational paratext of printed literature – the page number – disappears, but the number of paratextual elements serving navigational functions increases. On basic e-reading devices, these navigational paratexts include the menus and sub-menus that allow readers to navigate to a particular place in the text or to move outside the text (typically to the Kindle store). At the more experimental end of the e-literature spectrum, works are typically presented as 'mosaic screens of several components organized according to spatial and temporal syntax' (Strehovec 2014, 53), as opposed to sequential pages. A variety of menus and instructions 'facilitate orientation and progress' (Strehovec 2014, 52), allowing readers not only to find their way into and through the text, but also to construct the text and its meaning. In light of these differences, scholars have proposed moving away from Genette's peritext–epitext distinction and replacing it with distinctions more apposite to the digital context, as we will see below.

Community-building

One of the most obvious differences between the digital literary context and the traditional print context is the level of interactivity associated with the paratext. With the exception of what we might term 'professional' readers – that is, established intellectuals or literary journalists whose views might form part of the allographic epitexts in Genette's model – readers' responses to print literature would in the past have been expressed only privately, to a small group of friends, and would not have become part of a text's paratext in any easily analysable sense. In the internet era, however, ordinary readers of both print and digital literature are able to post their responses to texts online, and these rankings, ratings and reviews form an important part of the text's threshold. In the case of e-books, reader responses are further encouraged and incorporated into a text's paratexts in even more significant ways: e-readers such as Kindles allow readers to add highlighting and notes to the text, and these become part of the 'accumulated response of a whole reading community' (Birke and Christ 2013, 78) that is by default visible to all readers of the text in question. Other readers' responses thus become 'part of the e-book's presentation' (Birke and Christ 2013, 79), with implications for authorship and authorisation, as we will see below. Other platforms take this interactivity still further: Pressman (2014, 346) argues, for example, that the Readmill e-reading application 'incorporates social recommendations, annotations, and geolocation services' into its peritext, or in other words 'design[s] community and dialogue directly into the paratext', while fanfiction sites include reader-generated statistics and interactive forums through which authors and readers can communicate both privately and publicly (see Hill and Pecoskie 2014). These interactive paratexts serve multiple functions simultaneously, not only building up the community around a text, author or genre, but also marketing the text, influencing readers' interpretations of the text and even, in some cases, shaping the evolving text itself.[10]

World-building/guiding interpretation

The shift towards a more interactive paratext would appear to go hand-in-hand with a lessening of paratextual features that can easily be classified as efforts, on the part of the author and his allies, to ensure a pertinent reading of the text, to return once again to Genette's theory. Indeed, some of the paratexts that can generally be seen to fulfil this function become less prominent when the books in question are accessed electronically rather than in print. E-books are programmed to open at the first page of the main body of the text, or at the page the reader had reached previously. Front covers, which communicate important messages about a book's content and go hand-in-hand with the publisher's commercial strategy, are therefore seen far less frequently than when a reader accesses a book in print; furthermore, even on iPads, which have the potential to reproduce colour covers, the original front cover is generally replaced with a generic one (see McCracken 2013, 111). Other parts of the publisher's peritext also become optional and non-default, in the sense that readers must actively think to click backwards to access them, rather than reading them or at least flicking past them. As McCracken (2013, 113–14) observes, some writers count on readers engaging with these paratextual elements before accessing the text, perhaps by 'play[ing] with reality and fiction in the dedication or epigraph': for e-book readers, these paratexts may remain hidden.

On the other hand, the greater active role that is conceived for the reader of more experimental digital texts means that many different elements become paratexts serving what Amy Nottingham-Martin (2014, 297) terms a 'world-building' function. Such paratexts enable a reader to gain new insights into characters or plot and thus shape the construction and comprehension of the narrative. Drawing on a term used by Genette, Birke and Christ (2013, 73) label such paratexts 'diegetic' and similarly suggest that they serve interpretive functions by adding to the fictional universe. Examples of world-building or diegetic paratexts are provided by Nottingham-Martin (2014, 300–4) in her analysis of the transmedia story *The 39 Clues*: here, both the collector cards and the alternate reality game that are part of the transmedia project are seen as paratexts that serve world-building functions (alongside various other functions), allowing the reader to fill in gaps in the narrative or adding verisimilitude. To give another example, in the case of the application e-book hybrid *The Silent History* studied by Smyth (2014), readers wishing to fully comprehend the Field Reports that form part of the e-book text are required to go to the physical location in which the Field Reports are set. In Smyth's (2014, 326) view, 'the physical world itself becomes a paratext, deliberately included within the bounds of the work by its authors'. The question of where the boundaries between text, paratext and context lie is one that recurs repeatedly in studies of contemporary, digital-based entertainment culture, leading some critics to suggest that the concept of the paratext reaches the limits of its usefulness in certain contexts, as we will see below.

Characteristics

If the preceding section provides an overview of discussions raised by consideration of Genette's fifth methodological question, 'to do what' (Genette 1997, 4) and simultaneously offers some responses to Genette's third question, the 'how', or 'mode of existence' of the paratext, this section introduces us to some of the terminology developed by scholars of digital literature in an effort to answer Genette's remaining three questions: where, when, and, most crucially, from whom.

Supplementing where with where to: from a static to a dynamic model

First, with regard to the *where* of the paratext, our discussions show that relying on a classification that distinguishes in a relatively straightforward way between text, peritext and epitext swiftly proves problematic in a digital context. For some texts, such as the online digital text *Inanimate Alice*, Gavin Stewart (2010) suggests that it is useful to distinguish instead between 'off-site paratexts' (60), 'on-site paratexts' (64), and 'in-file paratexts' (67), based on 'apparent location of the file (as designated by its URL)' (60). While this works well for the 'relatively centralized architecture' (72) of a text like *Inanimate Alice*, Stewart points out that it would be less useful for analysing 'more fluid and distributed types of digital texts' (72) such as transmedia projects which have multiple online texts on different sites.

In another reflection on the *where* of the paratext, McCracken (2013) effectively reformulates Genette's question as *where to*: she argues that, in light of the fact that paratexts can 'no longer be studied as singular fixed objects' (106) but 'exist spatially within particular dynamic viewing practices' (106), it is useful to focus on 'the centrifugal and centripetal motion to which they invite readers' (106). In this model, which, like Stewart's case study, is based on digital literature for which there is an identifiable core text, the core text is the centre, and the paratexts are the 'exterior and interior pathways leading readers both away from and more deeply into the words at hand' (106). Centrifugal paratexts might thus include blogs, readers' comments, or the author's webpage, or even the menu options that lead the reader to the e-book store. These same paratexts can, however, also operate centripetally, propel[ling] readers toward the central reading experience of the text itself' (110) and 'from there, further inward' (110), as readers engage with 'format, font changes, word searching and other enhancements' (107). McCracken's conceptualisation of paratexts as dynamic entities, moving the reader towards or away from the text, leads her away from the threshold metaphor developed by Genette and towards a space-based metaphor, speaking of texts and paratexts as existing in 'textual orbit' (110). This metaphor is strikingly similar to the one proposed by Steven Jones (2008) in the context of videogame paratexts, as we will see below.

Replacing when *with* what if: *a new view on paratextual temporality*

As we saw above, the digital text is far more fluid and transient than its print counterpart: it can be quickly and easily updated, with the result that any one digital text may go through many unsignalled iterations. The digital paratext is similarly ephemeral, particularly if we allow for webpages and websites to be considered as part of the paratext, as argued above. The transience of both text and paratext makes very difficult any temporal mapping of one to the other along the lines proposed by Genette. As Nottingham-Martin (2014) observes, it is hard to track when paratexts appear relative to what she terms 'anchor-texts' (290) in transmedia storytelling, because 'one of the affordances of digital media, especially web content, is that it can be updated nearly continuously, sometimes with no record of the previous content' (293). Nottingham-Martin also points out that digital texts offer multiple, non-obligatory points of entrance, and that readers may therefore not access some paratexts at all; for this reason, she suggests replacing Genette's temporal framework with a conditional one, or in other words, asking "'what if' the reader experiences a paratextual element before, simultaneously with, or after he or she encounters the anchor-text' (293), rather than trying to map when each paratext is published relative to the text in line with Genette's model. Stewart (2010, 71) makes a similar suggestion, but goes one step further by proposing that critics complement qualitative analysis with quantitative analysis, studying flows to digital text sites in an effort to understand which of the sometimes conflicting thresholds to the text are most frequently used. The issue of ascertaining which paratexts viewers actually access is also one which is increasingly preoccupying scholars in media studies, as we will see below.

Replacing authorship with authorisation and editorialisation

In the introduction to their 400-page edited volume on the applications of para-textual theory to digital contexts, Desrochers and Apollon (2014a, xxii) identify the status and function of the author as 'perhaps the thorniest element of Genette's theory, especially in digital culture'. As we will see below, the issue of the connection between authorship and paratexts is one that is also raised repeatedly in other media contexts, with the majority of scholars choosing to weaken the link between authorial intention and paratextual status. Georg Stanitzek (2005, 34) suggests that attempts to apply Genette's framework to contexts other than the traditional book force to the surface questions which Genette 'attempted to exclude systematically from his conception of the paratext', motivating a reconsideration of some of the weaker aspects of Genette's theory in the process. He sees Genette's refusal to engage with Foucault's interrogation of the function of the author as providing a case in point (see Stanitzek (2005, 35) for further discussion). As noted in Chapter 2, this issue is one that is also of paramount importance to any attempt to adapt Genette's theory to translation, and we shall return to it at several moments in the remainder of this book. In this section, I shall outline two of the most interesting solutions proposed by scholars of digital literature in relation to this issue.

Authorisation

When addressing the phenomenon of reader-produced material which may serve as a threshold to digital texts or influence other readers' interpretations of them, digital culture scholars are unanimous in their agreement that such material can and should be considered part of a text's paratext. While some argue this point on the basis of the spatial or functional characteristics of such material, discarding the relevance of any notion of authorship,[11] others build a case for considering material posted on platforms specifically designed for the purpose of enabling reader interaction as part of the paratext. Thus, in the case of transmedia projects, Nottingham-Martin (2014, 296) argues that the nature of such projects '"authorizes" readers to contribute to the narrative in an active way, which implicitly also "authorizes" readers in the sense of granting them a kind of authorial and authoritative status'. Similarly, in her study of e-books, McCracken (2013, 112) considers popular highlighting and reader comments to be part of an electronic text's paratext on the basis that the platforms on which these take place are built into the devices by the publisher. In their study of fanfiction, Heather Hill and Jan Pecoskie (2014, 156) take this argument one stage further, removing the need for a publisher or other text-creator to issue the authorisation and arguing instead that it is the nature of the genre itself that creates this authorisation:

> Certainly Genette (1997) argues that epitexts and peritext must be con-structed with authorial intention (p.2) . . . but the fact that the [fanfiction] community itself is an authorial platform negates the confines of Genette's definition of authorial intention and widens its parameters.

Editorialisation

One of the most detailed discussions of the question of authorship is found in Vitali-Rosati's (2014) contribution to Desrochers and Apollon's volume. In this essay, Vitali-Rosati argues that the theory of the death of the author that was proclaimed by Foucault and Barthes in the 1960s and 1970s 'did not provide the conditions for a shift towards a world without authors because of its inherent lack of concrete editorial practices different from the existing ones' (111), linked with the economic model in which printed works circulate. He goes on to posit that the 'birth and diffusion of the Web . . . have allowed the concrete development of a different way of interpreting the authorial function' (111), making the death of the author now possible. In order to demonstrate this, Vitali-Rosati pinpoints the two main functions of the author, based on Genette's own analysis. These are, first, to legitimate the text and what it says by taking responsibility for it and, second, to 'produce the uniqueness of the text' (115). In the context of the web, Vitali-Rosati (111) argues that these functions are fulfilled by a 'set of editorialization elements', making authors no longer necessary. To understand his position, we need to understand what he means by 'editorialization'. As Vitali-Rosati (2016) explains in another publication, he is using this term not as a derivative of the English term *editorialise*, with its sense of expressing an opinion in an editorial, but as a neologism from the re-semanticised French term *éditorialisation*. In French, he explains, the word has acquired a broader meaning and refers to the 'set of dynamics that produce and structure digital space' (104). For example, in the case of Amazon,

> the editorialization of content . . . is the result of the dynamic interaction of the Amazon algorithm, the platform's graphics and ergonomics, the databases, the users' actions, and all sorts of practices that take place within the space. The totality of these interactions – always in motion and always changing – is what structures the space.
>
> *104*

In the digital milieu, it is editorialisation which 'makes a text accessible and determines its context' (Vitali-Rosati 2014, 113), rather than the traditional print publisher, working in collaboration with or in the interests of the author, as in Genette's model. Examples of editorialisation elements include the indexation of a text by search engines using metadata, which 'allows readers to trust and find the text' (Vitali-Rosati 2014, 123), and social networks, which vouch for a text's quality and interest. Vitali-Rosati (2014, 113) concludes that 'paratext, as the set of online editorialization devices surrounding a text . . . and providing its meaning, can completely replace the traditional authorial function, which seems obsolete in this context'. The efforts of Vitali-Rosati, Nottingham-Martin, McCracken and others to adapt Genette's framework to e-books and internet-based literature have many points in common with the work of scholars in media studies, particularly in the domains of film, television and videogames; it is to these that we now turn.

Paratexts of film, television and videogames

Writing in 2010, Jonathan Gray (2010, 4) called for a 'relatively new type of media analysis' which would focus on the media world's equivalent of book covers such as opening credit sequences, trailers, posters and promotional campaigns. Gray adopts Genette's terms *paratexts* and *paratextuality* to denote such supposedly peripheral elements, arguing like Genette that they play a crucial role in meaning-making for the films and other media products to which they are thresholds. We should note that Gray was not the first to assert the relevance of Genette's concept of the paratext for film and television studies, even if it was his book that prompted the boom in interest in studying media paratexts in the UK and the US. Earlier efforts to draw links between Genette's paratextual framework and audiovisual genres can be found in de Mourgues (1994) as well as in important studies by German scholars such as Klaus Kreimeier and Georg Stanitzek (2004) and Alexander Böhnke (2007). In many respects, these studies represent more focused attempts to engage with the detail of Genette's theory; unlike Gray (2010), they address some of the key difficulties associated with adapting Genette's concept of the paratext to audiovisual contexts, notably his conceptualisation of the paratext as subservient to the text and its link to authorial intention. Böhnke (2004, 228), for example, views both of these aspects as severely restricting the transferability of the concept to the audiovisual realm and argues that they need to be dropped. Although Gray does not reference any of these earlier studies, the explicit conclusions reached by Böhnke and others regarding the adaptations that are needed if Genette's concept of the paratext is to be adequate for media studies anticipate his position, as we will see below.

In addition to these studies on film and television, Gray's seminal publication followed on from two significant studies of the videogame industry, both of which stressed the usefulness of Genette's concept to understanding the contemporary mediascape. Thus Mia Consalvo's (2007) study of the phenomenon of cheating suggests that, whereas the concept of intertextuality is unable to account for the videogames system as a whole, Genette's conceptualisation of the paratext constitutes 'a better way to think about the game industry and the text (and industries) that surround it' (21). Jones's enquiry into the meaning of videogames, published the following year, reaches a similar conclusion (see Jones, 2008, 7). Like Gray and the majority of other media scholars, Consalvo and Jones adopt the spirit rather than the letter of Genette's framework, broadening Genette's definitions of the paratext to allow it to encompass a wide range of material, including material produced by fans rather than by the makers of the product or text itself.

We should note that, in Gray's framework, a paratext is not something which serves as threshold to a text, but to a work, and that it is paratext and work together which make a text. In other words, Gray uses the term *text* in a different manner to Genette, adopting a Barthesian view of text as something that is neither concrete nor finite, but constructed by readers, 'experienced only in an activity of production' (Barthes 1977, 157). However, as Gray (Brookey and Gray 2017, 102) acknowledges in a later reflection on developments in media-related paratextual analysis, this terminology has not been widely taken up, with most media studies scholars opposing *paratext* to *text* rather than to *work*. In this section, and for the sake of consistency with discussions elsewhere in this volume, I therefore use *text* in a manner parallel to Genette, rather than in the Barthesian sense preferred by Gray.

Elements

The list of tangible paratexts relevant to television shows, films, videogames and 'natively digital texts' (Pesce and Noto 2016, 2) such as web documentaries is long, and reflects what Sara Pesce and Paolo Noto (2016, 3) term the 'extraordinary quantity of paratextual materials circulating on- and off-line'. An indicative but not exhaustive list is as follows:

- posters or billboards
- trailers
- opening credit sequences
- DVD covers and other packaging material
- DVD bonus material
- prequels and sequels
- podcasts
- interviews
- websites
- spoilers
- recaps
- idents[12]
- iPhone apps
- merchandise and toys[13]
- alternate reality games[14]
- spinoff videogames[15]
- internet memes[16]
- animated GIFS[17] (often produced by users)
- fan videos
- blogging
- reviews
- audience discussions
- pop-up ads
- online commentaries
- live tweeting (e.g. during TV shows)
- gaming magazines
- gaming strategy guides
- technological cheat devices such as enhancers (genies, sharks) and mod chips
- fan-created games.

In addition to these tangible paratexts, intangible aspects such as the genre of a film can also function paratextually,[18] in much the same manner as the factual paratext identified by Genette.

Functions

Many of the functions of media-related paratexts are similar to the functions of literary paratexts discussed by Genette. For example, media-related paratexts such as trailers offer viewers 'the possibility of either stepping inside [the text] or turning back' (Genette 1997, 2), while paratexts such as TV recaps foreground particular aspects of the show to ensure a 'pertinent reading' (Genette 1997, 2) of what follows. Other media-related paratexts, like certain literary paratexts, may seem at first glance to serve a particular function but in fact also serve others: for example, the commentaries that are often supplied as DVD bonus material, rather like the extensive additional material that forms part of literary scholarly editions, serve on one level to guide interpretation of the text, but on another are commercial in intent, included to encourage purchase of the DVD or book in question.[19]

Media studies scholars also focus, however, on paratextual functions that are distinct from those analysed by Genette. Paul Benzon (2013, 93), for example, examines the complex functions of the compulsory paratexts to DVDs in the present cultural and temporal context, explaining that they 'hedge in multiple directions against the obsolescence of the very product to which they are appended'. Other scholars focus on the links between paratexts and brands, often as part of broader enquiries into the phenomenon of branding in media, something which is growing in importance in line with the increase in channels and online digital services and the associated pressure for media corporations to win and keep viewers. Catherine Johnson (2012), for example, studies idents and interstitials as well as various 'extension[s] of programme content' (144) such as websites, additional short films, and promotional blogs, noting the usefulness of 'think[ing] about the television programme as part of a network of paratexts' (146).[20] Other functions highlighted in the context of media-related paratexts include examining the effects of paratexts on a fictional world's 'life expectancy' (Pesce and Noto 2016b, 1); assessing the connections between paratexts and ways of remembering or nostalgia (see, in particular, the essays in the second part of Pesce and Noto's (2016a) volume); and exploring the 'orienting' function of paratexts (Mittell 2015, 261–91).

Characteristics

Some of the media-related paratexts listed above offer relatively clear parallels with the literary paratexts studied by Genette: DVD covers and packaging operate in much the same way as book covers and other parts of the publisher's peritext (see Birke and Christ 2013, 71), while interviews, reviews and online commentaries are comparable to the authorial and allographic epitexts discussed by Genette. Other media-related paratexts, however, are markedly different from literary paratexts, notably in their authorship, substance, temporality and relation to the text. Rather than taking a chronological approach to media scholarship on paratexts, structuring discussion along the lines of these points of divergence offers a useful way of pinpointing the ways in which media theorists have developed and expanded Genette's framework.

Authorship

While user-generated paratexts would not count as paratexts under Genette's model, since they have no direct connection to the author of the text, media studies theorists tend to federate all peripheral and threshold matter under the term *paratext* and introduce a range of sub-categories to reflect the type of originator.[21] The labels given to these sub-categories vary from theorist to theorist, but the gist of the distinctions remains the same. Thus Gray (2010, 143) distinguishes between 'industry-created' and 'viewer-' or 'audience-created' paratexts, Jason Mittell (2015, 262) refers to 'official and unofficial paratexts' and also speaks more specifically of 'fan-created' paratexts, and Martha Boni (2016, 213) coins the term *grassroots paratexts* in opposition to *official paratexts*.[22] Slightly different terminology is developed by Consalvo (2007) in her study of videogames: she starts off initially considering as paratext 'all of the elements surrounding a text that help structure it and give it meaning' (21), but in the course of her analysis develops a distinction between the 'core game industry' (10) on the one hand and the 'paratextual industry' (10) on the other. In this dichotomy, the paratextual industries are those which produce non-authorised material, such as strategy guides, tip lines, cheat books, GameSharks and mod chips (9). In other words, in direct opposition to the constraints on the paratext imposed by Genette, the paratexts of Consalvo's analysis are precisely those that do not have a connection with authorial intention.[23]

It is important to note that none of the coinages outlined above involve the word *author*, or in other words, do not oppose the viewer-/audience-/user-/fan-created paratext to an author-created one. The absence of the word *author* is a reflection of the complexities of authorship pertaining to the texts themselves. As Mittell (2015, 88) explains, 'film scholars, critics, fans, and the industry itself have wrestled with authorship for decades', arriving at a mode of authorship attribution which he suggests might be termed 'authorship by responsibility' (88), as opposed to the model of 'authorship by origination' (87), generally imagined for literary texts. The mode of attribution for television series is different again, and can be conceptualised as 'authorship by management' (88), a model which 'emphasizes the additional role that television authors must take in helming an ongoing series rather than a stand-alone work' (89). Although these models of authorship permit individuals such as the director, producer or showrunner to be identified as the author of a particular film or TV series, Mittell stresses that 'given the intensely collaborative nature of the production process, such notions of authorship, even in its managerial conception, oversimplify the creative process and threaten to deny agency to the array of contributors who help make television' (95).[24] At the same time, Mittell argues that conceptions of authorship 'still function in our understanding of television narrative, are active within industrial, critical, and fan discourses, and serve an important cultural role' (95). In other words, as Mittell shows, authorship is a product of the way in which television series and other types of cultural entertainment are programmed and circulated, and serves a range of important functions, including those of branding and reputation-building.

Given the multiplicity of people involved in creating and circulating filmic and televisual texts and the severing of the link between authorship and origination, it is not surprising that media studies scholars have opted for function- rather than originator-based criteria for deciding what might be considered to constitute a paratext, and that terminology used to denote originators is based on broad group-ings (industry, corporate, viewer, etc.) rather than on terms which might denote individuals (e.g. director-produced paratext, screen-writer-produced paratext, etc.). Such an approach allows scholars to fully acknowledge and interrogate the meaning-producing and meaning-changing power of all paratext producers, rather than restricting analysis to those working with the official sanction of a production company.

Ephemerality

The notion of ephemerality is particularly relevant to the study of media-related paratexts in two ways: first, many media paratexts are short in duration; second, many media paratexts are only available for a short period. An example of the first type of brevity is provided by channel idents, which are typically shown on screen for fifteen to twenty-five seconds (Grainge 2011b, 91). However, as Charlie Mawer, in interview with Paul Grainge (2011b, 94), points out, idents are likely to be watched thousands of times, bringing their brevity into contrast with the amount of time in total that any one individual might spend watching them. The second type of brevity is encapsulated by the bus shelter, which, in Gray's (2016, 32) words, 'over its lifetime may host hundreds of posters for movies but each for no more than a week or two'. The ephemerality of these types of elements means that historically far less scholarly attention has been paid to them than to 'the more solid and sub-stantial film and television content' (Grainge 2011a, 10).

Yet this lack of attention does not match the amount of finance typically invested by production companies in these apparently peripheral elements (see Ellis 2011, 68), and also has consequences for the validity of media scholarship, as Gray (2016, 32) explains:

> To some, the disappearance of ads, trailers, toys, merchandise, press cover-age, and more may seem wholly unproblematic. After all, textual analysis as a technique regularly fetishizes a solitary engagement with 'the thing itself,' excluding the static and noise introduced by paratexts . . . But . . . paratexts matter. The ads that graced my hypothetical bus shelter did not just gesture at films: they created meaning for them.

Gray illustrates this point with a discussion of *Mad Men*, showing that, while many academic articles focus on it as a feminist text, many of the paratexts that currently surround the show are reducing or even 'outright destroy[ing]' (Gray 2016, 37) the show's feminism by presenting the main actresses as objects of sexual desire. Gray (2016, 39) argues that, given that 'by and large . . . most libraries hold on to the product itself, not the paratexts', analysts trying to make sense of what a text like *Mad Men* '*was* and what it *did* in social, cultural terms' in the future will not be able to access all of the relevant material; he concludes that the reliability of their analyses – and indeed any current efforts to analyse media products from the past – must therefore be cast into doubt.[25]

Temporality

Unlike Genette's framework which distinguishes systematically and with relatively little difficulty between *original, later* and *delayed* paratexts, as discussed in Chapter 1, the paratexts associated with the contemporary entertainment industry may be accessed at different moments relative to the text by different viewers, similar to the paratexts of digital literary texts discussed above. Gray (2010, 23) foregrounds the contrast between paratexts which 'grab the viewer before he or she reaches the text and try to control the viewer's entrance to the text' and those which 'flow between the gaps of textual exhibition, or that come to us "during" or "after" viewing'. The former, which Gray (2010, 23) terms 'entry-way paratexts', span elements such as genre, critical reviews, advertising, hype, previews, trailers, spinoff merchandise, and so forth. As both Jones (2008, 152) and Consalvo (2007, 8) observe, the paratexts that proliferate in anticipation of new videogames are particularly numerous, far exceeding those that precede the publication of a literary text.

The paratexts which appear during the viewing or playing of the text, which Gray (2010, 23) terms 'in medias res paratexts', encompass such things as bonus materials, websites, fan discussion forums, alternate reality games, spinoff novels, and mini-episodes, all material through which viewers can continue engaging with a series or regular show in between the actual episodes. The presence of in medias res paratexts, in particular, has profound effects on meaning creation for the text itself: rather than asking what a text *is*, Gray (2010, 41) suggests that we need to know how it *happens*. With regard to serial programmes and films, for example, Gray (2010, 42) argues that 'it would be ludicrous to think that we simply tuck away our interpretative efforts into small corners of our brains, waiting until after the series finale to make sense of a text'. On the contrary, much of our sense-making goes on in the moments between shows, moments which 'are often filled with paratexts' (Gray 2010, 42) such as online discussions or tie-in products. Jones (2008) formulates a similar argument in relation to videogames, suggesting that, far from being contained, as it were, in the text itself, meaning is created in the processes of game-playing and engaging with the 'teeming cloud of dynamically intermediated paratexts' (46):

Video gamers already know in the most practical, mundane ways that meanings are social and collaboratively constructed, that they reside not in self-contained objects, narratives, plots, or dramatic arcs, but in procedurally-enabled dynamic interactions, cooperative and competitive, improvised in conjunction with other 'intelligences'.

173

Hierarchy

The proliferation of paratexts that is a feature of the present-day media landscape leads many theorists to question the supposed hierarchy between text and paratext that is a key feature of Genette's model. Thus Consalvo (2007, 8) argues that the paratextual system that appears in anticipation of and alongside videogames 'isn't the game industry but is closely related to it. To call it peripheral dismisses or ignores its centrality to the gaming experience'. She continues: 'Paratexts are . . . anything but peripheral, and they grow more integral to the digital game industry and player community with every year' (182). In a later publication, she takes this argument still further, analysing cases in which a supposedly peripheral or supplementary element becomes central, and arguing for 'flexibility in when a game text (or any other media text) might become a paratext and vice versa' (Consalvo 2017, 178). Gray (2010, 39) similarly argues that, in some cases, 'paratexts overtake and subsume their texts', providing as an example of such a process the phenomenon of 'fan vidding' (155). Here, fans take clips from a film or show and set them to lyrics of a background song in order to 'offer an interpretation of and/or argument regarding that show' (154); these vids not only shape viewers' interpretations of a particular show or a character within it, but can sometimes 'become texts in and of their own right, watched closely, parsed for meanings, eagerly anticipated, traded in fan communities, given commentary tracks, and becoming the basis for their own conventions' (159). In a similar vein, in her study of the world of *The Girl with the Dragon Tattoo* – which encompasses the *Millennium Trilogy* novels by Stieg Larsson, three Swedish films, a feature film by David Fincher, a graphic novel and a radio drama, as well as various ancillary media and derivative fan productions – Martha Boni (2016, 217) argues that:

> it is increasingly difficult to conceive of paratext in terms of a straightforward correlation to a primary text. Paratexts should no longer be considered just 'thresholds for the interpretation' (as in Genette's work): they have to be considered as separate mini-worlds building up a media 'ecosystem'.

Jones (2008, 69–70) proposes a similar shift in metaphorical conceptualisation, speaking of a 'cobbled-together universe' composed of official and unofficial elements:

> almost any successful game exists in a system of many worlds, only some of which are strictly story-worlds but all of which, I would argue, add to the sum total of the game's universe . . . If there is official story canon, then there is likely

to be unofficial apocrypha, sectarian dispute, Gnostic reinterpretation – and at the outer reaches, fan fiction and slash fiction, mashups and parodies – all of which may be imagined as numerous other small planets or satellites or artificial worlds orbiting along in the collectively cobbled-together universe that contains but is not entirely coextensive with that smaller subset of orderly authorial stories and characters, designs of maps and objects, not to mention the rules and formal constraints on potential gameplay events that are sometimes naively referred to as 'the game itself'.

Nevertheless, scholars in these disciplines do not tend to discard notions of centre and periphery completely. Instead, they stress that, while some paratexts may fit the more traditional view of something that is in service of a core text, others may not – or at least not for particular viewers or at particular moments in time.

Variability

The range and physically disparate nature of paratextual elements associated with films, television shows, and games make it unlikely that any given viewer will encounter the same range of paratexts as another viewer. In recent years, technological developments and more specifically the personalisation of on-demand television interfaces have rendered the question of variability in paratextual experience even more pressing. Gray outlines this issue in relation to Netflix, but it can also be seen to be relevant to other on-demand services as they switch to sign-in-only, personalised models:[26]

> We're all getting potentially really different experiences of texts and of the textual world based on what the various algorithms around us think they know about us. On my Apple TV, for instance, when I log into Netflix, there is no category or menu of Netflix Originals . . . the flow that Netflix gives me is not the flow that Netflix gives you or someone else.
>
> *Brookey and Gray 2017, 104–5*

As with studies of digital paratexts, the issue of variability makes it more apposite to replace the *when* of Genette's model with a *what if*, as well as emphasising the need to find empirical methods for investigating which paratexts are, in Gray's (Brookey and Gray 2017, 105) words, 'loud', rather than 'quiet', which cannot be avoided and which are less likely to be accessed by significant numbers of viewers.

Tensions between industry-created and viewer-created paratexts

The move in media studies to extend the reach of the paratext to encompass viewer-created paratexts in addition to industry-created ones, as outlined above, leads inevitably to the possibility that paratexts might come into conflict with each other in a way that is far less likely under Genette's model. Indeed, Gray (2010, 39) characterises the dynamic of today's paratext-rich media landscape as primarily conflictual rather than complementary, stating, for example, that 'with all sorts of random paratextual or intertextual collisions threatening the encoded meaning of texts, and with devious and critical paratexts or intertexts working to hijack their meaning-making processes, the industry requires a strong frontline of paratexts'. The issue of tensions between paratexts is often brought to the fore by scholars working in fan studies, who stress the ways in which fans are active participants in the processes of meaning production and negotiation that surround a text (see, for example, Henry Jenkins' (1991) seminal work, *Textual Poachers*). In a similar vein, Consalvo's (2007) study of cheating in videogames, mentioned above, devotes considerable attention to conflicts between the paratextual industries and the core game industry, suggesting, for example, that 'hardware was the first consistent area of trouble for the paratextual industry' (64), with the game development industry fighting back against companies involved in developing modifications for games without their authorisation. In an interesting twist on this state of affairs, however, Consalvo also considers the phenomenon of what she terms the 'growing corporatization of the paratextual industries' (12), whereby game industry companies purchase websites and other paratexts developed by fans (see Consalvo 2007, 175–90).

Paratexts of print and online newspapers

In comparison with the high levels of interest in the paratext in the domain of digital and media culture, take-up of the concept in the domain of news analysis has been much less pronounced. The Danish scholar Finn Frandsen (1992) was the first to adapt paratextual theory to news analysis, and it is within Nordic scholarship, and to a lesser extent German scholarship, that engagement with the concept of the paratext in this field of study has found some level of exploration. Frandsen's discussion builds on the two seminal works published by Teun A. van Dijk, *News as Discourse* (1988b) and *News Analysis* (1988a), even though van Dijk himself does not apply the term *paratext* to material found in newspapers.[27] Frandsen (1992, 148) critiques 'that part of van Dijk's "new, interdisciplinary theory of news in the press" . . . which concerns what I call the paratextual structure of the news text'. He goes on to specify that he is taking the paratext to denote 'the headline system of news text (superheadline, main headline, subheadline) as well as the so-called lead' (149), though subsequently argues that any material which functions as a threshold between reader and news text can also be considered paratextual, including – and even particularly – material which derives from section editors rather than the journalist who authors the news article itself (153).

Following on from Frandsen, a number of Scandinavian scholars have drawn on the concept of the paratext in an effort to draw attention to the importance of considering the format and structure of newspapers as part of an analysis of news discourse. Yngve Benestad Hågvar (2012), for example, considers content taxonomies (e.g. 'News', 'Sports', 'Opinion') and section names to be paratexts,[28] and explores the differences between these paratexts in print and online editions of Norwegian newspapers. Hågvar situates the study of paratexts within the field of format studies, which is interested in 'how a medium organizes its contents physically and semiotically' (28), and draws on a theoretical framework developed by Ledin (2000), also based on Frandsen.[29] Hågvar explains that Ledin's format analysis model 'combines multimodal *paratext* analysis with *layout* analysis' (2012, 28, italics in original), thereby aiming to describe, respectively, 'the *thresholds* and *construction* of "semiotic rooms"' (28, italics in original). Ledin's model proposes a categorisation of paratexts based on their levels of generality, their scope and their function (see Hågvar 2012, 28–9).

What is particularly interesting about Hågvar's study is his exploration of the way in which the paratexts – or perhaps what might more accurately be labelled the 'paratextual structure' – of online newspapers actually shape the way in which the texts themselves are written. Hågvar provides the example of a news story about an American mass murderer being sentenced to death. The online newspaper *Dagbladet.no* reported on this story under the 'Celebrity' section, foregrounding the celebrity status of the murderer in both the headline and the opening sentence of the report itself. In contrast, another online paper, *VG Nett*, published the story in their Foreign Affairs section, referring to the murderer in the headline simply as a 'serial killer' rather than as a 'dating show suitor' and foregrounding instead the foreign location of the events (see Hågvar 2012, 32). Furthermore, the very existence of a paratextual tab such as 'Celebrity' influences the generation of texts by journalists or, as Hågvar (30) puts it, 'the fixed nature of the menu invites a continuous production of texts within each section'. This sets the relationship between paratext and text in newspaper contexts somewhat at odds with the relationship envisaged by Genette, in which the paratext is 'only an assistant, only an accessory of the text' (Genette 1997, 410). Here, the paratextual structure and the existence of the paratextual tabs are the primary and prior feature, and the texts are produced to match this paratextual frame.

As in studies of digital culture, distinguishing between text and paratext in certain news contexts can prove difficult. This difficulty is indirectly illustrated by Ulrich Schmitz's (2014) study of print and online newspapers. While Schmitz posits a relatively straightforward distinction between text and paratext in printed newspapers, defining paratexts as 'side texts, which accompany the main text in an inviting, describing, orientating, commenting or subsidiary way' (290), he shows less certainty in distinguishing between them in the case of online newspapers. Schmitz initially makes reference to 'paratextual tabs at the top and bottom of the entire site [of the *Rheinische Post* <*www.rp-online.de*>]' (291) and appears to consider everything else as texts, rather than paratexts, counting seventy-seven texts on the scrollable site. However, Schmitz later refers to these texts as 'paratexts', writing that 'to a larger extent (especially at the bottom of the page) there are only paratexts, i.e. titles of categories, headlines, the link "mehr" [more], and similar link labels or pictograms' (294), and reflecting generally that 'the majority of the front page consists of paratexts and visual characters (e.g. pictograms)' (294). Schmitz's uncertainty over which elements of online newspapers are to be considered 'text' and which 'paratext' indicates the need for more extensive and systematic reflection on the adaptation of Genette's concept of the paratext to the domain of contemporary mass media, a need which is openly acknowledged by Hågvar (2012, 29).

Concluding remarks

As the above discussion makes clear, scholars in digital, media, and communication studies have moulded the notion of the paratext to fit the material at hand, moving quite some distance from Genette's constraining parameters in the process. The extent of the changes to Genette's original conceptualisation of the paratext are encapsulated by the new metaphors proposed in place of Genette's metaphor of the threshold, which see texts and paratexts as part of an 'ecosystem' (Boni 2016, 217) or universe (Jones 2008, 69; McCracken 2013, 110). For the most part, Stanitzek's (2005, 41) optimism about the continuing relevance of the concept of the paratext, expressed over a decade ago, has been shared: as Pesce and Noto (2016a, xxxviii) observe, 'even as the digital revolution causes upheaval and disruption in the evolution of our conceptual tools, . . . something, in this notion of paratext, remains astonishingly relevant'.

Yet these sentiments have not been unanimous. Thus Birke and Christ (2013, 79), for example, suggest that the heuristic value of the paratext concept may reach its eventual limits with regard to '"digital-born" narrative – narrative texts that are created in and for digital media and that are, presumably, at least one step further removed from concepts of the work, the author, and the text as object than are those texts that are merely digitized'. They warn that 'speaking of paratext in interlinked digital environments . . . leaves scholars at the impasse that Genette himself warned of, namely that of "rashly proclaiming that 'all is paratext'"' (80) and conclude that, in such an environment, 'we need new concepts and a new vocabulary'. A similar position is taken by Annika Rockenberger (2014, 253), who questions the way in which Genette's concept has been applied to videogame studies, particularly the fact that it has become, in her view, 'a vague umbrella term with an extremely broad extension, covering almost everything somehow "related to," "referring to," or "surrounding" the primary object (the "video game itself")'. Rockenberger (2014, 253) proposes an alternative terminology which uses 'framings' as 'the higher-order umbrella term' and restricts the use of paratext to 'messages or communicative signals' that meet the criteria of being functionally subservient to the game proper and authorised by 'entitled members of the game's production collective'. The choice presented by Rockenberger – namely to extend Genette's concept as the majority of scholars have done, or to constrain the concept within the parameters established by Genette and look to other terms to denote the material, functions or activities that are excluded from the concept as a result – is, as she argues, 'not a matter of truth and verification but a matter of practical adequacy' (Rockenberger 2014, 271). This is, in many respects, the best summary of the choice that this book is seeking to make with regard to translation studies – and we will return to it in Part III.

Notes

1 For a discussion of this issue, see, for example, Poldsaar (2010).
2 See McCracken (2013, 105–6) for an overview of these developments.
3 For explicit reflection on this issue in relation to e–books, see Smyth (2014, 330).
4 On the latter, see Genette's (1997) description of the text as having a 'relatively immutable identity' (408) – a description which he qualifies in a note: 'very relatively, of course, and very diversely: one has only to think of those medieval works of which no two texts are absolutely alike' (408n10).
5 See also the chapters in Desrochers and Apollon (2014a), most of which sketch a working definition of the paratext based on Genette at the outset.
6 It should be noted that Pressman is writing as the founder of a software strategy and design company (see Pressman 2014, 335). The term *secondary orality* is borrowed from Ong (2012).
7 The suggested typology of functions is intended merely as a way of giving structure to this introduction of a vast and potentially bewildering array of paratextual elements. Alternative typologies of function for digital literature can be found in Nottingham-Martin (2014, 296–7) and Birke and Christ (2013, 67–8), and will be discussed further in Part III.
8 Regarding webpages, see, for example, Stewart (2010) on the production company page for the digital text *Inanimate Alice;* regarding websites, see, for example, Smyth (2014) and McCracken (2013).
9 We should note that printed books sometimes also adopt this practice, including at the end of a book the first chapter of another book by the same author.
10 On this last point, see Hill and Pecoskie (2014, 150–1).
11 See, for example, van Dijk (2014, 25).
12 An ident is 'a short sequence shown on television between programmes to identify the channel' (English Oxford Living Dictionaries n.d.).
13 For a compelling theorisation of the paratextual relevance of toys and action figures, see Suzanne Scott (2017).
14 Alternate reality games are 'a transmedia form of fictional play that is often (though not always) tied into marketing campaigns' (Jones 2008, 11). Jones further explains: 'In ARGs, players engage in an elaborate game of make-believe out in the world; they may use websites, TV shows or ads, payphones, text-messages via cell-phone, even mailed objects, as tokens and forms of expression and communication' (2008, 11).
15 Note, however, that games scholars generally consider games to be texts which have their own range of paratexts.
16 An internet meme is a 'concept or idea that spreads "virally" from one person to another via the Internet' (Beal n.d.).
17 An animated GIF (Graphics Interchange Format) file is 'a graphic image on a Web page that moves – for example, a twirling icon or a banner with a hand that waves or letters that magically get larger' (TechTarget n.d.)
18 Gray (2010, 6) touches on this point, but most of the focus on paratextuality in media studies to date has been on tangible rather than intangible paratexts.
19 Genette does not make this point directly, although he does make witty reference to the voluminous nature of the Pléiade series (Genette 1997, 403). On DVDs, see Benzon's (2013, 93) argument that the 'paratextual surplus' of DVDs 'serve[s] a stark economic imperative'.
20 We will return to the connection between branding and paratexts in Chapter 6.
21 For a succinct justification of this move, see Brookey and Gray (2017, 102–3).
22 It should be noted that these uses of the terms *official* and *unofficial* are different from Genette's: as explained in Chapter 1, Genette's official, semiofficial and unofficial paratexts all refer to material that is connected in some way with the author.
23 It is worth noting that this focus on viewer- or fan-produced paratexts results in a certain level of overlap with enquiries into participatory culture. This phenomenon has been

explored in particular in works by Jenkins (1991, 2006, 2008), and includes the study of fan videos, massively multiplayer online role-playing games (MMORPGs) and web discussion forums, often with an emphasis on the tensions and controversies associated with them. Consalvo's notion of 'paratextual industries' also overlaps with what Grainge and Johnson (2015) term 'promotional screen industries'.

24 Gray (2016, 35) similarly stresses that 'most directors and showrunners are single agents in a large network of authorship, where the media corporation that owns their property controls much of the rest of that network'.

25 A similar point is made by Boni (2016, 219) in relation to the paratexts of *The Girl with the Dragon Tattoo*, particularly in light of the short-lived paratexts that were part of a 'viral' campaign.

26 For a discussion of the varying levels to which UK channels are personalising their on-demand interfaces, see Johnson (2017, 131).

27 The wording used by Frandsen (1992) in his chapter is rather misleading. For example, he writes that 'van Dijk is very cautious in his definition of the paratext' (149) and also includes a section entitled 'Objections to van Dijk's Concept of the Paratext' (152). However, an examination of van Dijk's work shows that van Dijk does not employ the term *paratext* or cite Genette anywhere. To be fair to Frandsen, after presenting a definition of the paratext based on van Dijk, he does stress that 'this wording cannot be found directly in van Dijk's two books' (149), but overall he does not make it clear that the concept of the paratext as such finds no direct expression in van Dijk at all.

28 From his summary of Ledin's framework, however, we can see that he also considers such elements as headlines, bylines and hyperlinks to be paratexts.

29 As Ledin's original book is in Swedish, a language in which I have no expertise beyond words picked up while watching Scandi-noir, this section limits itself to Hågvar's summary of Ledin's framework.

References

Aström, Frederik. 2014. "The Context of Paratext: A Bibliometric Study of the Citation Contexts of Gérard Genette's Texts". In *Examining Paratextual Theory and its Applications in Digital Culture*, edited by Nadine Desrochers and Daniel Apollon, 1–23. IGI Global.

Barthes, Roland. 1977. *Image/Music/Text*. Translated by Stephen Heath. Glasgow: Fontana-Collins.

Beal, Vangie. n.d. *Wepopedia: Internet meme*. Accessed 9 June 2017 from www.webopedia.com/TERM/I/internet_meme.html.

Benzon, Paul. 2013. "Bootleg Paratextuality and Digital Temporality: Towards an Alternate Present of the DVD". *Narrative* 21 (1): 88–104.

Bhaskar, M. 2011. "Towards Paracontent: Marketing, Publishing and Cultural Form in a Digital Environment". *Logos* 22 (1): 25–36.

Birke, Dorothee, and Birte Christ. 2013. "Paratext and Digitized Narrative: Mapping the Field". *Narrative* 21 (1): 65–87.

Böhnke, Alexander. 2004. "Wasserzeichen". In *Paratexte in Literatur, Film, Fernsehen*, edited by Klaus Kreimeier and Georg Stanitzek, 225–43. Berlin: Akademie Verlag.

——. 2007. *Paratexte des Films: Über die Grenzen des filmischen Universums*. Bielefeld: transcript Verlag.

Boni, Martha. 2016. "*The Girl with the Dragon Tattoo*: Paratexts in a Flexible World". In *The Politics of Ephemeral Digital Media: Permanence and Obsolescence in Paratexts*, edited by Sara Pesce and Paolo Noto, 213–27. New York and London: Routledge.

Bordalejo, Barbara. 2014. "Get out of my Sandbox: Web Publication, Authority, and Originality". In *Examining Paratextual Theory and its Applications in Digital Culture*, edited by Nadine Desrochers and Daniel Apollon, 128–42. IGI Global.

Brookey, Robert, and Jonathan Gray. 2017. "'Not Merely Para': Continuing Steps in Paratextual Research". *Critical Studies in Media Communication* 34 (2): 101–10.

Consalvo, Mia. 2007. *Cheating: Gaining Advantage in Videogames.* Cambridge, MA: MIT Press.

———. 2017. "When Paratexts Become Texts: De-centering the Game-as-Text". *Critical Studies in Media Communication* 34 (2): 177–83.

de Mourgues, Nicole. 1994. *Le Générique de film.* Paris: Méridiens-Klincksieck.

Desrochers, Nadine, and Daniel Apollon, eds. 2014a. *Examining Paratextual Theory and its Applications in Digital Culture.* IGI Global.

———. 2014b. "Introduction". In *Examining Paratextual Theory and its Applications in Digital Culture,* edited by Nadine Desrochers and Daniel Apollon, xxix–xxxix. IGI Global.

Ellis, John. 2011. "Interstitials: How the 'Bits in Between' Define the Programmes". In *Ephemeral Media: Transitory Screen Culture from Television to YouTube,* edited by Paul Grainge, 59–69. London: British Film Institute.

English Oxford Living Dictionaries. n.d. "ident". *English Oxford Living Dictionaries.* Accessed 21 June 2017 from https://en.oxforddictionaries.com/definition/ident.

Frandsen, Finn. 1992. "News Discourse: The Paratextual Structure of News Texts". In *Nordic Research on Text and Discourse: Nordtext Symposium 1990,* edited by Ann-Charlotte Lindeberg, Nils Erik Enkvist and Kay Wikberg, 147–60. Åbo: Åbo Akademis förlag.

Genette, Gérard. 1997. *Paratexts: Thresholds of Interpretation.* Translated by Jane E. Lewin. Cambridge: Cambridge University Press.

Grainge, Paul. 2011a. "Introduction: Ephemeral Media". In *Ephemeral Media. Transitory Screen Culture from Television to YouTube,* edited by Paul Grainge, 1–19. London: British Film Institute.

———. 2011b. "TV Promotion and Broadcast Design: An Interview with Charlie Mawer, Red Bee Media". In *Ephemeral Media: Transitory Screen Culture from Television to YouTube,* edited by Paul Grainge, 87–101. London: British Film Institute.

Grainge, Paul, and Catherine Johnson. 2015. *Promotional Screen Industries.* Abingdon and New York: Routledge.

Gray, Jonathan. 2010. *Show Sold Separately: Promos, Spoilers, and other Media Paratexts.* New York and London: New York University Press.

———. 2016. "The Politics of Paratextual Ephemeralia". In *The Politics of Ephemeral Digital Media: Permanence and Obsolescence in Paratexts,* edited by Sara Pesce and Paolo Noto, 32–44. New York and London: Routledge.

Hågvar, Yngve Benestad. 2012. "Labelling Journalism: The Discourse of Sectional Paratexts in Print and Online Newspapers". *Nordicom Review* 33 (2): 27–42.

Hill, Heather L., and Jan Pecoskie. 2014. "Iterations and Evolutions: Paratext and Intertext in Fanfiction". In *Examining Paratextual Theory and its Applications to Digital Culture,* edited by Nadine Desrochers and Daniel Apollon, 143–58. IGI Global.

Jenkins, Henry. 1991. *Textual Poachers: Television Fans and Participatory Culture.* New York: Routledge.

———. 2006. *Fans, Gamers, and Bloggers: Exploring Participatory Culture.* New York: New York University Press.

———. 2008. *Convergence Culture: Where Old and New Media Collide.* New York: New York University Press.

Johnson, Catherine. 2012. *Branding Television.* London and New York: Routledge.

———. 2017. "Beyond Catch-up: VoD Interfaces, ITV Hub and the Repositioning of Television Online". *Critical Studies in Television* 12 (2): 121–38.

Jones, Steven E. 2008. *The Meaning of Video Games: Gaming and Textual Strategies.* New York and London: Routledge.

Kreimeier, Klaus, and Georg Stanitzek, eds. 2004. *Paratexte in Literatur, Film, Fernsehen*. Berlin: Akademie Verlag.

Ledin, P. 2000. *Veckopressens historia: Del II [History of the Weekly Press: Part II]*. Lund: Svensk sakprosa.

McCracken, Ellen. 2013. "Expanding Genette's Epitext/Peritext Model for Transitional Electronic Literature: Centrifugal and Centripetal Vectors on Kindles and iPads". *Narrative* 21 (1): 105–24.

Mittell, Jason. 2015. *Complex TV: The Poetics of Contemporary Television Storytelling*. New York: New York University Press.

Nottingham-Martin, Amy. 2014. "Thresholds of Transmedia Storytelling: Applying Gérard Genette's Paratextual Theory to *The 39 Clues* Series for Young Readers". In *Examining Paratextual Theory and its Applications in Digital Culture*, edited by Nadine Desrochers and Daniel Apollon, 287–307. IGI Global.

Ong, Walter J. 2012. *Orality and Literacy: The Technologizing of the Word*, 3rd edition. London: Routledge.

Pesce, Sara, and Paolo Noto, eds. 2016a. *The Politics of Ephemeral Digital Media: Permanence and Obsolescence in Paratexts*. New York and London: Routledge.

——. 2016b. "The Politics of Ephemeral Digital Media: Permanence and Obsolescence in Paratexts". In *The Politics of Ephemeral Digital Media: Permanence and Obsolescence in Paratexts*, edited by Sara Pesce and Paolo Noto, 1–9. New York and London: Routledge.

Poldsaar, Raili. 2010. "Foucault Framing Foucault: The Role of Paratexts in the English Translation of *The Order of Things*". *Neohelicon* 37: 263–73.

Pressman, Corey. 2014. "Post-Book Paratext: Designing for Haptic Harmony". In *Examining Paratextual Theory and its Applications in Digital Culture*, edited by Nadine Desrochers and Daniel Apollon, 334–48. IGI Global.

Ricoeur, Paul. 1991. *From Text to Action: Essays in Hermeneutics, II*. Translated by K. Blamey and J.B. Thompson. Evanston, IL: Northwestern University.

Rockenberger, Annika. 2014. "Video Game Framings". In *Examining Paratextual Theory and its Applications in Digital Culture*, edited by Nadine Desrochers and Daniel Apollon, 252–86. IGI Global.

Schmitz, Ulrich. 2014. "Semiotic Economy, Growth of Mass Media Discourse, and Change of Written Language through Multimodal Techniques. The Case of Newspapers (Printed and Online) and Web Services". In *Mediatization and Sociolinguistic Change*, edited by Jannis Androutsopoulos, 279–304. Berlin and Boston: De Gruyter.

Scott, Suzanne. 2017. "#Wheresrey?: Toys, Spoilers, and the Gender Politics of Franchise Paratexts". *Critical Studies in Media Communication* 34 (2): 138–47.

Smyth, Patrick. 2014. "Ebooks and the Digital Paratext: Emerging Trends in the Interpretation of Digital Media". In *Examining Paratextual Theory and its Applications in Digital Culture*, edited by Nadine Desrochers and Daniel Apollon, 314–33. IGI Global.

Stanitzek, Georg. 2005. "Texts and Paratexts in Media". *Critical Inquiry* 32 (1): 27–42.

Stewart, Gavin. 2010. "The Paratexts of *Inanimate Alice*: Thresholds, Genre Expectations and Status". *Convergence* 16 (1): 57–74.

Strehovec, Janez. 2014. "E-literary Text and New Media Paratexts". In *Examining Paratextual Theory and its Applications in Digital Culture*, edited by Nadine Desrochers and Daniel Apollon, 46–62. IGI Global.

TechTarget. n.d. *animated GIF (Graphics Interchange Format)*. Accessed 20 June 2017 from http://searchmicroservices.techtarget.com/definition/animated-GIF-Graphics-Interchange-Format.

van Dijk, Teun. 1988a. *News Analysis: Case Studies of International and National News in the Press*. Hillsdale, NJ: Lawrence Erlbaum.

——. 1988b. *News as Discourse*. Hillsdale, NJ: Lawrence Erlbaum.

van Dijk, Yra. 2014. "The Margins of Bookishness: Paratexts in Digital Literature". In *Examining Paratextual Theory and its Applications in Digital Culture*, edited by Nadine Desrochers and Daniel Apollon, 24–45. IGI Global.

Vitali-Rosati, Marcello. 2014. "Digital Paratext, Editorialization, and the Very Death of the Author". In *Examining Paratextual Theory and its Applications in Digital Culture*, edited by Nadine Desrochers and Daniel Apollon, 110–27. IGI Global.

——. 2016. "Digital Architectures: The Web, Editorialization and Metaontology". *Azimuth: Philosophical Coordinates in Modern and Contemporary Age* 4 (7): 95–111.

PART II
Case studies

4

AUTHORISED TRANSLATIONS AND PARATEXTUAL RELEVANCE

English versions of Nietzsche

In this chapter, I return to the idea that translations can be considered to be paratexts to the work in the original language, as evoked by Genette and discussed in Chapter 1. Genette's (1997, 405) suggestion that the paratextual relevance of a translation is particularly strong when there is a close connection between translator and author can perhaps best be illuminated in theoretical terms by analogy with another form of textual transfer, namely that from written text to audiobook. In an article exploring the development of e-books and digital paratexts, Patrick Smyth (2014, 324) makes a cogent case for viewing audiobooks as paratexts to original works when those audiobooks are narrated by the author:

> From one perspective, [audiobooks] are simply an alternate way of presenting or bounding a central text. This is a particularly useful way of looking at recorded books narrated by their authors rather than by professional actors. This practice . . . is paratextual in the sense that it facilitates another level of interpretation – when reading his or her own work, an author can give emphasis or nuance to particular sections of the text, or may provide characterization or emotional interpretations that go beyond what listeners might experience were they to consume the book in a more conventional manner.

If we imagine a scenario in which an author translates his or her own work into another language, or has significant input into that process, it should be possible to recognise, in the translation, places where emphasis has been given to particular aspects, nuances introduced, or new insights given into characterisation and so on. This is presumably the mode of reading that Genette is suggesting we follow when he argues the case for translations being a kind of paratext, and it raises the question of whether authorised translations can lay claim to particular paratextual relevance. In this chapter, I ask what the notion of 'authorised translation' means and take the

English translations of Nietzsche's works as a case study through which to explore the questions raised by the phenomenon in more detail.

Authorisation of translations

Although the term *authorised translation* has a long history of use in English, notably in connection with Bible translation, definitions of the term are difficult to find. Specialist reference books such as the *Dictionary of Translation Studies* (Shuttleworth and Cowie 1997), the *Routledge Encyclopedia of Translation Studies* (Baker and Saldanha 2008) and the *Handbook of Translation Studies* (Gambier and van Doorslaer 2013) contain no dedicated entry for the term, although mention is made of authorised translations, notably the Authorised Version of the Bible, in a number of places (see, for example, Baker and Saldanha (2008, 24, 346) and Valdeón (2013, 113)). The term is also absent from general dictionaries and encyclopedias.

This absence of clear definition allows for a significant degree of latitude in use of the term, in line with the loose range of meanings of the adjective *authorised*. According to the *Oxford English Dictionary*, when the adjective *authorised* is related to 'an action, undertaking, product, etc.', it means 'legally or duly sanctioned; having official or formal approval' (*Oxford English Dictionary* 2017). When applied to translation, this definition leaves open the key question of agent: legally or duly sanctioned by whom (or by which institution)? Having the official or formal approval of whom? In order for the term *authorised translation* to convey adequate meaning, it would need to include this information alongside the fact (or claim) that the translation has been authorised; invariably, however, the term *authorised translation* is used on its own in the most prominent parts of translation paratexts, and information on the agent behind the authorisation has to be uncovered from a careful reading of other paratexts, if indeed it is present at all.

Reliance on the semantic value of *authorised* as an adjective allows for still further ambiguity when related to translation, however. The second and third meanings of the adjective given in the OED are:

2. Of a person: that has been given authority; placed in a position of authority; formally appointed to a particular role or duty.
3. That is acknowledged as authoritative; thoroughly established; highly esteemed.

Oxford English Dictionary 2017

Although proper use of the second meaning of *authorised* would require it to collocate with *translator*, rather than *translation*, it is perfectly feasible to imagine the term *authorised translation* being used in such a way as to imply that the translation has been produced by an authorised translator, thus making the end product authorised. In other words, when we see the term *authorised translation*, the term could be suggesting that the translation has undergone any one of three processes; namely,

1) Someone (or some institution) has given the translation formal approval.
2) The translator, editor or publisher has been formally appointed by someone (or some institution) to undertake the translation.
3) The translation has come to be regarded as authoritative or highly esteemed by an unspecified person, group of people or institution.

If we were to undertake a history of authorised translations – something which, to my knowledge, has yet to be done[1] – we would see that the term is also used in conjunction with a fourth process, namely:

4) The translator or editor claims authorised status for the translation through use of the term *authorised translation* in the translation's paratexts.

In this fourth scenario, authorisation is not formally given by any external body; rather, the translator appeals to some kind of connection with an institution or individual – very often the author – to make a case for his or her translation having special status. When the term *authorised translation* is used in this way, it is used performatively, or at least aspires to be: the translator or editor hopes that by labelling the work as authorised, it will take on the status of an authorised product, even if the grounds on which authorisation is claimed are not always explicitly laid out or may be tenuous. As we will see in our case study, this performative act is vulnerable to challenge and reversal.

In this chapter, I will explore the case of the so-called 'first' authorised English translation of Nietzsche's works, examining the grounds on which authorisation was originally claimed, and exploring the way in which those grounds became problematic for the reception of Nietzsche's work in England. In the final part of the chapter, I reflect on connections – or lack of – between authorisation and paratextual value.

Nietzsche: the 'first authorised' English translation

The 'Complete Works of Friedrich Nietzsche First Complete and Authorised English Translation in Eighteen Volumes', edited by Oscar Levy, was published in the UK between 1909 and 1913. Oscar Levy was a German-Jewish physician who settled in London in 1894 and became part of the New Age circle, a group of writers and intellectuals centred around A.R. Orage (see Stone 2002, 12). Levy described himself as a convert to Nietzsche's thought, and drew on private funds to finance the publication of the English translation (Stone 2002, 13).

The status of the Levy series as the authorised translation of Nietzsche's works is made clear on the front cover of each volume, each one displaying in identical format the words 'The Complete Works of Friedrich Nietzsche: The First Complete and Authorised English Translation Edited by Dr Oscar Levy', followed by a picture of Nietzsche, the volume number and the title of the work (see, for example, Figure 4.1).

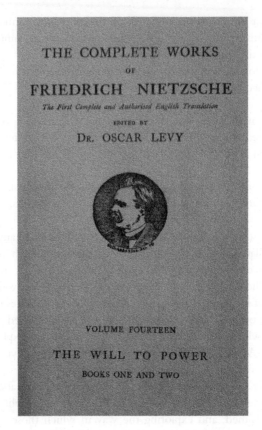

FIGURE 4.1 Front cover of *The Will to Power*, volume 14 in *The Complete Works of Friedrich Nietzsche*, edited by Oscar Levy

The name of the translator appears only on the inside title page, rather than on the more prominent front cover. This implies that it is the fact that the translation belongs to the authorised series that is of utmost importance, rather than the name or expertise of the translator in question. The claim to authorisation is repeated at the end of each book through the reproduction of a standard template giving the list of translations in the series, under the heading 'The works of Friedrich Nietzsche: First Complete and Authorised English Translation'. This template is gradually developed as the works are published, and in the back matter to *Early Greek Philosophy and Other Essays*, which appeared in 1911, is supplemented by a paragraph which directly asserts the quality of the translations: 'It is claimed for these translations that they have been written by accomplished German scholars, who have spared no pains to render the poetical, passionate, racy, and witty style of Nietzsche in adequate English' (Nietzsche 1911, back matter). While this descriptive paragraph underlines the quality of the translations, it does not engage with the notion of authorisation as such, and the series thus claims authorised status for itself without outlining explicitly the process through which authorisation was acquired, or indeed engaging with the complexities of such a notion, particularly in the context of a deceased author.

If there is any such outline, it is to be found in Levy's 'Editorial Note' to the first volume in the series. Here, Levy appears to be basing the claim for the translations' authorised status on the way in which the rights for the translations were acquired, foregrounding his direct connections to Nietzsche's sister, Elisabeth Förster-Nietzsche, holder of the copyright to Nietzsche's work and controller of the Nietzsche archive:

> The Editor, during a recent visit to Mrs. Förster–Nietzsche at Weimar, acquired the rights of translation by pointing out to her that in this way her brother's works would not fall into the hands of an ordinary publisher and his staff of translators: he has not, therefore, entered into any engagement with publishers, not even with the present one, which could hinder his task, bind him down to any text found faulty, or make him consent to omissions or the falsification or 'sugaring' of the original text to further the sale of the books.
>
> *Levy 1910a, viii*

Connections to Förster-Nietzsche are also emphasised in the template in the back matter of the translations, mentioned above: *The Birth of Tragedy* is advertised as being 'with Biographical Introduction by the Author's Sister', and *Thus Spake Zarathustra* is described as being 'with Introduction by Mrs Förster-Nietzsche'. Further appeals to material by Förster-Nietzsche and reproductions of her perspective on Nietzsche's life and works can be found in the prefaces to *Beyond Good and Evil* (Common 1923, xiv),[2] *The Will to Power* (Ludovici 1914, vii, ix–x) and, more briefly, *Ecce Homo* (Ludovici 1911, xiv).

Levy's account of his trip to Weimar implies that he is the first person to acquire such English translation rights, and also suggests that the direct line between himself and Nietzsche's sister guarantees the translations' authenticity. What Levy crucially fails to mention, however, is that authorised translations of several of Nietzsche's works were already in existence: Alexander Tille's translation of *Thus Spake Zarathustra* was published in 1896 by Henry and Co in London and by MacMillan & Co in New York, and subsequently republished by Fisher Unwin in London in 1899; Thomas Common's translation of *The Case of Wagner* was also published in 1896 by Henry and Co in London and by MacMillan & Co in New York, and subsequently republished by Fisher Unwin in London in 1899; William Haussmann's translation of *A Genealogy of Morals* was published in 1897 by MacMillan & Co in New York (Henry and Co having ceased publishing by this point) and in 1899 by Fisher Unwin in London; Johanna Volz's translation of *The Dawn of Day* was published in 1903 by Fisher Unwin in London and by MacMillan & Co in New York; Helen Zimmern's translation of *Beyond Good and Evil* was published in 1907 by The Darien Press in Edinburgh and by MacMillan & Co in New York.[3] These translations were originally envisaged as part of the 'Sole Authorised English and American Edition' and, in the case of the publications by Henry and Co and Fisher Unwin, are labelled explicitly as such in the front matter, as Figures 4.2 and 4.3 illustrate.[4]

The back matter of the 1896 volumes repeats the claim to authorisation, and lists the other volumes that are planned in the series (see Figure 4.4).[5]

By stating that the translations are being '[i]ssued under the supervision of the '"Nietzsche Archiv" at Naumburg', the publishers indicate that the claim to be the 'sole authorised edition' is based on the fact that the official holder of the rights to Nietzsche's works has agreed to the translations, and also (through use of the word 'supervision') has some level of involvement in the way in which they are carried out.[6]

Helen Zimmern's translation of *Beyond Good and Evil*, which was completed at the same time as *The Case of Wagner* and *Thus Spake Zarathustra*, and was supposed to form one of the volumes in the 'sole authorised' series, as confirmed by Figure 4.4 above, was subject to long publication delays. These were caused initially by the collapse of Henry and Co and then, depending on whose account is believed, by problems finding another publisher owing to Nietzsche's unpopularity in Britain (Levy 1924 [1913], ix–x) or to Elisabeth Förster-Nietzsche's obstructive behaviour (Common 1915, 115). When the translation was finally published in 1907 by 'The Good European Society', a

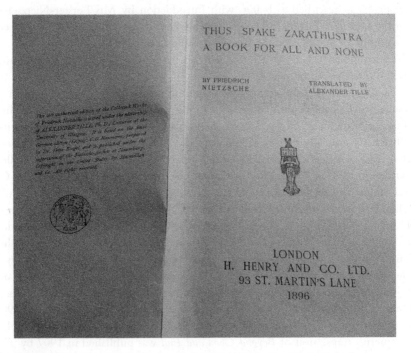

FIGURE 4.2 Front matter of *Thus Spake Zarathustra* (Henry and Co, 1896)

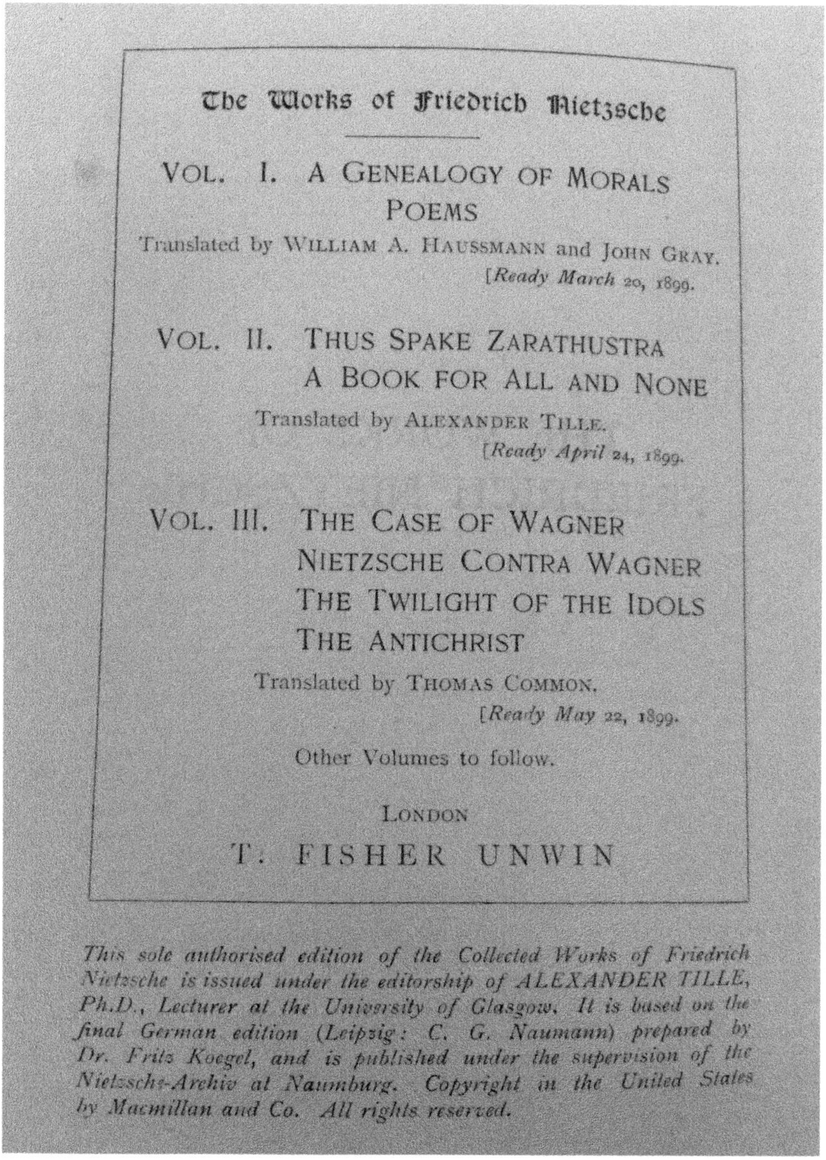

The Works of Friedrich Nietzsche

VOL. I. A GENEALOGY OF MORALS
POEMS
Translated by WILLIAM A. HAUSSMANN and JOHN GRAY.
[*Ready March* 20, 1899.

VOL. II. THUS SPAKE ZARATHUSTRA
A BOOK FOR ALL AND NONE
Translated by ALEXANDER TILLE.
[*Ready April* 24, 1899.

VOL. III. THE CASE OF WAGNER
NIETZSCHE CONTRA WAGNER
THE TWILIGHT OF THE IDOLS
THE ANTICHRIST
Translated by THOMAS COMMON.
[*Ready May* 22, 1899.

Other Volumes to follow.

LONDON

T. FISHER UNWIN

This sole authorised edition of the Collected Works of Friedrich Nietzsche is issued under the editorship of ALEXANDER TILLE, Ph.D., Lecturer at the University of Glasgow. It is based on the final German edition (Leipzig: C. G. Naumann) prepared by Dr. Fritz Koegel, and is published under the supervision of the Nietzsche-Archiv at Naumburg. Copyright in the United States by Macmillan and Co. All rights reserved.

FIGURE 4.3   Front matter of *A Genealogy of Morals* (Fisher Unwin, 1899)

'one-man operation in the person of Thomas Common' (Diethe 2014, 383),[7] the front matter did not present the work as part of the 'sole authorised edition', but rather claimed authorisation for the individual volume on the title page, as Figure 4.5 shows.

The reason for the disappearance of the 'sole authorised edition' label presumably lies in the complex disagreements and uncertainties that surrounded the English

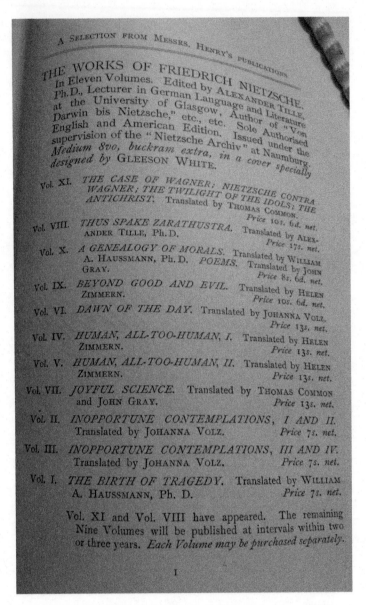

A SELECTION FROM MESSRS. HENRY'S PUBLICATIONS

THE WORKS OF FRIEDRICH NIETZSCHE. In Eleven Volumes. Edited by ALEXANDER TILLE, Ph.D., Lecturer in German Language and Literature at the University of Glasgow, Author of "Von Darwin bis Nietzsche," etc., etc. Sole Authorised English and American Edition. Issued under the supervision of the "Nietzsche Archiv" at Naumburg. *Medium 8vo, buckram extra, in a cover specially designed by* GLEESON WHITE.

Vol. XI. *THE CASE OF WAGNER; NIETZSCHE CONTRA WAGNER; THE TWILIGHT OF THE IDOLS; THE ANTICHRIST.* Translated by THOMAS COMMON.
Price 10s. 6d. net.

Vol. VIII. *THUS SPAKE ZARATHUSTRA.* Translated by ALEXANDER TILLE, Ph.D.
Price 17s. net.

Vol. X. *A GENEALOGY OF MORALS.* Translated by WILLIAM A. HAUSSMANN, Ph.D. *POEMS.* Translated by JOHN GRAY.
Price 8s. 6d. net.

Vol. IX. *BEYOND GOOD AND EVIL.* Translated by HELEN ZIMMERN.
Price 10s. 6d. net.

Vol. VI. *DAWN OF THE DAY.* Translated by JOHANNA VOLZ.
Price 13s. net.

Vol. IV. *HUMAN, ALL-TOO-HUMAN, I.* Translated by HELEN ZIMMERN.
Price 13s. net.

Vol. V. *HUMAN, ALL-TOO-HUMAN, II.* Translated by HELEN ZIMMERN.
Price 13s. net.

Vol. VII. *JOYFUL SCIENCE.* Translated by THOMAS COMMON and JOHN GRAY.
Price 13s. net.

Vol. II. *INOPPORTUNE CONTEMPLATIONS, I AND II.* Translated by JOHANNA VOLZ.
Price 7s. net.

Vol. III. *INOPPORTUNE CONTEMPLATIONS, III AND IV.* Translated by JOHANNA VOLZ.
Price 7s. net.

Vol. I. *THE BIRTH OF TRAGEDY.* Translated by WILLIAM A. HAUSSMANN, Ph.D.
Price 7s. net.

Vol. XI and Vol. VIII have appeared. The remaining Nine Volumes will be published at intervals within two or three years. *Each Volume may be purchased separately.*

I

FIGURE 4.4 Back matter of *Thus Spake Zarathustra* (Henry and Co, 1896)

translations following Förster-Nietzsche's assertion of control over the Nietzsche Archive, and which are outlined in Thatcher (1970) and Common (1915). These disagreements seemingly made presenting the translation as part of the 1896 edition impossible, even though the translation itself had been undertaken under the auspices of that agreement.[8] The grounds on which authorisation for Zimmern's translation is claimed are not made explicit anywhere in the front or back matter,

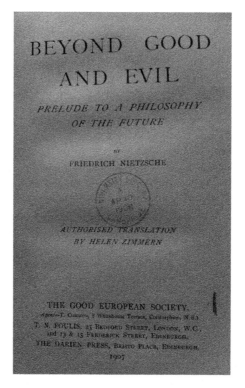

FIGURE 4.5   Front matter of *Beyond Good and Evil*, translated by Helen Zimmern (The Darien Press, 1907)

but an implicit justification can be found in the introduction to the translation, written by Common:

> Nietzsche was personally acquainted with Miss Helen Zimmern – her important book on Schopenhauer brought her under his notice – and, as appears from his letters, he had her in view as a translator of his works: this led her to undertake the task of rendering this volume into English.
>
> *Common 1907, xiv*

What is striking about this statement, to my mind, is not so much the shift in the grounds for authorisation as the fact that more is not made of this direct connection between Zimmern and Nietzsche, which is both well documented and far from inconsequential. A German Jew who had emigrated with her family to England as a child, Zimmern came to wider attention – including that of Richard Wagner – after the publication of her biography of Schopenhauer in 1876 (Young 2010, 391). She first met Nietzsche in Bayreuth through contact with Wagner (Diethe (1996, 99; Young 2010, 391), and corresponded with him later that same year.[9] She overlapped with Nietzsche in Sils Maria in the summers of 1884 and 1886 (Diethe 1996, 99). According to a variety of sources, she and Nietzsche were frequently to be found engaged in deep conversation: when Meta von Salis and her mother went to Sils Maria in September 1886, for example, 'they arrived in the Alpenrose Hotel to find Nietzsche sitting in a corner talking to Helen Zimmern' (Diethe 1996, 84; see also Young (2010, 432)); elsewhere it is reported that Nietzsche 'frequently walked with her [Zimmern] beside Lake Silvaplana and discussed his current work' (Creffield 2004). In late 1888, when Nietzsche started to seek out translators for *Götzen-Dämmerung* and *Ecce Homo*, he wrote to Peter Gast (Heinrich Köselitz), asking his opinion of Zimmern as a possible translator: 'she introduced Schopenhauer to the English, why not his antipode?' (Nietzsche to Köselitz, 9 December 1888, in Nietzsche (1984, 514, my translation)). He also told his publisher, Constantin Georg Naumann, that he was in discussion with Zimmern, 'an excellent author' (Nietzsche to Naumann, 17 December 1888, in Nietzsche (1984, 530, my translation)) with regard to the English translation of *Ecce Homo*, mentioning her also to Franz Overbeck in a letter dated 29 December 1888, this time as the translator he is envisaging for *Götzen-Dämmerung* (see Nietzsche 1984, 559). To Zimmern herself, he drafts a letter in early December 1888, explaining that he is waging an attack on Christianity in two parts: first in *Ecce Homo*, which is to be published simultaneously in German, French and English; and then in *The Antichrist*, asking Zimmern directly if she will take on the English translation of these works (see Nietzsche to Zimmern, circa 8 December 1888, in Nietzsche (1984, 511)). This letter was made available to the editors of the *Nietzsche Briefwechsel* only in draft form and it is not clear whether it was ever actually sent; what is clear is that Nietzsche also wrote Zimmern a shorter letter, dated 17 December 1888, asking her to translate Peter Gast's essay, *Nietzsche-Wagner* (which had appeared in the journal *Der Kunstwart* and with which Nietzsche was delighted), 'for one of the big newspapers' (Nietzsche to Zimmern, 17 December 1888, in Nietzsche (1984, 536, my translation)). He explains that it is absolutely necessary for him to become known in England now, since it is his intention to 'destroy Christianity' (Nietzsche 1984, 536, my translation), something which will require access to the freedom of the press of America, England and France. In contrast to the direct proposition expressed in the draft letter, Nietzsche offers to send her the manuscript 'wenn Sie Lust haben' (Nietzsche 1984, 536) [if you like]. He also says he will send Zimmern a copy of *Götzen-Dämmerung*, suggesting: 'you could potentially introduce this piece in England' (Nietzsche 1984, 536, my translation). Although Nietzsche's mental collapse just weeks later would mean that these discussions with Zimmern never reached a definitive conclusion, it is clear that Nietzsche saw her as a suitable translator of his work into English, valuing her reputation as a writer, her insight into his work, and her potential to open doors for his work in England (he boasts in his letter to Naumann that she writes for *The Times*, amongst other papers).

In light of the fact that Zimmern was the only one of any of the English translators of Nietzsche to have been directly approached by him to translate his work, Common seems to make rather weak use of this potential grounds for describing Zimmern's translation as 'authorised'. This may have been a result of hesitations over the quality of Zimmern's translation, since he follows this outline of

Nietzsche's and Zimmern's connections with the defensive statement that he and others have spent 'a great deal of labour . . . in making the version as satisfactory as possible' (Common 1907, xiv). Whatever the reason, the contrast between the prominent advertising of the translation's authorised status on the title page and the opaque grounds on which authorisation is being claimed is stark.

In light of the existence of both Zimmern's 'authorised translation' and of the four volumes of Tille's 'sole authorised edition', Levy's labelling of his 1909–13 series as the 'First Complete and Authorised Translation' appears deeply problematic.[10] According to the article that Thomas Common published in his own quarterly, *The Good European Point of View*, in 1915, Levy's behaviour towards the translators associated with the 1896 series was far from ethical: Common accuses him of 'trying to deauthorise Dr Hassumann's original copyright-preserving translation of "The Genealogy of Morals" by substituting in its place the inferior, careless translation of one of his creatures' (Common 1915, 116), and of doing the same for *The Case of Wagner*. He also criticises Levy's behaviour towards the two women involved in the original project, 'humiliat[ing] or attempting to humiliate' Johanna Volz by 'superseding her originally authorised translation of "The Dawn of Day" with another one' (Common 1915, 118), and refusing to allow Helen Zimmern to translate *Ecce Homo* and the second volume of *Human, all too Human*, both of which had been assigned to her by the Nietzsche Archive, and, in the case of *Ecce Homo*, which 'Nietzsche *himself* had wished her to translate' (Common 1915, 118, italics in original).

When the 1907 edition of Zimmern's translation of *Beyond Good and Evil* is compared to the version that appeared in Levy's series (this being one of the original translations that he did not replace with a new one), the deauthorisation of the earlier edition can be seen not only in the removal of the label from the title page, but also in the decision not to include status-enhancing information about Zimmern in the paratexts. In the 1907 edition, the back matter features a selection of books by Zimmern, as shown in Figure 4.6. This information serves not only to advertise these books, but also to highlight her status as an author and intellectual.

In line with the other volumes in the series, the Levy version includes no back matter at all, and the front matter paratexts foreground the identity of the series rather than that of the individual translators, as noted above. The introduction by Common, with its information about Zimmern's connection to Nietzsche, does remain, but the part of the paragraph that deals with the improvements made to Zimmern's translation by other people is strengthened by giving the name and status-enhancing information of the German scholar who contributed to the process.[11] I do not have space to explore the extent to which Levy's treatment of Zimmern was guided by her gender, but playing down her achievements as an author in her own right and guaranteeing the quality of her work by stressing the contribution and status of three men is certainly in line with Levy's views on women.[12]

Returning to the question of authorisation, and to Common's (1915) criticism of Levy's behaviour, Common not only criticises Levy for his dishonourable behaviour towards the first translators, but also addresses the issue of whether

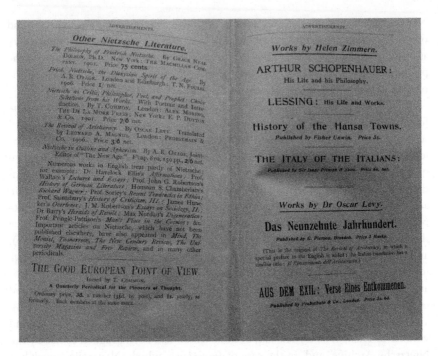

FIGURE 4.6 Back matter of *Beyond Good and Evil*, translated by Helen Zimmern (The Darien Press, 1907)

or not Levy's edition can truly claim to be an 'authorised' one. It is worth citing this part of his article in full, as it helps us interrogate the notion of authorisation and what it might have been considered to mean in the context of the Nietzsche translations:

> With regard to the boasted authorisedness of Dr Levy's edition, Mrs Förster-Nietzsche could confer no authorisation whatever on the greater part of the works of which the copyright had lapsed long ago. And if she insists on rejecting Naumann's authorisation, and our copyright-preserving translations derived therefrom, as she does when angry, there is still less that she could authorise. She could, perhaps, legally authorise 'The Will to Power' and 'Ecce Homo,' which were not included in Naumann's authorisation, and of which the copyright had not lapsed, but that is about all the authorisation she could confer. Any other authorisation in Dr Levy's edition has been conferred by his getting hold of some of the translations originally authorised by Naumann, whose authorisation, however, Mrs Förster-Nietzsche foolishly repudiates. It is not honourable, therefore, to claim authorisation for the other volumes; and Dr Levy's edition generally has far less direct authority than what was conferred on Messrs Henry's edition.
>
> *Common 1915, 117*

Common's dispute of the 'authorisedness' of Levy's version is founded on a copyright-based view of authorisation, with the question of whether or not a translation is authorised ultimately coming down to whether the rights for the translation were sold or granted by someone who had the authority to do so. Common argues that while Naumann, Nietzsche's German publisher, was in such a position, Elisabeth Förster-Nietzsche is not; the translations that were agreed with Naumann are therefore 'authorised', whereas those that were agreed with Förster-Nietzsche, with the possible exception of the volumes that had not already formed part of the earlier agreement, were not. In this line of logic, authorisation has nothing to do with the way in which the translations were carried out, and makes no appeal to any notions of faithfulness or reliability to the author. An authorised translation, in this model, holds no exclusive claim to paratextual relevance in Genette's sense; closeness to the author's original intentions is no more guaranteed in an authorised translation than a non-authorised one, and the authorised volume has no more potential to shed light on the author's intentions than any other.

This copyright-based view of authorisation contrasts somewhat with the grounds for authorisation that were laid out by Levy in the introductory essay to the first volume in the series, discussed above. Here, Levy not only outlines the formal agreement through which the series was established, but also appeals to notions of faithfulness and authenticity by stressing that the direct agreement means that the translations have not been tampered with in any way. Of course, for the direct line to Elisabeth Förster-Nietzsche to guarantee authentic access to the author's own thought and works, Förster-Nietzsche would need to be a reliable guardian of her brother's *Nachlass* (unpublished correspondence, manuscripts etc. left behind after his death) and an informed interpreter of his thought. As we will see, Förster-Nietzsche was neither of these things; and Levy's decision to claim authorisation on the basis of his direct connection to Förster-Nietzsche would fundamentally undermine the authority of his series.

Rescuing Nietzsche from the authorised translation

Although doubts about the reliability of Förster-Nietzsche were already being voiced as Levy published his series,[13] it was particularly in light of political developments in Germany in the 1920s and 1930s that the Levy translations' links to Förster-Nietzsche would prove deeply problematic. While Nietzsche himself had always been critical of anti-Semitism – as well as of German nationalism – under the leadership of Förster-Nietzsche the Nietzsche-Archiv openly welcomed Fascism. Key individuals associated with the archive published books connecting Nietzsche's thought with National Socialism,[14] the archive received financial backing from leading National Socialists, and Förster-Nietzsche herself welcomed Hitler to the archive on several occasions (see Diethe 2003, 140–58). By the end of the Second World War, the Nazification of Nietzsche undertaken both by the National Socialist Party and by the Nietzsche-Archiv itself was so complete that Nietzsche was widely regarded internationally as a proto-Fascist thinker and treated with the utmost suspicion.

It was against this backdrop that Walter Kaufmann, a professor at Princeton University, attempted to rehabilitate Nietzsche by developing a strong counternarrative to the one forged by Elisabeth Förster-Nietzsche and others at the Nietzsche-Archiv. This included discrediting *The Will to Power* as the culmination of Nietzsche's thought, distancing Nietzsche from his sister and her actions, and situating Nietzsche within a European and American network of thinkers. The key arguments of Kaufmann's counternarrative were formulated in a monograph published in 1950, *Nietzsche: Philosopher, Psychologist, Antichrist*. From a Genettian perspective, this work can be seen as a crucial epitext to the new translations of Nietzsche's works that were to follow. In the Prologue, Kaufmann (1963 [1950]) begins the process of disentangling the 'real' Nietzsche from the version created by his sister, sketching the 'satyr play' (16) through which Förster-Nietzsche came to be chief, and for a long time unquestioned, interpreter of her brother's thought, inverting her brother's philosophy 'through a prolific career of writing and editing' (17) that included holding back publication of *Ecce Homo* and creating *The Will to Power* from the notes left behind after Nietzsche's descent into madness and death.[15] Kaufmann (19) argues that Förster-Nietzsche ultimately 'laid the foundation' for the association of Nietzsche with proto-Fascism. Against Förster-Nietzsche's inversion of her brother's thought, Kaufmann stresses Nietzsche's documented antipathy towards his sister's husband, Bernhard Förster and his political views,[16] citing from Nietzsche's letters in which he labels himself an 'incorrigible European and anti-anti-Semite' (49) and expresses his horror at the way in which the political Right had already started to appropriate him and his work for their cause, partly because of his family connections to Förster.[17]

Kaufmann's rehabilitation of Nietzsche was achieved not only through his 1950 book – which went to three editions and is still in print today – but also through his translations of many of Nietzsche's works,[18] which reflected his views of Nietzsche in their translation choices and their paratextual material. In the introduction to *The Will to Power*, for example, Kaufmann cites from his own book directly and at some length, reproducing his explanation of how Elisabeth Förster-Nietzsche assembled *The Will to Power* and falsely represented it as Nietzsche's *magnum opus*, and laying the blame for the Nazification of Nietzsche squarely at Förster-Nietzsche's door: 'by bringing to her interpretation of her brother's work the heritage of her late husband, she prepared the way for the belief that Nietzsche was a proto-Nazi' (Kaufmann 1968, xix).

While Kaufmann's paratexts thus set out to distance Nietzsche from his sister, they do not include any direct critique of the paratexts of Levy's series. Given that many of the paratexts of Levy's series set up interpretative frameworks based on Förster-Nietzsche's accounts, this seems surprising. In his preface to the English translation of *The Will to Power*, for example, the translator Anthony Ludovici, argues that the books written by Nietzsche between 1883 and 1886 (*Beyond Good and Evil*, *The Genealogy of Morals*, *The Twilight of Idols* and *The Antichrist*) 'must be regarded as forming part of the general plan of which *The Will to Power* was to be the *opus magnum*' (Ludovici 1914, viii), thus directly reproducing Förster-Nietzsche's version of events. He admits that 'we have no warrant, save his sister's own word and the internal evidence at our disposal' (Ludovici 1914, vii) for viewing Nietzsche's works in this way, but it is clear from what follows that his appeal to 'his sister's own word' is intended to underscore the reliability of this interpretation, rather than foreground its untrustworthiness. Ludovici goes on to paraphrase at length Förster-Nietzsche's account of how the notion of the will to power first came to Nietzsche when he was serving in the German army, an account which Förster-Nietzsche had related in her book *Der junge Nietzsche [The Young Nietzsche]* (1912), and which Diethe (2003, 138) describes as a 'myth'.[19] Förster-Nietzsche's account of Nietzsche's inspiration for *The Will to Power* is fully discredited by Kaufmann in *Nietzsche*,[20] yet no reference is made to Ludovici's introduction in Kaufmann's own introduction to his translation of *The Will to Power*.

When we consider that the authorised nature of the Levy series was premised on closeness to Förster-Nietzsche, Kaufmann's silence on this feature of the Levy series seems surprising. Yet Kaufmann is not silent on the shortcomings of the Levy series overall. Significantly for our purposes, Kaufmann centres his critique of the Levy translations on the quality of the translations themselves. For example, in his preface to *Thus Spake Zarathustra*, Kaufmann (1978) criticises Common's translation at considerable length, even while admitting that 'the problems encountered in translating *Zarathustra* are tremendous' (xix). Kaufmann (1974) also criticises the early translation of *Gay Science* (*The Joyful Wisdom*), on the basis that it was 'inadequate' (3) and 'even had the title of the book wrong' (3). Ludovici's translation of *The Will to Power* also comes under fire, Kaufmann (1968, xx) picking out two mistranslations in support of his view that the translation is not even 'roughly reliable'. He is also critical of Helen Zimmern's translation of *Beyond Good and Evil* (see Kaufmann 1966, xiv), and summarises his view of the quality of all of the existing translations succinctly in the Introduction to *The Portable Nietzsche*, stating: 'The new translations were made because the older ones are unacceptable' (Kaufmann 1975 [1954], 3).

Through this detailed criticism of the translations, Kaufmann appears to be demonstrating that the Levy translations do not deserve their 'authorised' label, although he never makes this point directly. What is interesting about this approach is that it suggests that, in Kaufmann's view, readers' views of what it means for a translation to be authorised have primarily to do with issues of translation quality and reliability, rather than with the question of who authorised the translation in legal terms. To put this another way, while Levy's series bases its claim to authorisation on the second of the scenarios outlined in the first part of this chapter (the translator, editor or publisher has been formally appointed by someone (or some institution) to undertake the translation), Kaufmann bases his demolition of the claim to authorisation on the third scenario, by showing that the translations themselves should not be held in high esteem.

Reflections: authorisation, translations and paratextual relevance

This study of Nietzsche translations has shown that, while the label 'authorised translation' might give rise to expectations that the translation in question will carry some degree of paratextual relevance, latitude around usage of the label rules out any possibility of assuming such a thing. In the case of the Levy series, we have seen that the grounds for authorisation was the connection to Nietzsche's closest surviving relative, who claimed for herself a high level of insight into Nietzsche's thought and controlled access to his unpublished manuscripts. Already intrinsically less reliable than a direct connection to an author, in the abstract this kind of authorisation need not rule out the possibility that the translation is guided, albeit indirectly, by the author or at least done in line with his or her wishes. In the case of these translations, however, reliance on Förster-Nietzsche resulted in authorised translations which were deeply flawed, conveying Förster-Nietzsche's interpretation of Nietzsche rather than Nietzsche's own positions, and in so doing obstructing the target readers' understanding of Nietzsche's work. The fact that the translations carried the 'authorised' label may even have made this misinterpretation of Nietzsche more acute, the label itself offering reassurance of quality and reliability and closing down any questioning of the degree to which the translation really possesses those qualities. In the case of *The Will to Power*, for example, a reader picking up the 'authorised translation' is unlikely to question such basic things as the composition of the source text or the very existence of such a volume in the source language at all. Our case study thus indicates that the 'authorised translation' label can in fact contribute to readings of the author's work that are deeply unreliable, becoming in effect a barrier to an informed reception of that author in the target culture.

This leads us to consider another sense in which translations function as paratexts – one which, to my mind, is more frequently the case than the kind of scenario envisaged by Genette. In the case of the Nietzsche translations, we have seen that both the Levy and the Kaufmann translations make considerable use of paratextual sites (notably, translator's or editor's prefaces) in order to shape the way in which the translated texts themselves are read. In this sense, the paratexts of the translated versions operate in the same way as paratexts to original works, as described by Genette. Yet the translated book as a whole (that is, the text and paratext combined) also fulfils a paratextual function in the sense that it offers a threshold to the author, and the author's reputation. This is not the same as functioning as a paratext to an original *text*, for the majority of readers of a translation will never access the text in its original language. But the translated book shapes readers' views of the original author, his or her oeuvre, reputation and relevance to their own concerns. The paratexts of the translated versions play an important role in this process, but so too do translation choices, as well as external factors such as the order in which an author's works appear in translation. If we were to apply this idea to the case of the Nietzsche translations, we could point to key translation choices pertaining to notions of *Zucht* and *Züchtung*,[21] or to the order in which the pre-Levy translations appeared,[22] all of which had a bearing on how Nietzsche's philosophical thought was understood, and on his reputation in England and America. Viewing translations as paratexts in this way has the advantage of stressing the process of interlingual transfer in the reception of ideas across cultures and foregrounding the fact that many readers access ideas in a form that is mediated by a translator and others involved in the publication of translations. As this is something that is all too frequently overlooked by scholars in domains that include philosophy,[23] there is undoubtedly value in this approach.

However, broadening out the concept of the paratext in this way – so that it becomes a threshold to an author, an idea of an author or a view of their philosophical thought – is not without risk. To remain with the example of the Nietzsche translations, if we are seeking to understand how the translations functioned as thresholds to Nietzsche, we would not want to stop at the translated texts with their peritexts: we would also want to explore interpretations of Nietzsche published in the scholarly and general press; the reputations of the translators and editors and the ways in which their own actions or their nationality had a negative bearing on the views of Nietzsche; political contexts which affected reception of German scholarship in general and Nietzsche in particular; and so on.[24] And we would want to do all of this in diachronic fashion, capturing the changing dynamics of the target culture and the relationship between source and target culture over time. In other words, if we view translated works as paratexts to something called 'Nietzsche', we would swiftly find ourselves erasing the boundaries between text, paratext and context, and studying 'paratext' in this broader sense would become indistinguishable from studying reception. This raises important questions around the definition of *paratext* to which I shall return in Part III.

Notes

1 Though see Hermans (2007, 1–25) for a discussion of connections between authentication and equivalence.
2 Common (1923, xiv) writes that *Beyond Good and Evil* was 'meant as a prologue or prelude to his great, never-completed work on which he was then engaged, "The Will to Power: An Attempt at a Transvaluation of all Values". The circumstances under which the work was written are very fully set forth in Chapter XXX (pp.588–635) of *Das Leben Nietzsches* [by Elisabeth Förster-Nietzsche]'. Even more tellingly, he explains that 'it was during this period that Nietzsche's sister was married and went with her husband to Paraguay, thus leaving her brother more solitary than ever. The spirit of solitude which broods over the book, discloses itself especially in the last chapter' (Common 1923, xiv).
3 This summary has been devised by checking the information provided in Common (1915) against online library catalogues, bookseller websites, and the front and back matter of individual volumes. It finds confirmation in research carried out by van Ham (n.d.), whose online report also presents relevant information held in a range of archives.
4 The statement also appears in the front matter of the American edition of *The Case of Wagner*. The American edition of *Thus Spake Zarathustra* would appear not to contain this paragraph, at least insofar as the scanned copy available via archive.org shows. I have unfortunately not been able to check this against a hard-copy version or to find confirmation of whether the statement appears in the other early American editions.
5 The list that appears in the back matter of *The Case of Wagner*, published first, is shorter, containing only the first five volumes listed in *Thus Spake Zarathustra*, and anticipates that all of the volumes listed would appear by February 1897.
6 According to Common (1915, 113), the first agreement was a direct one between Naumann and three translators – Common, Haussmann and 'a Canadian lady, Miss Greenshields', made in 1894; the agreement with Henry and Co followed in 1895, and was 'specially to include our authorised translations'.

7 An account of the delays in publication is provided by Common (1915) and summarised in Thatcher (1970).

8 In light of the antipathy in England towards Tille by 1907 (see Manz 2007) and the fact that Tille had left academia by this point, it was perhaps also no longer advantageous or accurate to present the translation as being part of a series under Tille's editorship.

9 See Zimmern to Nietzsche, 25 April 1876 (Nietzsche 1979, 315–16), in which Zimmern thanks Nietzsche for giving her a copy of *Unzeitgemäße Betrachtungen*. According to Young (2010, 405), Nietzsche included Zimmern in the list of people who were to receive complimentary copies of *Beyond Good and Evil* on its publication in 1886.

10 In the sense that Tille's edition was not complete, Levy's claim could be argued to be technically correct. However, the wording used by Levy implies that his is the first authorised version, and in this regard is misleading.

11 In Levy's version, the paragraph reads as follows, the material in italic representing additions to the 1907 version: 'We here take the opportunity to thank Mr Alfred E. Zimmern of New College, Oxford, and a German friend of his, *Mr W. Drechsler, Rhodes Scholar of Worcester College*, for reading very carefully some of the first proofs and suggesting improvements. Dr Oscar Levy has also read many of the proofs and made valuable suggestions' (Common 1923, my emphasis).

12 On the latter point, see Levy's (1910b, xii) comments on the 'female mind' in his introductory essay to the series. That Levy did not consider women to be suitable readers of Nietzsche's work also emerges in the obituary of Levy written by his close collaborator, Anthony Ludovici. Ludovici (1946–7, 50) writes that 'many who wished to attempt the approach [to Nietzsche's works], Levy, in spite of his zeal as an impresario and for compassionate reasons alone, often gently turned away. Needless to say, many such were women whom, in his chivalry, he wished to spare the pain of it all.' Although this assertion must be treated with some suspicion, coming as it does from a man who was himself an ardent anti-feminist (Stone 2002, 33–61), it may well help to explain why Levy chose not to rely on connections between Zimmern and Nietzsche to build a case for authorisation.

13 Writing in 1915, Common (1915, 114) describes Förster-Nietzsche as 'a most violent and thoroughly self-willed creature, [who] has with almost witchlike perversity insisted on mismanaging the affairs of the Nietzsche Archive'; he subsequently refers to her in the same article as 'the pythoness of Weimar' (115). Just how widespread such views were during the period of the publication of Levy's series (1909–1913) is not clear; writing about the moment when Elisabeth Förster-Nietzsche took control of Nietzsche's *Nachlaß* in 1896, Diethe (2003, 87) states that Förster-Nietzsche 'had many detractors', but that 'most people were prepared to give her the benefit of the doubt for decades, awarding her manuscripts a respect for accuracy that they manifestly did not deserve'.

14 Examples include Alfred Baeumler's *Nietzsche: Der Philosoph und der Politiker* (1931) and Richard Oehlers' *Friedrich Nietzsche und die deutsche Zukunft* (1935), which 'displayed a photograph of Adolf Hitler as its frontispiece' (Diethe 2003, 156).

15 Although Nietzsche had announced at the end of *Zur Genealogie der Moral* (1887) that his next work would be *Der Wille zur Macht: Versuch einer Umwerthung aller Werthe*, at the time of his collapse in 1889 he had not yet written it (Diethe 2003, 93). All that existed of this work when Nietzsche's writing career ended were twenty-five different outlines for the work and 'sentences and paragraphs [scribbled] virtually at random' (Diethe 2003, 96) in nigh-on-illegible notebooks full of alterations, crossings out and corrections, the writing 'sometimes . . . back to front, or wrong way up' (Diethe 2003, 96). That these scribblings were even intended for eventual publication as opposed to being fragments rejected by Nietzsche is also open to question. Out of this, Förster-Nietzsche, in collaboration with Peter Gast (Heinrich Köselitz), one of very few people able to read Nietzsche's handwriting, swiftly created *Der Wille zur Macht*, '[giving] the impression that [this] was a work that Nietzsche had all but completed' (Diethe 2003, 95), and presenting the work as the culmination of Nietzsche's thought.

16 Bernhard Förster, whom Elisabeth married in 1885, was a zealous anti-Semite. In 1893 he set out to establish a 'colony of racially pure Germans' (Diethe 2003, 52) in Paraguay, Elisabeth moving out to join him after their marriage. The colony was a failure and Förster died in 1889, 'either through self-poisoning, or, as Elisabeth always asserted, through a heart attack' (Diethe 2003, 73).

17 See Kaufmann (1963 [1950], 49–50).

18 Kaufmann translated *Thus Spoke Zarathustra, Twilight of the Idols, The Antichrist*, and *Nietzsche contra Wagner* (all originally published in *The Portable Nietzsche*, 1954), *Beyond Good and Evil* (1966), *The Birth of Tragedy* and *The Case of Wagner* (1967), *Ecce homo* (1967) and, with Richard Hollingdale, *Genealogy of Morals* (1967). A new translation of *The Will to Power*, which included a commentary and facsimiles of the original manuscript, was published in 1968.

19 That Ludovici himself was something of an admirer of Förster-Nietzsche is clear: he translated Förster-Nietzsche's two biographical works on Nietzsche into English and his own philosophical work is described by Dan Stone (2002, 34) as an 'idiosyncratic blend of Förster-Nietzscheanism, Lamarckianism, social Darwinism, antisemitism, anti-feminism, monarchism and aristocratic conservatism'.

20 See Kaufmann (1963 [1950], 153).

21 For example, in his version of *Beyond Good and Evil*, Kaufmann translates these as 'discipline' or 'cultivation' rather than the ideologically loaded term *breeding*, even where the context might have supported a biological interpretation. See Nietzsche (1966).

22 Thatcher (1970, 38) suggests that one of the factors operative in the poor reception of Nietzsche in England in the late nineteenth century was the disapproval of the press, a disapproval which 'stemmed partly from the fact that Nietzsche's later works had been thrown on the public without the key the earlier ones would have provided'.

23 This is a point which is made by Diethe (2003, 102): 'it is truly astonishing that so many philosophers who claim to be able to interpret Nietzsche cannot actually read him in the original language and do not even see this as a disadvantage'.

24 An example of this broader type of survey can be found in Nicholas Martin's (2006) chapter on the process through which Nietzsche came to be regarded as responsible for the First World War and the German army's conduct during it.

References

Baker, Mona, and Gabriela Saldanha. 2008. *Routledge Encyclopedia of Translation Studies*, 2nd edition. London: Routledge.

Baeumler, Alfred. 1931. *Nietzsche: Der Philosoph und Politiker*. Leipzig: Reclam.

Common, Thomas. 1907. "Introduction". In *Beyond Good and Evil*, by Friedrich Nietzsche, translated by Helen Zimmern, vii–xv. Edinburgh: The Darien Press.

——. 1915. "Uprightness or Unscrupulousness". *The Good European Point of View*, 109–119.

——. 1923. "Introduction to the Translation". In *Beyond Good and Evil: Prelude to a Philosophy of the Future*, by Friedrich Nietzsche. Translated by Helen Zimmern, vii–xv. London: George Allen & Unwin Ltd.

Creffield, C. A. 2004. "Zimmern, Helen (1846–1934)". In *Oxford Dictionary of National Biography*. Oxford: Oxford University Press. Accessed 24 July 2017 from www.oxforddnb.com/view/article/55284.

Diethe, Carol. 1996. *Nietzsche's Women: Beyond the Whip*. Berlin and New York: Walter de Gruyter.

——. 2003. *Nietzsche's Sister and the Will to Power: A Biography of Elisabeth Förster-Nietzsche*. Urbana and Chicago: University of Illinois Press.

——. 2014. *Historical Dictionary of Nietzscheanism*, 3rd edition. Lanham, Boulder, New York, Toronto and Plymouth: The Scarecrow Press, Inc.

Gambier, Yves, and Luc van Doorslaer, eds. 2013. *Handbook of Translation Studies*, vol. 4. Amsterdam and Philadelphia: John Benjamins.

Genette, Gérard. 1997. *Paratexts: Thresholds of Interpretation*. Translated by Jane E. Lewin. Cambridge: Cambridge University Press.

Hermans, Theo. 2007. *The Conference of the Tongues*. Manchester: St Jerome Publishing.

Kaufmann, Walter. 1963 [1950]. *Nietzsche: Philosopher, Psychologist, Antichrist*. Cleveland, OH: The World Publishing Company.

——. 1966. "Translator's Preface". In *Beyond Good and Evil*, by Friedrich Nietzsche. Translated by Walter Kaufmann, ix–xvii. New York: Vintage Books.

——. 1968. "Editor's Introduction". In *The Will to Power*, by Friedrich Nietzsche. Translated by Walter Kaufmann and R.J. Holingdale, xiii–xxiii. London: Weidenfeld and Nicolson.

——. 1974. "Translator's Introduction". In *The Gay Science*, by Friedrich Nietzsche. Translated by Walter Kaufmann, 3–26. New York: Vintage Books.

——. 1975 [1954]. "Introduction". In *The Portable Nietzsche*, by Friedrich Nietzsche. Translated by Walter Kaufmann, 1–19. New York: The Viking Press.

——. 1978. "Translator's Preface". In *Thus Spake Zarathustra*, by Friedrich Nietzsche. Translated by Walter Kaufmann, xiii–xxii. New York and London: Penguin Books.

Levy, Oscar. 1910a. "Editorial Note". In *Thoughts out of Season. Part 1*, by Friedrich Nietzsche. Translated by Anthony M. Ludovici, vii–ix. Edinburgh and London: T.N. Foulis.

——. 1910b. "Nietzsche in England: An Introductory Essay by the Editor". In *Thoughts out of Season. Part 1*, by Friedrich Nietzsche. Translated by Anthony M. Ludovici, xi–xxviii. Edinburgh and London: T.N. Foulis.

——. 1924 [1913]. "The Nietzsche Movement in England: A Retrospect – A Confession – A Prospect". In *Index to Nietzsche: Compiled by Robert Guppy*, by Friedrich Nietzsche, ix–xxxvi. New York: The Macmillan Company.

Ludovici, Anthony M. 1911. "Translator's Introduction". In *Ecce Homo,*by Friedrich Nietzsche. Translated by Anthony M. Ludovici, vii–xiv. Edinburgh and London: T.N. Foulis.

——. 1914. "Translator's Preface". In *The Will to Power: An Attempted Transvaluation of all Values. Part 1*, by Friedrich Nietzsche. Translated by Anthony M. Ludovici, vii–xiv. Edinburgh and London: T.N. Foulis.

——. 1946–7. "Dr Oscar Levy". *New English Weekly* 30: 49–50.

Manz, Stefan. 2007. "Translating Nietzsche, Mediating Literature: Alexander Tille and the Limits of Anglo–German Intercultural Transfer". *Neophilologus* 91 (1): 117–34.

Martin, Nicholas. 2006. "Nietzsche as Hate-Figure in Britain's Great War: 'The Execrable Neech'". In *The First World War as a Clash of Cultures*, edited by Fred Bridgham, 147–66. Rochester, NY: Boydell & Brewer.

Nietzsche, Friedrich. 1911. *Early Greek Philosophy and Other Essays*. Translated by Maximillian A. Mügge. Edinburgh and London: T.N. Foulis.

——. 1966. *Beyond Good and Evil*. Translated by Walter Kaufmann. New York: Vintage Books.

——. 1979. *Nietzsche Briefwechsel Kritische Gesamtausgabe*. Edited by Giorgio Colli and Mazzino Montinari, vol. 2.6.1. Berlin and New York: Walter de Gruyter.

——. 1984. *Nietzsche Briefwechsel Kritische Gesamtausgabe*. Edited by Giorgio Colli and Mazzino Montinari, vol. 3.5. Berlin and New York: Walter de Gruyter.

Oehler, Richard. 1935. *Friedrich Nietzsche und die deutsche Zukunft*. Leipzig: Kröner.

Oxford English Dictionary. 2017. "authorized, adj". In *OED Online*. Oxford: Oxford University Press. Accessed 26 July 2017 from www.oed.com/view/Entry/13353.

Shuttleworth, Mark, and Moira Cowie. 1997. *Dictionary of Translation Studies*. Manchester: St Jerome Publishing.

Smyth, Patrick. 2014. "Ebooks and the Digital Paratext: Emerging Trends in the Interpretation of Digital Media". In *Examining Paratextual Theory and its Applications in Digital Culture*, edited by Nadine Desrochers and Daniel Apollon, 314–33. IGI Global.

Stone, Dan. 2002. *Breeding Superman. Nietzsche, Race and Eugenics in Edwardian and Interwar Britain*. Liverpool: Liverpool University Press.

Thatcher, David S. 1970. *Nietzsche in England 1890–1914*. Toronto and Buffalo: University of Toronto Press.

Valdéon, Roberto. 2013. "Nation, Empire, Translation". In *Handbook of Translation Studies*, vol. 4, edited by Yves Gambier and Luc van Doorslaer, 111–18. Amsterdam and Philadelphia: John Benjamins.

van Ham, Dirk. J. n.d. "Preliminary Research Note. *Friedrich Nietzsche, Early Translations*". Accessed 13 October 2017 from https://djvanham.home.xs4all.nl/CANON%20 EXTENDED/translations.htm.

Young, Julian. 2010. *Friedrich Nietzsche: A Philosophical Biography*. Cambridge: Cambridge University Press.

5

MAKING THE FOREIGN SERVE CHINA

Chinese paratexts of Western translation theory texts

In 2009, Maria Tymoczko (2009, 403) issued a call to internationalise translation studies, proposing to 'de-centre inherited Eurocentric conceptualisations that continue to be commonplace and even dominant in the field despite their decreasing relevance'. Delabastita (2013, 30) situates Tymoczko's concerns within a questioning movement in the discipline, which asks whether 'our current theories and methodologies . . . really have the "general" validity that their academic and theoretical status would imply'. Debates on Eurocentricity are not the preserve of translation studies scholars alone,[1] and in this respect can be seen as part of a more generalised anxiety which arises quite logically, as Delabastita (2013, 30) suggests, from 'our growing post-colonial sensibility, the greater presence and visibility of non-Western scholars in academia, and the overall erosion of Western hegemony'.[2]

Tymoczko's call for internationalisation appeared in a special issue of *The Translator* on *Chinese Discourses on Translation*, and several of the contributions in that volume reflect on the issue in the context of intellectual exchange between scholars based in the West and scholars in China.[3] As part of an enquiry into the Westernisation of translation studies in China, for example, Nam Fung Chang (2009, 312) notes that 'translation studies in the Chinese mainland is now dominated by Western models', a position that had been heavily criticised by Jinghao Zhang (2006) and others. While Chang (2009) points to the fact that Chinese discourse on translation is beginning to be introduced abroad through 'journal articles, book chapters, and anthologies of Chinese writings on translation' (313), he nevertheless concludes that China 'acts as an importer rather than exporter of repertoires' (313), and still remains peripheral. This situation is further confirmed by Ning Wang and Yifeng Sun (2008, 1), Martha Cheung (2009, 224) and Yangsheng Guo (2009, 255).

Although the number of publications that seek to bring Chinese and Western scholarship into dialogue has increased somewhat since these critiques, the imbalance in exchange of theories between China and the West is still striking. In China, scholars currently have access to two series of 'Western' or 'foreign' translation studies monographs in English, published in Chinese editions with the aim of making them both affordable and available for students. These are the Shanghai Foreign Language Education Press 'Foreign Translation Studies Texts' series (henceforth abbreviated to 'Shanghai FTST series'), which comprises 41 books, published between 2001 and 2012; and the Beijing Foreign Language Teaching and Research Press 'Foreign Translation Studies texts' series (henceforth 'Beijing FTST series'), which consists of 28 books, published between 2006 and 2008. Chinese scholars also have access to a third series, 'Contemporary Western Translation Studies' (henceforth 'Beijing CWTS series'), also published by the Beijing Foreign Language Teaching and Research Press, and which makes the texts themselves available in Chinese, as opposed to presenting the English texts in Chinese editions. Originally envisaged as a 10-book series, to date six volumes have been published, all between 2005 and 2009. While only one of these series labels itself 'Western' 西方的 (as opposed to 'foreign' 外国的), almost all of the books feature Anglo-Western scholarship.[4] In addition, there are 15 translations into Chinese of other translation theory texts, published by a range of publishing houses between 1986 and 2011.[5] Finally, there are three series of books on translation or interpreting practice and pedagogy, all published by Shanghai Foreign Language Teaching and Research Press: the 'Translation Teaching and Practice Series' (6 books, 2009–14), the 'Interpreting Practice Series' (8 books, 2008–11) and the 'Written Translation Practice Series' (6 books, 2008).

The body of scholarly publications on Chinese translation theory and traditions published in the West is steadily increasing, but far more limited. It now includes a significant number of journal articles as well as various edited collections (e.g. Chan 2004; Cheung 2006, 2009; Wang and Sun 2008; Valdeón 2017) and, perhaps most notably, a *Routledge Handbook of Chinese Translation* (Shei and Gao 2017).[6] There is, however, a crucial difference between these publications and the volumes of Western theory published in China: these publications are produced by Chinese scholars *for a Western audience*, often with the direct goal of making Chinese thinking on translation more visible in the West. Wang and Sun's (2008) volume, for example, aims to 'present a general but also up-to-date picture of translation studies in China' (2) or in other words is an 'attempt to globalise the research results made by domestic Chinese scholars on translation studies in the international context' (2). To represent a true parallel to the volumes of Western translation theory published in China, volumes published in the West would need to feature research published originally in China for a Chinese audience: if we think in terms of Master's-programme reading lists, for example, this might involve a work like Fukang Chen's 中国译学理论史稿 [*On Chinese Translation Theory*] (2002) or Yichuan Zhuang's 英汉翻译简明教程 [*An Introduction to English–Chinese Translation Studies*] (2002), widely included on reading lists in China, being made available in the UK or US and adopted onto reading lists there. To my knowledge, no such translations or English editions exist, and the overall global visibility of mainland Chinese translation studies scholars remains low (see, notably, Li 2017).

Before we take these – admittedly very stark – imbalances in translation flow as further proof of the ongoing Eurocentricity of translation studies, however, we need to examine the ways in which the importation of Western translation theory is conceptualised and presented to the target audience by the Chinese actors who play key roles in the importation. Examining the peritexts of the Chinese editions of Western translation studies texts offers an ideal site through which to do this. Before we proceed to an analysis of the peritexts, however, we need first to define Eurocentricity and to address the important and sometimes overlooked issue of agency within it.

Eurocentricity

Defined in basic terms as 'implicitly regarding European culture as pre-eminent' (Oxford Dictionaries n.d.), the notion of Eurocentricity has been unpacked by scholars in a variety of ways. It is a phenomenon which is closely connected with 'Orientalism', as famously analysed by Edward Said (2003 [1978]), the latter being defined as 'a Western style for dominating, restructuring, and having authority over the Orient' (Said 2003 [1978], 3). The aspects of Eurocentricity which are of most salience for this chapter can be summarised as follows:

- viewing European/Western theories and ideas as superior to non-Western ones
- assuming European/Western theories and ideas to be universally relevant or applicable
- considering theories and ideas developed elsewhere to have local rather than universal relevance, or to be useful at most in terms of offering refinement of so-called 'mainstream' (i.e. Western) theories and ideas.

Eurocentricity is generally viewed as something negative and destructive, which 'should have no place in scholarly research' (Delabastita 2013, 30): it ignores other ways of knowing, 'may entail the tendency to submit non-Western practices to Western theories in ways that fail to register and respect the former's cultural specificity' (Delabastita 2013, 30) and, in the most forceful interpretations, 'lies at the center of a predatory model of civilization that threatens to destroy the conditions that make life possible on Earth' (Lander 2002, 245).

Scholars of both Orientalism and Eurocentricity have argued that these ways of thinking are not exclusively the preserve of Westerners; on the contrary, they have been absorbed by many non-Westerners, resulting in an Orientalism that is 'self-impose[d] and internalize[d]' (Li 2016, 18). This self-imposition of Eurocentric ways of thinking is viewed by many as a type of colonisation of the mind, with disastrous consequences for non-Western nations. In the preface to a volume devoted to exploring non-Eurocentric paradigms in higher education, for example, Claude Alvares and Shad Saleen Faruqi (2012, xx) describe the book's aim as being 'to discover what needs to be done to liberate our minds and souls; to end this academic colonialism . . . We need to send Columbus packing back home. Not only the Columbus outside but also the Columbus within.'

These overwhelmingly negative critiques contrast with the far more positive language used to discuss processes of technology and knowledge transfer, even though what is actually transferred may not be dissimilar. Technology transfer is defined as 'the transfer of new technology from the originator to a secondary user, especially from developed to developing countries in an attempt to boost their economies' (Oxford Dictionaries n.d.). As Richard Hua Li (2003, 3) observes, 'traditionally, technology transfer was conceptualised as the transfer of hardware objects, but today also often involves information (e.g. a computer software programme or a new idea)'. Practitioners and academics alike underline the need for technology transfer to go hand in hand with 'knowledge transfer', based on the fact that knowledge is increasingly being recognised as a vital organisational resource (see Nonaka and Takeuchi 1995; Leonard 1998). The definition of technology transfer provided above presents the benefits of the transfer as accruing to the recipient; no mention is made of the motivations or positive outcomes for the 'originator', though in general, as Leonard (1998, 224) notes, these are linked to a desire to 'lower costs or to follow the market'. From the perspective of the recipient, technology and knowledge transfer are invariably construed positively; academic discussions generally focus on improving the effectiveness of technology and knowledge transfer and thus increasing the benefits for the recipients, rather than questioning or contesting the global power dynamics that form the backdrop to such transfers (see, for example, Leonard 1998; Li 2003; Buckley, Clegg and Tan 2004). In other words: there is no criticism of the 'Eurocentricity' of technology or knowledge transfer; although the flow of such transfers are from West to East, North to South, the appropriateness of non-Western nations taking on Western technologies and knowledge is not generally questioned by the receiving nations; the transfers are not seen as a threat to national identity or as the perpetuation of Western imperialism.

To some extent, this striking difference in attitude can be explained by the nature of the material exchanged: those things that are usually accused of Eurocentrism are ideas and theories, often operating at an abstract intellectual level – and theory, in the words of Arif Dirlik (2000, 74) has 'lost its innocence, as its universalist claims have been deconstructed in one intellectual realm after another . . . to expose the hegemonies built into all theories'. Technology and knowledge transfer, on the other hand, involve more concrete, practical know-how, resulting in products that can be bought and sold on world markets. To draw on Appadurai's (1990) characterisation of the various kinds of flows associated with globalisation, it would appear that, while things belonging to the 'ideoscape' (flow of ideas) are often construed as Eurocentric, things that belong to the 'technoscape' (flow of technology) are never seen this way, even though the flow of technology inevitably involves the flow of ideas, and the flow of ideas can lead to marketable products or increases in market share. The relevance of this discussion of the different discourses around ideoscape and technoscape will become clear when we examine the discourses used in the Chinese paratexts to Western translation theory texts, and in particular when we consider the extent to which they present Western theories as tools serving development rather than as theory.

There is another difference, however, and this concerns the level of agency imputed to the recipient in both kinds of process. While the recipients of Eurocentric views are often portrayed as powerless victims of Western hegemony (see, for example, Wang 1997, 159; Sun 2012, 39), the recipients of technology transfer are often the initiators of the transfer process – or at the very least, are viewed as exerting a 'pull . . . for new product development capabilities [which] exceeds the transfer *push* of managers in the developed nations' (Leonard 1998, 248). This point is of particular relevance when we consider the agency dynamics that underlie the processes by which Western translation theory is being imported to China in the form of Chinese editions or translations of Western works. Far from being imposed by the West, such publications undoubtedly concord with Toury's (2012, 18) observation that translations can usually be regarded as 'facts of the culture that would host them', in the sense that the publications are the initiative of Chinese, rather than Western, publishing houses.

Paratextual analysis

As outlined in the opening section of this chapter, there are six series of foreign translation studies texts available in China. Owing to space limitations, this study excludes the three Shanghai Foreign Language Teaching and Research series on translation pedagogy and practice, focusing instead on publications that focus more narrowly on translation theory. In terms of paratexts, the Shanghai FTST series provides a generic 'General Publisher's Note' and 'General Preface' (identical for all books in the series) as well as a brief anonymous introduction and back-cover blurb specific to each text. The Beijing FTST series, meanwhile, offers no generic general introduction, blurb, or other paratextual material relating to the series itself, but does include a lengthy reading guide as part of the paratext of each individual text. Unlike the introductions to the Shanghai FTST series, these guides are signed by high-profile Chinese academics and go beyond simple summaries of content to resemble academic articles. The Beijing CWTS series provides more detailed paratextual materials than the other two series, although there is a certain level of variation from book to book. In most cases, the paratext to the CWTS series includes an editor's 'General Preface' (giving a summary of the main content, the significance of the series and some background information on the author), a long introduction by the translator, offering critique and analysis in the style of an academic article, and a much briefer introduction by the author, translated into Chinese. The paratexts of translations which are published outside the scope of these theories range from very minimal (e.g. a two-paragraph translator's introduction to Wolfram Wilss's (2001) *The Science of Translation: Problems and Methods*) to much more extensive (e.g. two prologues, back-cover blurb, author's introduction, translator's introduction, publishing house introduction for Mona Baker's (2011) *Translation and Conflict: A Narrative Account*). The themes which emerge most consistently from the paratexts are presented below, and the implications of the findings are discussed in further depth in the concluding section.

Make the foreign serve China

The most salient theme that emerges in the paratexts is the notion that the publications are intended to benefit China. In some of the paratextual material, this argument is formulated in general terms and by making appeal to politically sanctioned sayings. In other places, the paratext authors spell out more specifically the ways in which access to foreign translation studies will be of use to domestic scholars.

The publisher's note that accompanies the 1999 Chinese version of two of Eugene Nida's books offers a clear example of the first type of statement, declaring that '在新书的编译过程中, 仍然本着 "洋为中用", 去粗存精原则' [the principles for editing this book are 'foreign used by the Chinese' and discard the useless and accept the good] (Tan 1999a, iv). The translator of this volume – who is also the author of the editor's note – also translated Mark Shuttleworth and Moira Cowie's *Dictionary of Translation Studies* for the Beijing CWTS series in 2005, and repeats similar sentiments in his introduction to that volume:

> 把马克•沙特尔沃思和莫伊拉合编的 *Dictionary of Translation Studies* 翻译成中文, 对于一个善于'古为今用, 洋为中用', 现在蒸蒸日上, 欣欣向荣的古老而又新兴的译学体系来说, 一定是一件既有理论价值又有实践意义, 值得花力气来做的工作。
>
> [It is theoretically and practically worthwhile translating Mark Shuttleworth and Moira Cowie's *Dictionary of Translation Studies* into Chinese for an old yet newly sprung translation system, which is good at 'mak[ing] the past serve the present and foreign things serve China', and which is currently developing vigorously in China.][7]
>
> *Tan 2005, x*

In both of these paratexts, Tan is evoking slogans which were originally coined by Mao Zedong in the late 1930s and early 1940s, and which have become common sayings in China over time. 'Make the past serve the present and foreign things serve China' references the policy presented by Mao in a speech to the Literature and Art Forum in Yan An in 1942 (see Mao 1991).[8] In this speech, Mao indicates that the People's Republic of China should use only what it needs from the outside world, remaining in full control of the process of cultural transformation and thus maintaining the so-called 'Chinese characteristics'. He also makes clear that the process of adoption of foreign ideas is not one of straightforward borrowing, but one that involves assimilation and critical application.[9] The idea of making the foreign serve China was also reinforced and reinterpreted by Deng Xiaoping at the end of the 1970s in a policy that 'promote[d] greater interaction between China and the rest of the world to foster modernization of China's industry, agriculture, defence and science and technology' (Guo 2009, 241). The other slogan, 'discard the useless and accept the good', was first formulated by Mao Zedong in his book 实践论 [*On Practice*] written in 1937 and published in 1950, generally seen as the founding text of Marxist philosophy with Chinese characteristics. The slogan was subsequently applied to art and other related disciplines, notably by the artist and theorist Jiang Kongyang (see Kongyang 1979). Both slogans thus have a long and weighty political history, and have become frequently used sayings in both scholarly and everyday discourse. By appealing to these widely accepted or even clichéd ideas, Tan situates the translated books within a familiar and politically uncontroversial mode of engaging with foreign ideas.

A variation on the idea of making the foreign serve China, this time evoking a philosophical angle, can be found in the 'General Preface' to Beijing's CWTS series. Here, the author appeals to the notion of Sinicisation, developed by He Lin:

> 翻译在历史上有沟通文化, 传播学术之功能, 促进了个民族的交流和
> 社会文明的进步。因此翻译又有繁荣文化, 启发创新之功效。尤其
> 值得指出, 翻译的一大价值是 '内化外学' 或者如哲学家贺麟先生所
> 说的 '华化西学' : '使西洋学术中国化, 灌输文化上的新血液, 使西
> 学成为国学之一部分'。我们不能指望懂外语的人从外文了解外域思
> 想 …… 在我国传承千年的翻译研究基础上, 借鉴西方现代翻译理论,
> 或可使中国翻译研究的话题模式更为丰满。这就是我们编选这套译
> 丛的基本出发点。
>
> [Translation can promote cultural and scholarly communication, which pro-motes cultural exchange between various nationalities and the progress of social civilisation . . . In particular, the great value of translation is 'inter-nalisation' or what He Lin called '华化西学' [Sinicisation], which is to Sinicise Western academia and make it part of Chinese academia . . . Only when foreign ideologies have been translated into Chinese can these new ideas and concepts be absorbed as our own knowledge to promote our research . . . Based on the 1,000-year-old domestic translation studies, 'bor-rowing' and referencing modern Western translation theories will enrich topics of Chinese translation studies.]
>
> *Beijing Foreign Language Teaching and Research Press 2005, 2*

He Lin (1902–92) was a translator, philosopher and educator, known in particular for his translations of Hegel's books into Chinese. In the 1930s and 1940s, he was well-known as a philosopher in his own right, publishing four books between 1934 and 1947. As Ci (2002, 188–9) explains, He did not attempt to build a philosophical system of his own, convinced as he was of the existence of one universal philosophical system, the essentials of which had already been found in Hegelian idealism. Instead, He saw his task as being to 'updat[e] the philosophy of the Lu-Wang school in the light of modern idealism in general and Hegel in particular' (Ci 2002, 188). Far from being a purely exegetical or academic task, He saw this as a means of revitalising Chinese culture and strengthening Chinese society (Ci 2002, 189); He Lin's Sinicisation, in other words, was a process through which the foreign could be made to serve China. In this preface, the author does not appear to be invoking He Lin's position on Western or Hegelian philosophy in specific terms (he or she is not arguing, for example, that Western theorists have uncovered universal truths), but rather suggests more generally that translation is useful for communication and progress.

Another variation on the idea of making the foreign serve China can be found in the introduction to the Chinese edition of Gunilla Anderman and Margaret Rogers' *Translation Today: Trends and Perspectives* (Mu and Zhu 2006), published as part of the Beijing FTST series. Rather than appealing to philosophical or political figures, the authors of the introduction appeal to a literary figure, Lu Xun, generally considered the greatest modern Chinese author:[10]

> 诚如鲁迅先生所言, '只看一个人的著作, 结果是不大好的: 你就得不到多方面的优点。必须如蜜蜂一样, 采过许多花, 这才能酿出蜜来, 倘若叮在一处, 所得就非常有限, 枯燥了'。 在如今的全球化背景下, 我们不仅要采'国产花', 也要采'洋花'。
>
> [As Lu Xun said, 'you will not learn much from learning one single book. As with the work by bees, the more flowers they adopt, the more honey they can make. If they focus on one flower, the honey will be very limited'. Against the background of globalisation, we must not only collect 'domestic flowers', but also pay attention to 'foreign flowers'.]
>
> *Mu and Zhu 2006, xi*

While the letter from which this Lu Xun citation is taken does not specifically evoke the notion of learning from 'foreign flowers' – it is simply an affirmation of the value of being widely read on a range of subjects rather than reading the works of only one literary author[11] – the author of this introduction uses Lu Xun's statement as a justification for engaging with ideas that have originated outside China. Later in the same introduction, the authors stress that the benefits of this foreign flower collection are for China, invoking the notion that the foreign should be put to use to serve Chinese interests: '我们也可以从他们的讨论中找到自己的切入点, 在国内乃至世界翻译研究领域做出自己的贡献' [We can also find starting points for our own research from their discussion, and make some contribution to the field of translation studies in China and the world] (Mu and Zhu 2006, xi).

Mu and Zhu's suggestion that the 'foreign flowers' can provide an impetus for domestic research is an idea which recurs frequently. The anonymous preface to the Shanghai FTST series' edition of Steiner's *After Babel*, for example, argues that the book's publication '将有力促使我国语言和翻译研究事业的进一步繁荣和发展' [in our country will effectively promote the further development of our language and translation studies and research] (Shanghai Foreign Language Education Press 2001b, ii), and a very similar formulation is found in the anonymous preface to Lefevere's *Translation, Rewriting, and the Manipulation of Literary Fame* (see Shanghai Foreign Language Education Press 2010, ii). More detailed formulations of this sentiment can be found in the preface to the Shanghai FTST series' edition of Bassnett's *Translation Studies* (see Cao 2010, xv) and in the introduction to the Beijing FTST series' version of Tymoczko and Gentzler's *Translation and Power*:

我们以往的很多研究成果都是对别人的理论的套用, 当然, 这是中国翻译理论建构的必由之路。而且我们已经走过了早期的'挪用'阶段。我们希望, 未来的'套用' 更多的是范式创新精神的套用, 从而不断推出独特的研究范式, 为翻译研究作出我们都有的贡献。

[A large amount of existing research in China involves applying others' theories. It is a necessary step to copy and apply others' theories, but we have already passed the stage of 'borrowing theory'. So we sincerely hope that we will 'borrow' attitudes and spirits of innovation, rather than the content, from Western theories. This will allow us to create our own theories and make our own contribution to translation research.]

Wang 2007, xvi

According to other paratexts, an important means of strengthening Chinese translation studies is to offer Chinese scholars direct access to 'original works'. In the 'General Publisher's Note' to the Shanghai FTST series, for example, the publishers state that '学习翻译专业的研究生人数越来越多, 这种状况若继续存在,' [this series will satisfy the demand for original works required by translation education for Master's students of translation and translation theory studies] (Yang 2001, n.p.), indicating that the current lack of original works '国内引进的原版翻译著作匮乏 …… 将十分不利于学科的发展和翻译人才的培养' [blocks the development of the translation discipline and the cultivation of translators] (Yang 2001, n.p.). The lack of availability of 'foreign translation studies', particularly in Chinese rather than English, is also noted in the 'General Preface' to the Beijing CWTS series (see Beijing Foreign Language Teaching and Research Press 2005, 1). The problem of Chinese scholars relying on secondary sources rather than having recourse to the original works is expanded upon in the back-cover blurb of the Chinese edition of Alexander Fraser Tytler's *Essay on the Principles of Translation* (Beijing Foreign Language Teaching and Research Press, 2008):

1791年, Alexander Fraser Tytler 在Essay on the Principles of Translation一书中提出了著名的翻译三原则, 标志着西方译学研究从此走上了从理论推动理论的道路。故而, 这本书被誉为西方现代译学研究的开山之作。…… 在国内学界, '翻译三原则', 几乎是人人耳熟能详, 但遗憾的是, 国内读过原著者寥寥, 学界不得不转来转去地二手引用。希望本书的出版有助于研究者养成读原著的习惯。

[In 1971, Alexander Fraser Tytler put forward the famous Three Principles of translation in his *Essay on the Principles of Translation*. This marked the beginning of Western translation studies' theoretical journey, and this book is therefore acclaimed as the first work of Western modern translation studies . . . In domestic translation studies, almost everyone is familiar with the Three Principles of translation. However, it is unfortunate that very few Chinese readers have read the original work and scholars repeatedly cite second-hand references. I do hope the publication of this book can encourage Chinese researchers to get into the habit of reading original works.]

Beijing Foreign Language Teaching and Research Press 2008, back cover

Statements such as these, particularly in the more specific formulation that is found in the note to Tytler's essay, could be read as criticism of Chinese translation studies. If we read between the lines, then Chinese translation studies – at least in the years when these paratexts were written – could be viewed as derivative (dependent on foreign theories) and lacking in rigour (relying on secondary rather than original material). Many of the paratexts thus evoke some kind of gap or weakness in domestic translation studies, but the tone taken by paratext authors is uniformly affirmative of Chinese translation studies. The 'General Publisher's Note' to the Shanghai FTST series, for example, opens with the statement that '近些年国内研究已经取得了很大进步' [In recent years, domestic translation studies has made great progress] (Yang 2001, n.p.). The 'General Preface' to the Beijing CWTS series uses an almost identical phrase and supports this statement with statistics regarding the number of domestic translation studies-related publications (see Beijing Foreign Language Teaching and Research Press 2005, 1).

Alongside the affirmations of domestic translation studies is an emphasis on the importation of foreign translation studies being under the control of domestic scholars. Thus the Shanghai FTST General Publisher's Note explains that, in light of the scarcity of foreign translation studies texts, the Publishing House '上海外国语教育出版社约请了多名国内翻译研究著名学者分别开列出最值得引进的国外翻译研究论著的书目' [invited a number of famous domestic scholars of translation studies to list the foreign translation works which are the most worthy of introduction] (Shanghai Foreign Language Education Press 2001a, n.p.), while the 'General Preface' to the Beijing CWTS lists by name and affiliation a number of Chinese academics '帮助选编这个系列的学者' [who helped with the selection of the topics for this series] (Beijing Foreign Language Teaching and Research Press 2005, 4). The control and endorsement of the publications by domestic scholars is also made clear in the Beijing FTST series, each volume of which includes a lengthy reading guide by a named individual, usually a professor in translation studies from a university in China.

The emphasis on the value of domestic translation studies and the need to take inspiration from Western scholars rather than simply copying or adopting them uncritically is a prevailing concern of Chinese scholars, as Yifeng Sun explains:

> The overriding concern of many Chinese translation scholars is how to develop Translation Studies in China with its own theoretical system and methodology so as to claim to create the so-called Chinese characteristics. The feverish quest for identity is fundamentally about cultural politics but it is also meant to effectively analyze and provide more definitive answers to translation problems related to continuous cultural and political change in a country eager to establish its overall cultural promotion.
>
> *Sun 2012, 35–6*

Presenting the imported material as a means to an end, rather than an end in itself, allows the material to become part of this 'quest for identity' and thus presumably to find a high level of acceptance in the target culture. On the surface at least, this kind of discourse is opposed to a Eurocentric one, since it rejects the idea that Western theories are universally applicable or in themselves superior to Chinese traditions. Yet aspects of Eurocentric discourse are not entirely absent from the corpus, as we will see in the next section.

Eurocentrism(?)

From the entire corpus, only one paratext appears to convey the view that a set of ideas are important for China simply because they were developed in (a prestigious centre in) the West. In the translator's introduction to the translation of Danica Seleskovitch and Marianne Lederer's *Interpréter pour traduire*, the translator states:

> 两位作者在本书中详尽阐述了巴黎高等翻译学校的指导思想，教学原则，培训方法，教学大纲及授课计划。对于我国翻译教学的改革与提高，对于我国高级口译人员的选拔与培训等都是一份不可多得的珍贵资料，对于有志走向世界译坛的外语学员和年轻译员，又是一部切实可行的自修参考，对于从事口译工作多年和从事翻译教学多年的同志们，也不愧为是一部必备的案头读物和译事参考。从这个意义上讲，这本书又可谓是一部翻译教育家的教育思想概略和教学经验总结。
>
> [In this book, the two authors elaborate the guiding ideology, teaching principles, training methods, syllabus and teaching plans of the Advanced Translating School in Paris. Therefore, it is a rare and valuable reference book for selecting and training advanced translators and interpreters. It is also a useful self-learning book for students majoring in translation studies and for young translators. For those who have studied and worked in translation for years, it is a necessary book for reading and referencing. From this perspective, this book can be considered as a summary of ideas on educating and teaching by a translator educator.]
>
> *Sun 1992, iii*

Later in the introduction, the 'Advanced Translation School' is specified as ESIT, the École Supérieure d'Interprètes et de Traducteurs at the Université Sorbonne Nouvelle. The logic of Sun's argument appears at least superficially to be entirely Eurocentric: the translation school in Paris uses this material, and therefore knowing about it (and, by implication, adopting it) will improve translation teaching in China. However, this Eurocentricity is not unthinking: translation teaching in Paris is not held up as a model for the Chinese simply because it is teaching that takes place in a prestigious Western capital; on the contrary, as a paratext to another translation from this era makes clear,[12] the Chinese translator's motivation for translating the work of the Paris school arises from a deep and detailed knowledge of their pedagogic methods and training programme. Nevertheless, the overt, rather simplistic reasoning presented in this particular translator's introduction does appear to betray a certain Eurocentricity, even if it is not entirely without ambiguity when more fully contextualised. It is almost certainly not incidental that the only example of this kind of argumentative logic is found in a paratext that predates the most intense period of the nationalist backlash against Western translation studies described by Cheung (2009), Guo (2009) and others.

While other paratexts do not present a simple Eurocentric logic in this way, there are nevertheless elements of what might be interpreted as Eurocentricity in many of the paratexts. Whether or not they are construed in this way depends to a large extent on interpretations of the nature of Eurocentricity and its connection to narratives of modernisation and development. One of the elements of Eurocentricity that might be said to be manifested in the paratexts is a tendency to treat theories of translation developed in the West as 'translation studies', while theories of translation developed in China are presented as 'Chinese translation studies'. This can be seen in the following statement from the Chinese edition of Katan's *Translating Cultures: An Introduction for Translator, Interpreters, and Mediators*, which casts Western Translation Studies as 'translation theory and research', or in other words gives it the status of the discipline of translation studies:

> 据学者考证，西方的翻译理论和实践研究的历史，就已挖掘的文字记载，已达两千余年，与我国翻译史基本同步。但直到1976年在比利时的卢万举行的'文学与翻译论坛'上才由勒菲弗尔提出'翻译研究' (Translation Studies) 这一命题。作为一门独立学科, '翻译研究' 旨在关注 '翻译的生成与描写提出的问题'。
>
> [Some scholars have proved that translation theory and applied research has been developed for 2,000 years since it has the written records, which is actually at the same time with the history of this discipline in China. However, 'Translation Studies' as a subject was not proposed until 1976 by Lefevere at the 'Literature and Translation Forum' in Belgium. 'Translation Studies', as an independent discipline, aims to address problems related to translation.]
>
> *Shanghai Foreign Language Education Press 2004, n.p.*

In general, however, the paratexts tend to describe translation studies developed in the West as 'Western Translation Studies', thereby constraining its universality to some extent. Thus Nida is described as '奈达是现代西方学界最著名的翻译理论家之' [one of the most famous translators among contemporary Western scholars] (Tan 1999b, xxvi), and his theory as '西方理论界的一块明亮的珍宝' [a bright jade in Western translation thinking and theories] (Tan 1999b, xxvi); Munday's *Introducing Translation Studies* is said to be '本书是翻译学的入门教材，广获欧美高等院校采用' [the introductory textbook of translation studies, widely used by European and American research institutions] (Munday 2007, back-cover blurb) and offering a '全书综览现当代重要的翻译学说，加以阐述和评议' [comprehensive review of the most important contemporary translation theories in the West] (Munday 2007, back-cover blurb); Catford's *A Linguistic Theory of Translation* is recommended for scholars '本书是我国外语院校师生，翻译理论工作者和从事翻译实践的读者了解和研究西方现代理论的一本很有价值的参考书'

[who are interested in understanding and doing research on Western modern translation theory] (Mu 1991, v); and the back-cover blurb for Bassnett and Lefevere's *Constructing Cultures* states that the range of topics in the book includes '中西译论' [Chinese and Western thinking on translation] (Bassnett and Lefevere 2001, back-cover blurb).

This localising move draws on a concept – namely 'Western translation studies' – which appears to be widely and consistently used only by those who would consider themselves to occupy a place outside it. In addition to its prominence in the paratexts to Chinese editions of foreign translation theory texts, a survey of the first 300 hits on Google Scholar for the phrase (out of 812 in total) found that 293 of them were for work by Chinese scholars.[13] Definitions of the term are elusive, but if a parallel can be drawn with Chinese uses of the term 'West', then it would appear to refer primarily to work emanating from Northern Europe and North America, with a bias towards centres of power in which the English language is used. Like the term *the West, Western translation studies* always stands in opposition to something else. In the case of the paratexts in this corpus, that something else is 'Chinese' translation studies, itself a construct which generally refers to 'the mainstream viewpoints and positions in and of the Chinese mainland' (Guo 2009, 240–1).

Translation theory as knowledge transfer

Another way in which the potential threat of Western theories is neutralised in the paratextual discourse of the Chinese editions is through the choice of words used to denote the material that has been selected for publication in China. Rather than referring to the works in question as '研究' [research], or '理论' [theory], many of the paratexts show a strong preference for the terms '教科书' [textbook], '阅读书单' [reading list book] or '参考书' [reference book], all of which stress the educational function of the books and their role in higher education and translator training. The 'General Preface' to the Shanghai FTST Series, for example, states that the 'series will solve the age-old problem of the lack of original 阅读书单 [reading list books] in China' (Shanghai Foreign Language Education Press 2001a, n.p.), terminology which ties in which its emphasis on the publisher's role in '适应这种高层次人才培养和新学科建设的需要' [meet[ing] the needs of construction of modernisation and education reform] (Shanghai Foreign Language Education Press 2001a, n.p.). Many of the introductions to individual works in this and other series draw on similar terminology: André Lefevere's *Translating Literature*, for example, is described as '很好的文学翻译教科书，可以供我国高等院校翻译专业的师生使用' [a very good textbook for teachers and students in universities in China] (Sun 2006, xiii); Seleskovitch and Lederer's *Interpréter pour traduire* is described as '对研究生和年轻译者是一本好的参考书' [a good reference book for postgraduate students and young interpreters] (Sun 1992, ii); and Mark Shuttleworth and Moira Cowie's *Dictionary of Translation Studies* is denoted in even more pragmatic terms as a '工具书' or 'tool book' (Tan 2005, x). Referring to the imported texts in these ways indicates that what is being transferred is concrete, practical know-how. The language used in the paratexts thus aligns this type of importation with the more positive, ideologically neutral process of knowledge transfer, and ties in with the general preference in China for treating translation studies as an applied rather than theoretical discipline (see, in this regard, the Chinese Ministry of Education's official statement (State Council 2007) on the aims of the Master in Translation and Interpreting programme).

Concluding discussion

My analysis of the paratexts of imported Western translation studies texts in this chapter has revealed the dominance of discourses that stress the benefits of the imported texts for China. This would appear to suggest that, although imbalances of translation flow are indicative of Eurocentricity in the discipline of translation studies, the uses to which imported texts are put are not. Yet critics of development discourses such as Vincent Tucker would argue that the underlying logic of all the paratexts in this corpus falls prey to some extent to a Eurocentric discourse of development that equates modernisation with Westernisation:

> The words 'development' and 'modernization' were coined by spokespersons for the West to characterize the efforts of others whom they implicitly assumed to be destined to achieve their levels of consumption . . . Under the rubric of modernization, Westernization gained the status of a universal goal and destiny.
>
> *Tucker 1999, 7*

Far from questioning the foundations of the methods and concepts of Western translation studies, the dominant paratextual discourse of 'make the foreign serve China' is based on the premise that the approaches modelled by Western scholars represent the means by which Chinese translation studies can and should develop. This is a far cry from the more radical 'decentred consciousness' envisaged by Said (1985, 105–6), which is

> for the most part non- and in some cases anti-totalizing and anti-systemic. The result is that instead of seeking common unity by appeals to a centre of sovereign authority, methodological consistency, canonicity and science, they [the efforts to attain decentred consciousness] offer the possibility of common grounds of assembly between them.

To re-situate these discussions in the Chinese context more specifically, the paratexts can be seen as occupying a position that is closer to the philosophy of Bao Zunxin as opposed to that of the 'new Confucians' (Fewsmith 2001, 23). As Joseph Fewsmith (2001, 23) explains, the latter group 'emphasize[s] that "modernization is not the same as Westernization" and argue[s] that unless China finds the sources of its modernization within its own tradition, it will become detached from its "roots" and continue to face a "crisis of identity"'. In contrast, Bao Zunxin and others 'have argued that even though modernization is not the same as Westernization, absorbing the experiences of Western nations is an inevitable part of modernization and nothing to worry about' (Fewsmith 2001, 24).[14] The overwhelmingly pragmatic approach to Western theories taken in the paratexts suggests that the paratext authors concur with this latter view, regarding some level of absorption of Western models and approaches as a necessary step towards achieving greater success on both a local and a global level. The paratexts' stress on the connection between importing Western translation theory and furthering domestic translation studies (thereby enhancing its ability to contribute to the development of the discipline on an international level) suggests that the paratext authors do not accept the binary decision presented by Guo (2009, 256) in his analysis of the current predicament of the 'non-West':

> The 'non-West' peoples have been silenced for so long . . . that they may have lost their 'voice' and their 'self'. Consequently, they are caught in a dilemma. Either they participate in debates on theoretical issues by borrowing, learning or adopting the dominant language of the West, and thus risk becoming mere parrots, or they lapse further into silence.

The discourse in the paratexts suggests that the aim is indeed to borrow, learn and adopt the language of the West, but not in such a way as to become 'mere parrots'. Rather, in line with the alternative vision that Guo (2009, 256) goes on to present, the aim is to create a situation in which Chinese scholars make original contributions to translation studies, participating in a 'more open and hermeneutic space of intercultural dialogue'. On the global level at least, such an approach would seem to be a pragmatic acceptance of the status quo, particularly with regard to the situation that obtains in higher education. For the conditions in which academic dialogue takes place are strongly shaped by Western academic conventions: Western universities dominate global university ranking tables (the ranking system itself being biased towards the West, as Qi (2014, 26–7) observes), the majority of academic journals are published in the United States or Western Europe and 'are typically benchmark sites of theory and method in academic practices' (Qi 2014, 37), and 'textbooks written from a US or UK perspective are sold worldwide' (Altbach 2004, 11). Underlying and compounding Western hegemony is the dominance of the English language in research work across all disciplines, which 'gives a significant advantage to the US and the UK and to the other wealthy English-speaking countries' (Altbach 2004, 10).

Yet operating within the constraints of Western hegemony does not imply acceptance of them in the longer term. Neither those who play a role in the importation of Western translation theory to China nor those in the target culture who read those texts are passive recipients; as our analysis of the paratexts has shown, the process of importation – which is in some senses an inevitable aspect of globalisation and Western dominance thereof – is controlled by the receiving culture and encourages active, rather than passive, engagement at every turn. In addition, as many of the paratexts stress, the importation of Western theory takes place alongside the development of theories drawing on domestic traditions and concepts. To the extent that these two ideals are realised in practice, they open up opportunities for resistance, allowing Chinese scholars to 'move away from the margins' (Guo 2009, 248) by increasing their 'discursive power, exercised through a universally intelligible language'. In his analysis of globalisation and higher education, Altbach (2004, 6) argues that 'globalisation cannot be completely avoided. History shows that when universities shut themselves off from economic and societal trends they become moribund and irrelevant.' He goes on, however, to note that 'institutions and systems do possess great latitude in how they deal with globalisation' (Altbach 2004, 6). Chinese efforts to 'make the foreign serve China' against a backdrop of current dominance of Western translation studies represent part of that latitude, and underscore the complexities of the notion of an international translation studies and how it might be achieved.

Notes

1 For examples of similar debates in other academic disciplines, see Munck and O'Hearn (1999), Acharya (2011), and Qi (2014).
2 The opposition between 'Western' and 'non-Western' – and indeed the notion of the 'West' itself – is inherently problematic, as Tymoczko (2007, 2009) and numerous others have observed. For the purposes of this chapter, and in line with other scholars in translation studies who have discussed these issues, I take 'the West' to be a construct (Cheung 2009, 224n3), generally referring to 'traditional centres of power, mostly located in Northern Europe and North America' (Guo 2009, 239n1) but also taking the more symbolic form of the 'realistically unavoidable Other against which China has been trying to define itself, especially over the last two centuries' (Guo 2009, 249).
3 It should be noted, however, that by 'internationalisation' Tymoczko (2009, 403) stresses that she is referring to 'a conception of the international that includes all languages and all cultures', as opposed to bilateral relations between, say, China and the UK.
4 The term 'Anglo-Western' is taken from Shohat and Stam (1994, 6) and neatly encapsulates the tendency for dominant 'Western' scholarship to be written in English, or to find broad support in the West only once translated into English. For a lucid discussion of this issue, see Qi (2014, 14–40).
5 Tan (2009) lists a number of other translations published in the 1980s, notably *Selected Papers on Foreign Translation Theory* (1983), *Nida on Translation* (1984), Steiner's *After Babel* (1987) and two works by Russian theorists, Barchudarov's *Language and Translation* (1985) and Gachechiladze's *An Introduction to the Theory of Literary Translation* (1987) (see Tan 2009 for further discussion and publication details). These early publications would appear to no longer be in circulation, although new editions of Nida's and Steiner's works have been made available. The absence of translations and editions published later than 2012 is striking and something that undoubtedly merits further investigation.
6 The third edition of *Introducing Translation Studies* by Jeremy Munday also includes a summary of Chinese discourses of translation as part of its historical overview of pre-twentieth-century translation theory. See Munday (2012, 32–6, 44–5).
7 This and all subsequent translations of Chinese paratextual material were done by Sarah Fang Tang. As noted in the Acknowledgements, Sarah also contributed to the research for this chapter, identifying the corpus of Chinese translations and editions, providing summaries of paratextual material and commenting on drafts.

8 Brady (2003, 1) gives 1956 as the date on which Mao coined the expression, but the speech first appeared in print in the newspaper *Jiefang Daily* on 19 October 1943 and was published in the third volume of Mao's selected works in 1953.

9 See Dirlik (2000) for further discussion of the related question of Mao's views on the Sinicisation of Marxism.

10 In some respects, distinguishing between political and literary figures from the perspective of present-day paratexts is to invoke a false dichotomy. Lu Xun's status as a leading cultural figure has always been affirmed by the Chinese Communist Party; Mao Zedong apparently called him 'commander of China's cultural revolution' (see Peking Review 1966).

11 The sentence is taken from one of Lu Xun's letters to a friend, Yan Li-Min, in which Lu Xun advises Yan to read more widely, taking in maths, biology and other subjects as well as literature (see Xun 2005, 439).

12 See Delisle (1988, i–ii).

13 The search was carried out on 26 April 2017. Note that this does not equate to 293 independent uses of the phrase, since quite a number of these hits are for citations of existing articles.

14 For further discussion of these issues, see, for example, Gries (2004) and Li (2016).

References

Acharya, Amitav. 2011. "Dialogue and Discovery: In Search of International Relations Theories Beyond the West". *Millennium: Journal of International Studies* 39 (3): 619–37.

Altbach, Philip G. 2004. "Globalisation and the University: Myths and Realities in an Unequal World". *Tertiary Education and Management* 10 (1): 3–25.

Alvares, Claude, and Shad Saleem Faruqi. 2012. "Preface". In *Decolonising the University. The Emerging Quest for Non-Eurocentric Paradigms*. Edited by Claude Alvares and Shad Saleen Faruqi, xvii–xxi. Pulau Pinang: Penerbit Universiti Sains Malaysia and Citzens International.

Appadurai, Arjun. 1990. "Disjuncture and Difference in the Global Cultural Economy". *Theory, Culture & Society* 7: 295–310.

Baker, Mona. 2011. 翻译与冲突: 叙事性阐释 [Translation and Conflict: A Narrative Account]. Translated by Wenjing Zhao. Beijing: Peking University Press.

Bassnett, Susan, and André Lefevere. 2001. 文化建构: 文学翻译论集 [Constructing Cultures: Essays on Literary Translation]. Shanghai: Shanghai Foreign Language Education Press.

Beijing Foreign Language Teaching and Research Press. 2005. "总序 [General Preface]". In 翻译与翻译过程: 理论与实践 [Translation and Translating: Theory and Practice], by Roger T. Bell, 1–4. Beijing: Beijing Foreign Language Teaching and Research Press.

——. 2008. "出版说明 [Publisher's Note]". In 论翻译的原则 [Essays on the Principles of Translation], by Alexander Fraser Tytler, back cover. Beijing: Beijing Foreign Language Teaching and Research Press.

Brady, Anne-Marie. 2003. *Making the Foreign Serve China: Managing Foreigners in the People's Republic*. Lanham, MD: Rowman & Littlefield Publishers.

Buckley, Peter J., Jeremy Clegg, and Hui Tan. 2004. "Knowledge Transfer to China: Policy Lessons from Foreign Affiliates". *Transnational Corporations* 13 (1): 31–72.

Cao, Minglun. 2010. "导读 [Preface]". In 翻译研究 [Translation Studies], by Susan Bassnett, iii–xv. Shanghai: Shanghai Foreign Language Education Press.

Chan, Leo Tak-hung. 2004. *Twentieth-Century Chinese Translation Theory: Modes, Issues and Debates*. Amsterdam and Philadelphia: John Benjamins.

Chang, Nam Fung. 2009. "Repertoire Transfer and Resistance: The Westernization of Translation Studies in China". *The Translator* 15 (2): 305–25.

Chen, Fukang. 2002. 中国译学理论史稿 *[On Chinese Translation Theory]*. Shanghai: Foreign Language Education Press.

Cheung, Martha, ed. 2006. *An Anthology of Chinese Discourse on Translation: Volume One: From Earliest Times to the Buddhist Project*. Manchester: St Jerome Publishing.

——. 2009. "Introduction: Chinese Discourses on Translation". In *Chinese Discourses on Translation: Positions and Perspectives*. Special Issue of *The Translator* 15 (2), edited by Martha Cheung, 223–38. Manchester: St Jerome Publishing.

Ci, Jiwei. 2002. "He Lin's Sinification of Idealism". In *Contemporary Chinese Philosophy*, edited by Chung-Ying Cheng and Nicholas Bunnin, 188–210. Oxford: Blackwell Publishing.

Delabastita, Dirk. 2013. "Continentalism and the Invention of Traditions in Translation Studies". In *Eurocentrism in Translation Studies*, edited by Luc van Doorslaer and Peter Flynn, 29–42. Amsterdam and Philadelphia: John Benjamins.

Delisle, Jean. 1988. "致中国读者 [To Chinese Readers]". In 翻译理论与翻译教学法 *[Translation: An Interpretive Approach]*, by Jean Delisle. Translated by Huishang Sun, i–ii. Beijing: International Culture Press.

Dirlik, Arif. 2000. "Theory, History, Culture: Cultural Identity and the Politics of Theory in Twentieth-Century China". *Development and Society* 29 (2): 73–104.

Fewsmith, Joseph. 2001. *Elite Politics in Contemporary China*. London: Routledge.

Gries, Peter Hays. 2004. *China's New Nationalism. Pride, Politics, and Diplomacy*. Berkeley: University of California Press.

Guo, Yangsheng. 2009. "Theorizing the Politics of Translation in a Global Era. A Chinese Perspective". In *Chinese Discourses on Translation: Positions and Perspectives*. Special Issue of The Translator 15(2), edited by Martha Cheung, 239–59. Manchester: St Jerome Publishing.

Kongyang, Jiang. 1979. "建国以来我国关于美学问题的讨论 [Discussion of Chinese Aesthetical Problems in New China]". 复旦大学学报（社会科学版）*[Fudan Journal (Social Sciences Edition)]* 5: 16–25.

Lander, Edgardo. 2002. "Eurocentrism, Modern Knowledges, and the 'Natural' Order of Global Capital". *Nepantla: Views from South* 3 (2): 245–68.

Leonard, Dorothy. 1998. *Wellsprings of Knowledge: Building and Sustaining the Sources of Innovation*. Boston, MA: Harvard Business School.

Li, Hongmei. 2016. *Advertising and Consumer Culture in China*. Cambridge: Polity Press.

Li, Richard Hua. 2003. "From Technology Transfer to Knowledge Transfer: A Study of International Joint Venture Projects in China". *International Association for Management of Technology (IAMOT) Conference*. Nancy. Accessed 19 December 2017 from http://citeseerx.ist.psu.edu/viewdoc/download?doi=10.1.1.565.4558&rep=rep1&type=pdf.

Li, Xiangdong. 2017. "International Visibility of Mainland China Translation Studies Community: A Scientometric Study". In *Chinese Translation Studies in the 21st Century: Current Trends and Emerging Perspectives*, edited by Roberto A. Valdeón, 241–62. London and New York: Routledge.

Mao, Zedong. 1991. "Speech at the Forum on Literature and Art in Yan An". In *Selected Works of Mao Zedong*, by Zedong Mao, 847–79. Beijing: People's Publishing House.

Mu, Lei. 1991. "译序 [Translator's Introduction]". In 翻译的语言学理论 *[A Linguistic Theory of Translation]*, by J.C. Catford, v. Beijing: Tourism Education Press.

Mu, Lei, and Xiaoyan Zhu. 2006. "前言 [Introduction]". In 今日翻译：趋向与视角 *[Translation Today: Trends and Perspectives]*, by Gunilla Anderman and Margaret Rogers, vii–xi. Beijing: Beijing Foreign Language Teaching and Research Press.

Munck, Ronaldo, and Denis O'Hearn. 1999. *Critical Development Theory: Contributions to a New Paradigm*. London: Zed Books.

Munday, Jeremy. 2007. 翻译学导论 – 理论与实践 [*Introducing Translation Studies*]. Translated by Defeng Li. Shanghai: Commercial Press.

——. 2012. *Introducing Translation Studies: Theories and Applications*, 3rd edition. Abingdon and New York: Routledge.

Nonaka, Ikujiro, and Hirotaka Takeuchi. 1995. *The Knowledge Creating Company: How Japanese Companies Create the Dynamics of Innovation*. Oxford: Oxford University Press.

Oxford Dictionaries. n.d. *Eurocentric*. Accessed 31 August 2017 from https://en.oxforddictionaries.com/definition/Eurocentric.

——. n.d. *Technology Transfer*. Accessed 31 August 2017 from https://en.oxforddictionaries.com/definition/technology_transfer.

Peking Review. 1966. "Commemorating Lu Hsun – Our Forerunner in the Cultural Revolution". *Peking Review*, 4 November: 8–10. Accessed 5 September 2017 from www.marxists.org/subject/china/peking-review/1966/PR1966-45g.htm.

Qi, Xiaoying. 2014. *Globalized Knowledge Flows and Chinese Social Theory*. New York: Routledge.

Said, Edward. 1985. "Orientalism Reconsidered". *Cultural Critique* 1: 89–107.

——. 2003 [1978]. *Orientalism*. London: Penguin.

Shanghai Foreign Language Education Press. 2001a. "前言 [General Preface]". In 文化建构: 文学翻译论集 [*Constructing Cultures: Essays on Literary Translation*], by Susan Bassnett and André Lefevere, n.p. Shanghai: Shanghai Foreign Language Education Press.

——. 2001b. "前言 [Preface]". In 通天塔之后: 语言与翻译面面观 [*After Babel: Aspects of Language and Translation*], by George Steiner, n.p. Shanghai: Shanghai Foreign Language Education Press.

——. 2004. "出版前言 [Preface]". In 文化翻译: 笔译, 口译及中介入门 [*Translating Cultures: An Introduction for Translators, Interpreters, and Mediators*], by David Katan, n.p. Shanghai: Shanghai Foreign Language Education Press.

——. 2010. "前言 [Introduction]". In 翻译, 改写以及对文学名声的制控 [*Translation, Rewriting and the Manipulation of Literary Fame*], by André Lefevere, n.p. Shanghai: Shanghai Foreign Language Education Press.

Shei, Chris, and Zhao-Ming Gao, eds. 2017. *Routledge Handbook of Chinese Translation*. London and New York: Routledge.

Shohat, Ella, and Robert Stam. 1994. *Unthinking Eurocentrism: Multiculturalism and the Media*. London and New York: Routledge.

State Council. 2007. "国务院学位委员会决定设置翻译硕士学位 [The State Council decides to set up a Master of Translation and Interpreting]". *China National Committee for Translation & Interpreting Education*. Accessed 1 September 2017 from http://cnti.gdufs.edu.cn/info/1016/1230.htm#.

Sun, Huishuang. 1992. "译者说明 [Introduction]". In 口笔译概论 [*Interpréter pour traduire*], by Danica Seleskovitch and Marianne Lederer, i–vi. Beijing: Language and Culture University Press.

Sun, Jingli. 2006. "前言 [Introduction]". In 文学翻译: 比较文学背景下的理论与实践 [*Translating Literature: Practice and Theory in a Comparative Literature Context*], by André Lefevere, xii–xiv. Beijing: Beijing Foreign Language Teaching and Research Press.

Sun, Yifeng. 2012. "The Shifting Identity of Translation Studies in China". *Intercultural Communication Studies* 21 (2): 32–52.

Tan, Zaixi. 1999a. "出版说明 [Publisher's Note]". In 新编奈达论翻译 [*Translation of New Theory by Nida*], by Eugene Nida, iv. Beijing: China Translation & Publishing Corporation.

——. 1999b. "译者序 [Translator's Introduction]". In 新编奈达论翻译 *[Translation of New Theory by Nida]*, by Eugene Nida, x–xxvil. Beijing: China Translation and Publishing Corporation.

——. 2005. "译者序 [Translator's Introduction]". In 翻译研究词典 *[Dictionary of Translation Studies]*, by Mark Shuttleworth and Moira Cowie, ix–xxii. Beijing: Beijing Foreign Language and Teaching Research Press.

——. 2009. "The 'Chineseness' versus 'Non-Chineseness' of Chinese Translation Theory". *The Translator* 15 (2): 283–304.

Toury, Gideon. 2012. *Descriptive Translation Studies – and Beyond*, revised edition. Amsterdam and Philadelphia: John Benjamins.

Tucker, Vincent. 1999. "The Myth of Development: A Critique of Eurocentric Discourse". In *Critical Development Theory: Contributions to a New Paradigm*, by Ronaldo Munck and Denis O'Hearn, 1–26. London: Zed Books.

Tymoczko, Maria. 2007. *Enlarging Translation, Empowering Translators*. Manchester: St Jerome Publishing.

——. 2009. "Why Translators Should Want to Internationalize Translation Studies". In *Chinese Discourses on Translation: Positions and Perspectives. Special Issue of The Translator* 15 (2), edited by Martha Cheung, 401–21. Manchester: St Jerome.

Valdeón, Roberto A. 2017. *Chinese Translation Studies in the 21st Century: Current Trends and Emerging Perspectives*. London: Routledge.

Wang, Dongfeng. 2007. "导读 [Reading Guide]". In 翻译与权力 *[Translation and Power]*, edited by Maria Tymoczko and Edwin Gentzler, i–xvi. Beijing: Beijing Foreign Language Teaching and Research Press.

Wang, Ning, and Yifeng Sun. 2008. *Translation, Globalisation and Localisation. A Chinese Perspective*. Clevedon: Multilingual Matters.

Wang, Yuechuan. 1997. *Si, Yan, Dao [Thinking, Discourse and Methodology]*. Beijing: Peking University Press.

Wilss, Wolfram. 2001. 翻译学: 问题与方法 *[The Science of Translation: Problems and Methods]*, 2nd edition. Shanghai: Shanghai Foreign Language Education Press.

Xun, Lu. 2005. 鲁迅全集 *[Complete Works of Lu Xun]*. Beijing: People's Literature Publishing House.

Yang, Zijian. 2001. "借鉴和创造 （代序）[General Publisher's Note]". In 文化建构: 文学翻译论集 *[Constructing Cultures: Essays on Literary Translation]*, by Susan Bassnett and André Lefevere, n.p. Shanghai: Shanghai Foreign Language Education Press.

Zhang, Jinghao. 2006. "主次颠倒的翻译研究和翻译理论 [Misplaced Priorities in Translation Studies and Translation Theory]". 中国翻译 *[Chinese Translators Journal]* 5: 59–61.

Zhuang, Yichuan. 2002. 英汉翻译简明教程 *[An Introduction to English–Chinese Translation Studies]*. Beijing: Foreign Language Teaching and Research Press.

6

WALTER PRESENTS AND ITS PARATEXTS

Curating foreign TV for British audiences

Writing for the *Guardian* in 2004, Alex Cox (2004) opens his article on foreign-language films on British TV with the following remark:

> For the past few weeks, I've been playing an interesting game. In one way, it's interesting; in another, it's a bit boring – because the result is always the same. The name of the game is: 'Spot the foreign-language film on British terrestrial television.' And the score, as you've probably guessed, is zero.

Less than a decade later, Mark Jones (2013), writing for the same newspaper, begins his article on French TV drama *The Returned* with a very different observation: 'In recent years, quality European drama has become so familiar to British viewers that Nigel Farage may well be experiencing night terrors.' Jones (2013) supports his reflection with statistics, noting that 'from the 30 most-watched programmes since BBC4 started in 2002, 14 places are taken up by episodes of Scandinavian thrillers *The Killing, The Bridge* and *Borgen*', and contrasting this with the situation in previous years, in which 'aficionados of foreign television . . . had to hunt for imported boxsets and English subtitles'. A 2016 review of the French drama *The Passenger* suggests that subtitling has even reached the point where it has taken on a broadly positive set of associations. After criticising various weaknesses of the drama, Julia Raeside (2016) writes: 'The saving grace of The Passenger is its Frenchness and the panache with which it's shot. Like any subtitled offering from the continent, your brain imbues it with more sophistication than it might actually possess.' Subtitling, in this account, is no longer a turn-off for mainstream viewers, but has become a draw. Where the fact of subtitling once conveyed fear, mistrust, reluctance, hard work and other negative predispositions, since the mid- to late 2000s it would appear to have become much more positive, conveying sophistication and high quality. Part of this difference is intertextual, since the growing association between subtitled drama and high-quality drama depends on subtitled dramas that have gone before.

These differences could be conceptualised as changes in the 'factual' paratext, according to Genette's (1997, 7) definition, and as outlined in Chapter 1, whereby the fact that a show is subtitled forms part of the assumptions and attitudes that viewers bring to the text or which governs their decision of whether to watch it or not. Alternatively, they could be conceptualised as changes to the context against which the material paratexts themselves need to be interpreted. In Part III, I will make a case for the second of these options on the basis that it helps us to avoid the 'paratext's collapse into the vastness of "the context"' (Rockenberger 2014, 267). The important thing to note at this stage is that the connotative meaning of subtitling has undergone a radical shift in Britain in the last ten or fifteen years for a significant proportion of viewers. In this chapter, I present a case study of a recent on-demand digital TV initiative to provide subtitled foreign drama in Britain,[1] exploring how these changes in attitude towards subtitling are reflected in its paratexts and drawing on Catherine Johnson (2012) to explore connections between paratexts and branding. Appealing to Jonathan Gray's (2010) distinction between industry- and viewer-created paratexts, I will also explore the extent to which the initiative's paratextual strategies are affirmed or countered in the paratexts produced by journalists and on social media sites.

Case study: Walter Presents

In January 2016, in partnership with the Global Series Network, Channel 4 launched Walter Presents as part of its digital hub, All 4, making subtitled box sets available to viewers free of charge. While some of the Walter Presents shows are available only via the on-demand service or website, the first episode is sometimes shown on Channel 4 or More 4. The TV advert announcing the launch summarises the nature of the initiative as well as its key selling points:

> Walter Presents – A handpicked selection – of the best – the best stories – the best characters – the best drama – from around the world . . . – entire box sets – all completely free – whenever you want – trust Walter – we do – Walter Presents.
>
> *Channel 4 2016*

In addition to the obvious emphasis on quality ('the best stories – the best characters – the best drama'), the advert foregrounds the role played by 'Walter', stressing that he has handpicked the dramas, and encouraging viewers to 'trust' him. 'Walter' is Walter Iuzzolino, a former commissioning editor for factual TV shows including *Embarrassing Bodies* and *Country House Rescue* (Day 2016), one of the co-founders of the Global Series Network, and the force behind the new initiative.

Curation

The decision to name the digital service after Walter rather than give it a more neutral label was reportedly taken by Channel 4 (K. Abbott 2016), and reflects the importance of what Mark Lawson (2016) describes as the 'currently fashionable concept of "curated programming"'. Whereas curation used to be an activity primarily associated with museums and exhibitions, in recent years the meaning of the term has been extended to the domain of media and refers to efforts to 'select, organize, and present (online content, merchandise, information, etc.), typically using professional or expert knowledge' (Oxford English Dictionary [online] 2017).[2] This type of curation has arisen because of the overwhelming vastness of choice associated with the on-demand television era, as Chuck Tryon (2013, 126) explains:

> media industry observers have noted the difficulty of 'curating' the wide selection of movies and television shows available at any given time and on such a wide range of platforms. In an era beyond the networks, cable television, and the video store, identifying and tracking down movies and television shows presents a new challenge.

Iuzzolino himself stresses the importance of curation in an interview reported by Kate Abbott for the *Guardian*:

> In a landscape dominated by Netflix, which is 'buying literally everything' but not promoting it enough, says Iuzzolino, personal recommendations are key. 'When everyone wants your subscription money and there's a boring algorithm somewhere in Iowa trying to decide what you might like, a) they get it wrong and b) it's a supermarket way of looking at the world.' Walter Presents is a commercial channel, which generates revenue from advertising, but it is free to viewers and driven by a small team's tastes.
>
> *K. Abbott 2016*

Iuzzolino's contrast between Netflix's purely algorithm-driven recommendations and his own personal ones echoes the vision presented by key players involved in the reconceptualisation of BBC iPlayer in 2014,[3] and ties in with Channel 4's identity as a public service broadcaster. A key selling point of Walter Presents, then, is its personally curated nature: rather than being an undifferentiated mass of foreign dramas, these dramas have been watched, weighed up and approved of by a man whom we are encouraged to trust. Of course, Walter does not know us, and we do not know him, but the illusion of personal recommendation is carefully cultivated by the paratextual material that surrounds the foreign dramas made available through this platform. Some of this material operates as paratext to the entire body of dramas made available through the service, or in other words serves as paratext to the Walter Presents initiative. These include the television advert discussed above, the 'Meet Walter' video available on the Walter Presents website,[4] as well as the plethora of interviews and articles about Iuzzolino that stress his personal involvement in the new service. Other material serves as paratext to each individual series: this includes one- to two-minute introductory video presentations by Iuzzolino and the ten- to twenty-word summaries of the series that appear on the Walter Presents website and the on-demand television menu pages.

In the introductory videos – which in some cases are embedded into the first episode of the series as a form of video preface, while in others are available as separate clips – Walter speaks directly to the camera from inside what we are invited to presume is his own home, a half-full cafetière, a cup of coffee and a notepad and pen on the table in front of him (see Figure 6.1).

He tells the viewers about the series, comparing it to other dramas they might have liked and addressing the viewers directly and informally. In the presentation to *Deutschland 83*, for example, Walter repeatedly uses the phrase 'I've seen', shares his own 'personal' dislike of the 1980s, and tells viewers they would have to be 'insane' not to like the series (*Walter Presents: Deutschland 83* [video] 2016).

The personal connection between Walter and the viewer is further strengthened through Twitter. According to an interview with Sinead McCausland (2017), Iuzzolino states that he is on Twitter 'all the time':

> I'm responding and answering to questions and I care very much about the community of viewers that love what we do . . . [People] come to this because they know it's got a real personal touch, and we can never lose that, that personal connection.
>
> *McCausland 2017*

A brief analysis of the Walter Presents UK Twitter account shows, however, that contrary to this emphasis on personal connection, much of the Twitter interaction

FIGURE 6.1 Still from the Walter Presents introductory video to *Deutschland 83*. Reproduced with the kind permission of Global Series Network Limited

is straightforwardly promotional, consisting of tweets promoting particular shows or citing favourable press reviews, or retweeting endorsements by other Twitter users. Where Iuzzolino does post responses to comments by other Twitter users, these tend to be brief, affirming a positive opinion expressed by a viewer or giving a short informational response to a query. In terms of function, then, the Twitter activity linked with Walter Presents serves more to cultivate the *image* of Walter Presents as a personally curated service – there is, after all, a real person behind the initiative – rather than to facilitate genuine dialogue between Iuzzolino and the viewers. In this sense, the Twitter account, like the presentations accompanying each series and the advert announcing the launch of the service, represents part of the effort to set up a strong brand for Walter Presents.

Branding

In her study of the development of branding in the contexts of US and UK television, Johnson (2012) argues that 'the emergence of digital television in the late 1990s consolidated the role of branding as a central strategy in the changing media landscape' (74). This was in large part a 'strategic response to a period of enhanced competition' (117), although in the case of public service broadcasters – most notably the BBC – branding also aimed to communicate the values of the broadcaster to the public in the face of political pressures (84–6). Unlike the consumer goods industry, where the focus is generally on developing brands for products, Johnson (4) argues that in the television industry there are 'three areas where branding might be adopted by television broadcasters: corporations, channels/services and programmes'. With Walter Presents, the branding operates in an area midway between the second and third levels of generality outlined by Johnson, or in other words beneath the broader levels of the Channel 4 and All 4 brands but above the specific level of the individual series available on the platform such as *Spin* or *Deutschland 83*. The key qualities that the brand looks to convey have been noted

FIGURE 6.2 Walter Presents logo. Reproduced with the kind permission of Global Series Network Limited

above, and can be summarised as international, high-quality, hand-picked, on-demand television dramas. The brand has its own logo, consisting of the letters 'wp' inside a circle, as shown in Figure 6.2. The nature of the logo – handwritten, and incorporating Walter's first name – reinforces the message that the series has been personally curated.

The logo features prominently on the menu pages of the on-demand service, with each box set being represented by a still from one of the episodes with the logo superimposed in the top right-hand corner (see Channel 4 2017a).[5] Where the box sets are listed alongside UK box sets on other on-demand menu pages, the logo serves a dual function, helping viewers to identify and navigate to Walter Presents dramas as well as reinforcing the Walter Presents brand. The brand is further strengthened by the superimposition of the logo on the still for each episode selection button on the subsequent on-demand menu page, as well as on the episodes available through the Channel 4 website. An animated version of the logo, which mimics the handwriting process and thus reinforces the idea that the dramas are hand-picked by an individual, is used in the opening and conclusion of each of the series presentations by Iuzzolino, as well as at the beginning and end of each episode in a series.

The logo plays an important role in drawing together series that have no formal link to each other save the fact that Walter has selected them, affirming in shorthand the quality and appeal of each of the dramas. To a certain extent, this obviates the need to create a brand for each individual series, something for which the individual series would in any case not be well suited, owing to their relative brevity.[6] With regard to what might be termed the higher-level brands, namely those associated with All 4 and Channel 4, the Walter Presents brand can be seen to work alongside these rather than replacing them: the Walter Presents logo is preceded by the Channel 4 ident in each episode; the words 'From Channel 4' appear at the bottom of the animated Walter Presents logo itself; the online and on-demand Walter Presents pages are reached via the All 4 platform and website, with its associated prominent branding. The structure of the All 4 on-demand portal and website also reflect the possibility that not all potential viewers of Walter Presents will be familiar with the Walter Presents brand: on the on-demand site, viewers reach the Walter Presents portal by selecting the generic category 'World Drama' (Channel 4 2017a) and are only then presented with the Walter Presents name and logo, while on the website viewers select 'World Drama' (Channel 4 2017b) and are presented with a selection of box sets featuring the WP logo but are only taken to the Walter Presents website if they select one of the box sets and then click 'Want more World Drama'. Nevertheless, the prominence given to Walter Presents itself is striking, resulting in a strong framework of paratextual branding for the subtitled programmes. In the next section, I will explore the ways in which the foreignness of the dramas is incorporated into the Walter Presents branding strategy, asking what this suggests about viewers' perceived attitudes towards subtitled drama at the present moment, thus contributing to the discussion of the shift in such attitudes initiated in the first part of this chapter. In the final section, I will explore the ways in which paratextual material created by viewers potentially undermines this strategy for presenting foreignness, as well as the Walter Presents brand more generally.

Industry-created paratexts: presenting foreignness and the fact of subtitling

In this section, I consider the extent to which the foreignness of the dramas and the fact of subtitling are foregrounded in the industry-created thresholds through which viewers access the dramas that feature on Walter Presents. More specifically, I examine the interfaces of the All 4 on-demand TV platform and the Walter Presents website, the written summaries of individual drama series and the video introductions given by Iuzzolino. In this case study, I consider as paratext any element that provides a threshold either to a particular drama series or to the Walter Presents service itself. The series and the service themselves thus form the 'texts'. In the case of the series, *text* therefore denotes the tangible, finite entity that is the complete drama itself, whereas in the case of the service *text* is used to denote the more abstract and mutable Walter Presents concept. The usefulness of viewing both types of entity as texts with their associated paratexts will become clear as the chapter progresses.

Interfaces

As noted above, the Walter Presents TV portal is available via the All 4 on-demand service and is accessed via the 'World Drama' category option. This category sits alongside ten other categories, which include 'Drama', 'Comedy', 'Entertainment', and so on (see Channel 4 2017a). While the short description of the 'Drama' category makes no mention of place – 'Original and compelling drama that stands the test of time' – the short description of 'World Drama' reads: 'Walter Presents a handpicked selection of the best international drama'. The use of the labels 'world drama' and 'international drama' to denote foreign subtitled series represents both a foregrounding and a euphemising of foreignness. On the one hand, although both terms could, in purely semantic terms, refer to drama from all over the world, in English, as well as other languages, the fact that 'world drama' is opposed to 'drama' in the category options shows that they are being used to denote something non-mainstream and to some degree exotic.[7] While this foregrounding of difference is negated to a certain extent by the fact that the Walter Presents dramas actually appear in the 'Drama' category listings as well, the fact that they retain the WP logo when listed under the more generic category means that they continue to be marked as different from the mainstream. On the other hand, the fact that the terms 'world' and 'international', which are vague with regard to language implications, are preferred over the terms 'foreign-language' or 'subtitled', glosses over the fact of language difference to a certain degree.

The tendency to downplay the fact that the Walter Presents dramas are in foreign languages is also evident on the Walter Presents website. With two exceptions, the website groups the dramas thematically rather than by language, ordering them under the headings 'Most Popular', 'Hot & Sexy Sizzlers', 'Feel Good Dramedy', 'Sinister Sharp Shockers', 'All-out Action', 'Drama Queens' and 'Critically Acclaimed Thrillers' (Channel 4 2017b). The exceptions are the headings 'French Fancies' and 'Chilling Nordic Noir' (Channel 4 2017b), both of which appear to be using explicit mentions of geographical origins to indicate genre rather than to flag up the language, or range of languages, used in the drama. The thresholds on the structure of the webpage thus encourage viewers to select what they want to watch based on their preferences for certain types of drama rather than on the language in which the drama is expressed. Nowhere on the website is any mention made of the fact that the dramas are subtitled, something which is quite remarkable when viewed against the backdrop of longstanding UK TV listing practices, according to which the fact of subtitling always finds explicit mention.[8]

Series summaries

While the website prioritises genre over language with regard to its overall structure, the ten- or eleven-word summaries that appear underneath the clickable image for each drama almost always mention geographical origin. To take the example of the dramas under the 'Most Popular' heading, the summaries read as follows:

> *Locked Up*: Spain's sexy and provocative prison drama returns for a new series
>
> *Case*: Looking for a moody drama? Watch this grim Icelandic noir
>
> *Black Widow*: The Dutch Olivia Colman. Watch an award-winning gangster thriller
>
> *Spin*: The rave-reviewed French House of Cards returns for its final series
>
> *Channel 4 2017b*

The same tendency to mention geographical origin can be observed in the slightly longer summaries provided on the on-demand TV portal (see Channel 4 2017a). Just six out of the thirty-five summaries do not mention the country in which the drama was made and, of those six, three mention the name of a place or person that would enable the viewer to deduce the approximate geographical origin of the drama ('Macarena Ferreiro' for *Locked Up*, 'Alpine village' for *The Returned*, 'Dunkirk' for *Reborn*). What is remarkably consistent across all of the summaries is a foregrounding of place rather than language: *Magnífica 70* is a 'Brazilian drama' rather than a 'drama in Brazilian Portuguese'; *The Invisibles* is a 'comedic fantasy drama from the Czech Republic' rather than a 'comedic fantasy drama in Czech', and so on. This ties in with the striking absence of all mention of subtitling noted above.

   Another strategy used in the Walter Presents summaries is the comparison of the foreign drama or actors to references with which the target audience is presumed to be familiar. Thus, in the examples cited above, the lead actor (Monic Hendrickx) of *Black Widow* is described as 'the Dutch Olivia Colman' (Channel 4 2017a), and *Spin* is referred to as the 'French House of Cards' (Channel 4 2017a). Other examples from the website include the summary of German drama *Hotel Adlon* as 'Period drama that plays like Downton Abbey. Or, as The Sun puts it: "Mr Selfridge with Nazis"' (Channel 4 2017b) and the description of *Magnífica 70* as 'Breaking Bad meets Boogie Nights in 1970s Brazil' (Channel 4 2017b).

Viewed from the perspective of translation theory, such a presentational strategy could be considered classically domesticating, 'leav[ing] the reader in peace as much as possible and mov[ing] the writer toward him' (Schleiermacher 2012, 49), to use Schleiermacher's distinctions on which Venuti's (1995) well-known dichotomy is based. Yet these types of comparison show themselves to be frequent in media promotional discourse even where no foreign culture is involved: new shows are often advertised as being the new or next version of some existing successful show, and academic research shows that film reviewers 'consistently assign films a comparative location in the existing film field' (Kersten and Bielby 2012, 191).

Intriguingly, this presentational strategy is not used at all in the summaries on the on-demand portal. Thus the on-demand summary of *Black Widow* reads: 'Carmen, the daughter of a crime lord, reluctantly takes charge of the family's drug-smuggling business in this complex Dutch crime drama' (Channel 4 2017a), while the summary for *Spin* is 'French political thriller following a tension-filled campaign and turbulent presidential term as two spin doctors go head to head' (Channel 4 2017a). The reasons for this discrepancy are not clear, although the consistency with which the two strategies (comparing versus not comparing) are followed on the two platforms indicates that it is deliberate. The comparisons made on the Walter Presents website frequently find their way into reviews and headlines in mainstream media or, in other words, into other paratexts to the series. The *Evening Standard*, for example, uses the heading 'The Dutch Olivia Colman' (Jones 2017) for its feature on *Black Widow*, while the *Guardian* draws on Iuzzolino's comparison of *The Swingers* to *Fatal Attraction* in its summary of the series.[9] The Walter Presents website summary of *Hotel Adlon* cited above reminds us that the borrowing of comparisons can go in both directions: in the case of that show, Iuzzolino repeats the *Sun*'s comparison of the show to *Mr Selfridge* alongside his own comparison of the show to *Downton Abbey*.[10]

Introductory videos

The tendency to draw comparisons between a new series and an existing one is also strongly present in the introductory videos presented by Iuzzolino. Iuzzolino suggests, for example, that the 1980s characters in *Deutschland 83* 'feel much closer to Mad Men than they do to Dynasty' (*Walter Presents: Deutschland 83* [video] 2016), selecting two US dramas as his points of comparison. In a similar vein, the video presentation of *Spin* repeats the comparison with *House of Cards* that is used in the written website summary, although also compares the show to the Danish drama *Borgen* (*Walter Presents: Spin* [video] 2016). This suggests that the popularity of foreign drama in the UK is now such that previously successful foreign dramas can be used alongside UK and US shows as intertexts to promote newly imported series. This also lends support to the argument made above that, while comparing foreign series to UK/US ones might to some extent be viewed as a strategy for reducing the foreignness of the dramas, it may also simply be part of a more general practice for selling any new show, whatever its origin. In other words, if *Spin* is compared to *Borgen*, this cannot have anything to do with attempting to mitigate *Spin*'s foreignness or subtitled nature, since *Borgen* is also a foreign subtitled drama. This presentational strategy is thus more about setting the new show within the context of the broader canon of shows that have been successful on UK TV and suggesting that the new show has its own rightful place within that canon.

In this respect, comparative strategies are a means of affirming the quality of the new series and go hand-in-hand with another key promotional strategy consistently used by Iuzzolino in the video introductions. We see this strategy at work in all of the videos: it consists essentially in emphasising the high quality of the series by noting that the series has won awards, or by stressing the calibre of the directors or actors. Thus *Spin* is 'multi-award-winning' (*Walter Presents: Spin* [video] 2016) and has an 'all-star cast'; the creator of *Elite Squad*, Olivier Marchal, is an 'award-winning monster talent' (*Walter Presents: Elite Squad* [video] 2017); and the introduction to *Valkyrien* opens with the statement that 'Sometimes a piece of telly comes along which totally transforms the landscape, raising the bar for everyone else' (*Walter Presents: Valkyrien* [video] 2017).

In addition to these enthusiastic affirmations of a show's quality, the introductory videos offer brief summaries of the plot and main characters, and comment on the tone or style of the series. As with the written summaries, there is no explicit mention of the fact that the shows are subtitled, and the foreignness of the series finds little mention beyond the odd comparative evocation along the lines of the ones used in the written summaries.[11] Nevertheless, in these introductory videos, the fact that the shows are subtitled does emerge through the clips that accompany Iuzzolino's commentary: while the majority of the clips are very short ones taken from action or sex scenes, some of them do contain small amounts of dialogue and correspondingly include subtitles. Overall, however, Iuzzolino's silence on the question of subtitling – a silence which is maintained in all of the official paratexts for Walter Presents – appears to be designed to convey the clear and consistent message that subtitling is a non-issue. In the next section, I shall analyse a range of viewer-created paratexts to the Walter Presents service and individual drama series in an effort to discover whether Iuzzolino's message is a reflection of British attitudes to subtitling or alternatively still in some respects aspirational.

Viewer-created paratexts

While shows such as *Lost* have an extensive viewer-created paratext,[12] the Walter Presents service and the drama series curated on it have much smaller viewer-created paratexts. Nevertheless, the viewer-created paratexts that do exist can function as significant 'entryway paratexts' (Gray 2010, 23), influencing potential viewers' decisions about whether or not to watch a particular show. They also function as a site where the strategies used in the industry-created paratexts for presenting the subtitled nature of the dramas can be directly and indirectly contested. In this section, I consider four different types of viewer-created paratexts, focusing in particular on the extent to which the foreignness of the dramas is foregrounded and on challenges to the Walter Presents brand.

Press reviews

For this case study, I analysed all reviews of the Walter Presents initiative or of a specific Walter Presents series that were published in the online versions of UK newspapers and magazines between August 2015 and April 2017. The publications that featured reviews during this period were the *Evening Standard, Guardian, Independent, Metro, NME, Radio Times, Telegraph, Drama Quarterly* and *Royal Television Society*. Of the nineteen reviews identified, seventeen explicitly mention that the shows are subtitled or in a foreign language.[13] In many cases, this fact is foregrounded: nine of the reviews highlight in their headline or sub-headline the fact that the drama is in a foreign language,[14] while a further eight use the headline or sub-headline to indicate the show's foreign geographical origin without stating explicitly that the show is subtitled.[15] Two of the reviews which do not mention the foreign-language nature of the drama in the headlines foreground it very prominently in the body of the article: both of these reviews appear in the *Evening Standard* in the short-review format 'Five things you need to know about . . .', and the fact that the show is subtitled is listed in first place in one of the reviews and second place in the other:

> Take a look at Locked Up . . . Here are five things you need to know:
>
> **1) It's in Spanish**
>
> As with all of Channel 4's Walter Presents series, this is a foreign language drama – so be prepared to read subtitles unless you're fluent in Spanish. Don't let that put you off – Walter Presents has already given us the thrilling Deutschland 83, which was in German, and you'll be so caught up in the fray of the drama that you'll forget about the subtitles within minutes.
>
> *Travis 2016, bold in original*

> Need a new gripping drama to get swept up in? Channel 4 are on the Case . . . Here are five things you need to know:
>
> **2) It's in Icelandic**
>
> Don't be shocked – yes, this Icelandic drama is in Icelandic. If you're the sort of person who usually runs a mile at the sight of a subtitle, give it a chance – as anyone who's delved into a Scandi-noir thriller before will attest, you forget you're reading them within the first five minutes.
>
> *Travis 2017, bold in original*

Unlike the industry-created paratexts, these reviews – which position themselves unambiguously as entryway paratexts – acknowledge that the fact that the shows are in a foreign language may be a turn-off for potential viewers. Similarly, a review of *Locked Up* that appears in the *Telegraph* presents the show as something which 'crackles with wit, even with subtitles' (O'Donovan 2017), repeating this sentiment in both the title and the body of the article.

Other reviews make subtitling into a point of discussion whilst suggesting that negative predispositions towards subtitling are a feature of the past. Caroline Corcoran's (2015) article on the Walter Presents initiative, for example, opens by sketching the shift in fortunes of subtitled drama in the UK:

> Fifteen years ago, if you'd mentioned to a colleague that you'd spent Saturday night glued to a subtitled European drama, you'd have been quietly declared pretentious, dull and, possibly, a little odd. Skip to today and foreign-language dramas aren't even on-trend, they're fully mainstream. Now we are as likely to discuss the latest Danish thriller over a morning flat white at our desks as we are a new season on HBO.

Mark Lawson (2016), writing for the *Guardian*, uses the sub-headline of his article to paint a similar picture: 'A few years ago, a French TV drama about complex machinations inside the Elysée Palace would have been scoffed at. But now foreign-language shows are a real draw and getting even more airtime thanks to C4's innovative project.' Similarly, Elizabeth Day (2016), writing for the *Telegraph*, argues:

> In recent years, Britain has fallen for foreign television. First, Scandinavian detective procedurals familiarised us with world drama . . . Before that point, we were scared of subtitles. They were associated with interminable European films, the kind Iuzzolino describes as 'dripping tap' because there is always a long shot of a leaking faucet in an empty room. Subtitles were dull. Subtitles were elitist. Subtitles required an expensive ticket to a half-empty cinema where the man who sold you the ticket was probably dressed in a polo neck and reading Sartre. But now all that has changed.

Almost all of the reviews, then, draw attention to the fact that the dramas available through the Walter Presents platform are subtitled. Furthermore, the platform itself is frequently labelled a 'foreign-language drama' collection, platform or service,[16] in contrast with Channel 4's designation of the service as providing 'world' or 'international' drama, discussed above. Although the citations given above show that the fact that the Walter Presents dramas are subtitled is generally presented positively, it is nevertheless striking that reviewers feel the need to make it clear that the shows are subtitled, in contrast with the strategy observed in the industry-created paratexts.

While the viewer-created paratexts discussed so far are those that are produced by 'professional television viewers' (Gray 2011, 115), those that will be discussed in the remainder of this section are created by ordinary viewers, or in other words people who have no obligation to write about a show but choose to do so, often anonymously. The value of examining these audience-created paratexts is twofold: on the one hand, they offer evidence of popular attitudes towards subtitling, enabling us to gauge the extent to which the attitudes towards subtitling that are evident in the industry-created and professional viewer-created paratexts are shared by the population at large;[17] on the other, as paratexts that function in their own right as thresholds to the Walter Presents shows, they illustrate the alternative framings through which some viewers come to the dramas.

Facebook

The Walter Presents Facebook group was set up by a fan,[18] and has no formal link to Iuzzolino or Channel 4. Overall, the tone in the Facebook group discussions is positive, and mention of subtitles is rare. One user comments that she watched the first episode of *Locked Up* and 'for the first minute I wondered if I would be able to follow it with the subtitles but very quickly I was hooked as it just gripped me!' (H. Abbott 2016), but this only elicits one further comment on subtitling (to the effect that the viewer 'knew [they] wouldn't be an issue' as he 'love[s] world cinema' (Starkey 2016)). The remaining ten comments focus instead on how much they liked *Locked Up* and similar dramas. The only other mentions that are made of subtitling in the Facebook group are in relation to practical difficulties in accessing subsequent series of the Walter Presents shows as quickly as users would like (see, for example, Johnson (2016) and the same user's reply to a query posted by Wichert (2016)). To a certain extent, the absence of commentary on the subtitled nature of the Walter Presents dramas on the Facebook group confirms the position that Iuzzolino himself appears to anticipate: once viewers have grown accustomed to viewing subtitled dramas, it is the quality of the series itself (and very often its addictiveness) that is uppermost in viewers' minds; subtitles become normal and therefore do not need to be mentioned.

YouTube

The TV advert promoting the launch of Walter Presents, discussed above, is currently available both on the Walter Presents website – or in other words as part of the industry-created paratextual apparatus – and on the separate platform, YouTube. YouTube also serves as an alternative platform for the introductory videos made by Iuzzolino for individual dramas. Whereas the industry-created paratextual framework offers viewers no opportunity to respond to the advert or the introductory videos, the YouTube platform does. YouTube thus opens up a space in which a viewer-created paratext can be built up beyond the control of the Walter Presents brand. Unlike the Facebook group, which draws together fans of Walter Presents shows, the viewers of the YouTube trailers are not necessarily people with any allegiance to the Walter Presents platform, and their contributions are thus less likely to function as 'value co-creation' (Aronczyk 2017) for the brand and more likely to challenge or undermine it.

Overall, the number of comments on the Walter Presents videos is low: the greatest number of comments on any one video is twenty-eight, and many of them have no comments at all.[19] Unlike the generally favourable comments posted to the Facebook group, almost all of the comments on YouTube are either neutral or negative. In parallel with the Facebook comments, however, very few of the YouTube comments focus on subtitling. To give examples of these two trends, the first comment that appears underneath the TV advert is 'Fuck you Walter and fuck your shit shows' (LEGO TUBE 2016). The other comments on this video (there are eleven in total) are neutral, focusing on the soundtrack to the video and how to get access to the dramas. Similarly, of the twenty-nine comments on the most viewed of all the Walter Presents videos (Iuzzolino's introduction to *Heartless*, with over 36,000 views at the time of writing), only one is clearly positive, whereas eight are negative. The negative comments include reasonably measured reactions as well as offensive statements targeted at Iuzzolino, like the one posted by LEGO TUBE cited above.[20] Only one commenter mentions the fact that the shows are not in English.[21]

While the number of comments posted in response to the YouTube videos is so low that we cannot extrapolate from them to make any generalisations about British viewers' attitudes towards subtitling,[22] the overall absence of comment on the fact that the dramas are in a foreign language does nevertheless suggest that subtitling is perceived fairly neutrally. In this sense, these viewer-created paratexts confirm the attitudes towards subtitling that the industry-created para-texts assume people to hold, somewhat in contrast with the viewer-created paratexts produced by professional television viewers, discussed above. In terms of the paratext that these comments on YouTube videos create, however, it is clear that viewers accessing the Walter Presents videos through this route are presented with a more ambiguous and negative threshold to the Walter Presents initiative than those who come to it through the industry-created paratexts. The extent to which this actually impacts on viewers' decisions to enter the text or turn back, or on their perception of the show itself, is difficult to ascertain. Nevertheless, the permanence of the comments is striking and renders them far more powerful than they would be in any real-world forum. In the real world, if we were sitting next to LEGO TUBE on the sofa and watching the Walter Presents advert on the TV, LEGO TUBE's denigratory reaction to the advert and to Walter would have disappeared as swiftly as it was expressed; in the online world, however, LEGO TUBE's comments appear together with the TV advert itself and are present, repeatedly, to every subsequent viewer of the advert. If the user has a high ranking in the YouTube system,[23] as LEGO TUBE appears to, the comment will appear above all other comments, immedi-ately below the advert. If the video is commented on relatively infrequently, as is the case for the Walter Presents videos, the top comment can retain its position for a very long time.

Discussion forums

Other types of site unconnected to the industry-created paratexts but which can operate as part of the Walter Presents paratext are discussion forums, such as those hosted by the leading entertainment site Digital Spy. Any user can start their own discussion threads or post to existing ones, as long as he or she conforms to the rules set out by the host site. A search for 'Walter Presents' on the Digital Spy site reveals sixty-one hits over a period of one year (14 June 2016–14 June 2017). The discussions show that the forum functions not only as a virtual place for viewers to exchange ideas about dramas that they have already seen, but also as an entryway paratext that helps potential viewers decide whether or not to watch a particular series. For example, one forum user posted the question 'Is it worth watching The Team then?' (tartan-belle 2017), prompting a range of opinions on the drama. In the course of the discussion, another user wrote 'Posters [to the discussion forum] have whetted my appetite for Dept Q . . . I will give that a go . . .' (Marispiper 2017), referring to a Danish drama shown on BBC4.

Like the You Tube comments, the comments on the Digital Spy forum reveal a range of attitudes towards the Walter Presents initiative and the dramas shown through it. Most of the discussions concern plot lines, reactions to the dramas, and queries about the availability of the programmes or of forthcoming series. There are very few comments on the fact of subtitling and no comments at all that indicate that subtitles were in any way a barrier or turn-off. On the contrary, the same user who said that posters had whetted his or her appetite for *Dept Q* expressed dislike of the drama *The Team*, calling it 'second rate' and reflecting, 'I think I fell into the trap of thinking "subtitles = good"' (Marispiper 2017). This comment represents an interesting corroboration of the sense expressed through some of the newspaper articles discussed above that subtitling now carries a broadly positive set of connotations, as opposed to the negative ones it held ten or fifteen years ago.

The main point of irritation that emerges through the discussion forum has to do not with the fact of subtitling, but with the way in which Channel 4 makes the shows available: users are frequently critical of the fact that it is only the first episode of a series that is broadcast, with the remainder being made available via the on-demand platform, a fact that is foregrounded in the thread entitled 'Warning: another Walter Presents Drama next week' (WhoAteMeDinner 2017). The warning here has not to do with the foreignness or subtitled nature of the dramas, but with the frustration that some viewers feel with this broadcasting format. As with the YouTube comments, the forum users also express a certain dislike of Walter, resulting in a similar undermining of Channel 4's careful cultivation of the curated programming brand in the industry-created paratexts.[24]

Concluding remarks

The findings of this case study can be summarised in a series of short reflections on Gray's (2010, 25) statement that 'paratexts condition our entrance to texts, telling us what to expect'. First, where a paratext conveys the information that the text is subtitled, precisely what such information 'tell[s] us to expect' is far from constant: as we have seen in this study, while only around a decade ago such information appears to have told UK viewers to expect highbrow impenetrability, it now tells them to expect high-quality drama that makes for addictive viewing. Second, we have seen that the industry-created paratexts to Walter Presents adopt a strategy of deliberately *not* telling audiences directly that the texts are in a foreign language, placing the emphasis instead on the idea that the dramas have been personally curated and vetted for quality. This selective approach to information is a typical feature of paratexts and a key way in which paratext creators 'condition our entrance to texts', to return to Gray's assertion. In this context, the elision of the foreign-language nature of the dramas may reflect the positive changes in attitude to subtitling outlined above; alternatively, it could perhaps be an acknowledgement that earlier negative attitudes towards subtitling may still persist, with the idea that euphemising rather than emphasising foreignness is less likely to put people off watching the dramas. Third, our case study has also shown that the elision of foreignness in the industry-created paratexts stands in contrast to the approach taken in press reviews, which consistently bring the fact that the dramas are in a foreign language back into focus, countering the message that subtitling is a non-issue even while asserting a positive view of it. In other respects, however, press reviews reproduce the industry-created paratextual messages, notably by focusing positively on Iuzzolino and the curated nature of the Walter Presents service. Other types of viewer-created paratexts, meanwhile, tend to parallel the industry-created paratexts in terms of their lack of emphasis on subtitling, but vary considerably in terms of their stance towards the Walter Presents brand. In summary, these contrasts between the messages conveyed in the industry- and viewer-created paratexts foreground the plurality of paratextual messages and underline the importance of taking account of the full range of thresholds through which viewers come to translated audiovisual products in the digital age.

Notes

1 The initiative, Walter Presents, was extended to the US in March 2017 as a subscription service. I do not analyse the paratexts of the US version in this chapter.
2 For an overview of the genealogy of the term 'curation' and its use in present-day contexts, see Snyder (2015).
3 See Grainge and Johnson (2018).
4 For this and all subsequent references to material on the website, see Channel 4 (2017b). The website is frequently updated and altered and the analysis presented in this chapter is based on the appearance of the website in June 2017.
5 In some cases, the logo is accompanied by the expansion of the acronym. The reasons for this variation are not clear. Where the logo is not included (see, for example, the drama *The Returned*), Iuzzolino's introduction to the drama is available but not the drama itself.
6 In her study of television programme branding, Johnson (2012, 159) observes that the programmes that are developed as brands 'have three central characteristics: longevity; transferability; and multiplicity'. The examples of programme brands that she provides – *The Apprentice, American Idol, Dr Who, Lost* – indicate that longevity is to be understood

as extending over many years. The Walter Presents dramas, in contrast, usually consist of around eight episodes.

7 It is worth noting that English-language drama from outside Britain (e.g. from the US) is not included under the 'world drama' listing. I could find no academic studies of the development of 'world drama' as a label, but it is likely that it developed as a strategy for unifying and marketing a range of cultural expressions considered to be in some way distant for UK and US consumers, much like the term 'world music' (see, on the latter, Connell and Gibson 2004, 349–53). In the case of world music, the sense of distance is premised on sounds and genres that are non-Western (but see Connell and Gibson (2004, 350) for a nuancing of this point), while in the case of world drama, the sense of distance would appear to be based on language (i.e. non-English).

8 The Radio Times archives, which contain the BBC listings from 1923 to 2009, reveal that the fact that a show is in a foreign language is always made clear through the formula 'in Spanish (or French, German etc.) with English subtitles'. The listings from 2004 to 2006 for the French series *Spiral*, for example, invariably state 'In French with English subtitles' (BBC Four 2006). A cursory survey of *Radio Times* listings at the time of writing (June 2017) shows that this formula is still consistently used, with other mainstream publications following the same pattern.

9 On the latter, see K. Abbott (2016) but note that in the *Guardian* piece, the title of the series is given as 'The Neighbours'.

10 The wording in the *Sun* review indicates that they are in fact borrowing the comparison from another source, rather than coining it themselves: 'This Berlin-based family saga has been likened to a German Mr Selfridge with Nazis' (TV Magazine 2017). I was not able to find the full comparison (Mr Selfridge with Nazis) in any online sources, and wonder whether the 'Mr Selfridge' part of the comparison did in fact come from Iuzzolino originally (see Holly Williams's piece in the *Independent* in 2015, which cites Iuzzolino's description of *Hotel Adlon* as 'Mr Selfridge – but stronger and better' (Williams 2015)). It would not be inconceivable for the *Sun* to have borrowed that comparison and added their own sensationalising flourish to it.

11 In the introductory video to *Spin*, for example, Iuzzolino suggests that 'if *House of Cards* and *Borgen* were set in France, this is what they would look like' (*Walter Presents: Spin* [video] 2016).

12 See Mittell (2015).

13 The two reviews which do not use the term *subtitle* or *foreign-language* still make the geographical origin of the show clear, but do so in a manner which echoes the strategies used in the industry-created paratexts. Thus *Deutschland 83* is referred to in a *Guardian* review as a 'new drama' (Tate 2016) (rather than a 'foreign-language' or 'subtitled' drama) in the sub-headline, and is described as a 'new imported German drama' (Tate 2016), rather than 'drama in German' or 'German-language drama'. Similarly, in an *Evening Standard* review, *Blue Eyes* is referred to simply as a 'political Scandi-noir thriller' (McKay 2016).

14 See Arnell (2015), Corcoran (2015), Sherwin (2015), Kemp (2016), Lawson (2016), Radio Times (2016), Razaq (2016), Bartleet (2017), O'Donovan (2017).

15 See K. Abbott (2016), Day (2016), McKay (2016), Oltermann (2016), Raeside (2016), Tate (2016), Allen (2017), Travis (2017).

16 See, for example, Oltermann (2016), Radio Times (2016) and Allen (2017). Other reviews such as K. Abbott (2016) and Razaq (2016) simply label Walter Presents a 'foreign drama' service, again in contrast with Channel 4's own preferred designations.

17 The idea that viewer-created paratexts are useful for gaining insight into text reception is taken from Gray (2010, 146) and will be discussed further in Chapter 8. It is important to note, however, that viewers who post their opinions on social media represent only a small sub-set of viewers. Research by Thelwell, Sud and Vis (2012) into YouTube video comments, for example, indicates that men are more likely to post opinions than women, and that negative comments are more likely to trigger debate than positive ones.

18 Tim Arnold, personal communication.

19 Correct at the time of writing (23 June 2017).
20 See *Walter Presents: Heartless* [video] (2016). The remainder of the comments are neutral in the sense that they are requesting information or giving clarification about the plot, number of episodes, or existence of another season. There are also some responses (also classed as neutral) on the question of which language the show is in and whether or not to expect an English version. Other possibly positive comments are too short to rule out sarcasm: one user comments 'Oooooooooh!' while another one writes 'You convinced me sir' and have not been classified as either positive, negative or neutral.'
21 See the question posted by DoppelgangerIsaacWhiteman (2016): 'On S1 Ep3, seems interesting so far. But why isn't it in English language, & will there be an English version soon on Netflix, if so when, & what language it [sic] that?'
22 In addition, the nationality of the commentators is not known.
23 See Simpson (2013) for an explanation of YouTube's commenting system.
24 WhoAteMeDinner (2017), for example, refers to Walter as 'that total bell-end'.

References

Abbott, Helen. 2016. "I watched the Spanish Prison thriller drama 'Locked Up' last night". 18 May. Accessed 6 November 2017 from www.facebook.com/groups/899789073442944/permalink/1019320008156516/.

Abbott, Kate. 2016. "'It's Better than The Sopranos': The Foreign TV You'll Be Bingeing on This Summer". *Guardian*, 8 April. Accessed 25 May 2017 from www.theguardian.com/tv-and-radio/2016/apr/08/sopranos-foreign-summer-tv-walter-presents-deutschland-83.

Allen, Aliyah. 2017. "Walter Presents to Premiere New Drama Case on Channel 4". *Royal Television Society*, 13 January. Accessed 1 November 2017 from https://rts.org.uk/article/walter-presents-premiere-new-drama-case-channel-4.

Arnell, Stephen. 2015. "Channel 4 Looks to Set Subs Standard with 4 World Drama". *Drama Quarterly*, 21 August. Accessed 1 November 2017 from http://dramaquarterly.com/c4-sets-subs-standard/.

Aronczyk, Melissa. 2017. "Portal or Police? The Limits of Promotional Paratexts". *Critical Studies in Media Communication* 34 (2): 111–19.

Bartleet, Larry. 2017. "Channel 4's Walter Presents – The Real Walter Talks us Through the 2017 Batch of Amazing Foreign-Language Telly". *NME*, 16 March. Accessed 1 November 2017 from www.nme.com/blogs/tv-blogs/2017-guide-channel-4s-foreign-language-tv-library-walter-presents-walter-2016889.

BBC Four. 2006. "Spiral". *Radio Times*, 25 May: 71. Accessed 6 June 2017 from http://genome.ch.bbc.co.uk/83ffe84860fe408aa7861821e4f51f29.

Channel 4. 2016. *Walter Presents/Launches January/All 4 [video]*. Accessed 25 May 2017 from https://youtu.be/q3y_1n9UOuE.

———. 2017a. "All 4". [On-demand TV portal]. Accessed 5 June 2017.

———. 2017b. *Walter Presents* [website]. Accessed 5 June 2017 from www.channel4.com/programmes/walter-presents.

Connell, John, and Chris Gibson. 2004. "World Music: Deterritorializing Place and Identity". *Progress in Human Geography* 28 (3): 342–61.

Corcoran, Caroline. 2015. "From Deutschland 83 to The Legacy and Gomorrah, British Viewers Can't Get Enough of Foreign-Language Dramas". *Independent*, 31 December. Accessed 18 May 2017 from www.independent.co.uk/arts-entertainment/tv/features/from-deutschland-83-to-the-legacy-and-gomorrah-british-viewers-cant-get-enough-of-foreign-language-a6792381.html.

Cox, Alex. 2004. "Shutting out Subtitles. How the Fate of Foreign-language Films on British TV was Sealed in a Budapest Swimming Pool". *Guardian*, 25 June. Accessed 18 May 2017 from www.theguardian.com/film/2004/jun/25/1.

Day, Elizabeth. 2016. "Walter Presents: Meet the Man who is Changing the Way we Watch TV". *Telegraph*, 19 November. Accessed 18 May 2017 from www.telegraph.co.uk/tv/2016/11/19/walter-presents-meet-the-man-who-is-changing-the-way-we-watch-tv/.

DoppelgangerIsaacWhiteman. 2016. "Re: An Introduction to Heartless/Walter Presents/All 4". Accessed 6 November 2017 from www.youtube.com/watch?v=ofDrYIZCEBw&lc=UgjwhZ-xBHzOz3gCoAEC.

Genette, Gérard. 1997. *Paratexts: Thresholds of Interpretation*. Translated by Jane E. Lewin. Cambridge: Cambridge University Press.

Grainge, Paul, and Catherine Johnson. 2018. "From Catch-up TV to Online TV: Digital Broadcasting and the Case of BBC iPlayer". *Screen* 59 (1): 21–50.

Gray, Jonathan. 2010. *Show Sold Separately: Promos, Spoilers, and other Media Paratexts*. New York and London: New York University Press.

———. 2011. "The Reviews are in: TV Critics and the (Pre)creation of Meaning". In *Flow TV. Television in the Age of Media Convergence*, edited by Michael Kackman, Marnie Binfield, Matthew Thomas Payne, Allision Perlman and Bryan Sebok, 114–27. New York and London: Routledge.

Johnson, Catherine. 2012. *Branding Television*. London and New York: Routledge.

Johnson, Melanie Clare. 2016. "I watched the first series of locked up within a week". 13 June. Accessed 6 November 2017 from www.facebook.com/groups/899789073442944/permalink/1034629206625596/.

Jones, Ellen. 2017. "Eight Foreign Language TV Drama Boxsets to Binge Online, from Black Widow to Suburra". *Evening Standard*, 15 March. Accessed 8 June 2017 from www.standard.co.uk/stayingin/tvfilm/eight-foreign-language-tv-drama-boxsets-to-binge-online-from-black-widow-to-suburra-a3490241.html.

Jones, Mark. 2013. "The Returned: How British TV Viewers Came to Lose their Fear of Subtitles". *Guardian*, 7 June. Accessed 18 May 2017 from www.theguardian.com/tv-and-radio/2013/jun/07/british-television-subititles.

Kemp, Stuart. 2016. "Subtitles, Sass and Sex: Why Foreign Programming is Booming". *Royal Television Society*, March. Accessed 18 May 2017 from https://rts.org.uk/article/subtitles-sass-and-sex-why-foreign-programming-booming.

Kersten, Annemarie, and Denise D. Bielby. 2012. "Film Discourse on the Praised and Acclaimed: Reviewing Criteria in the United States and United Kingdom". *Popular Communication* 10 (3): 183–200.

Lawson, Mark. 2016. "Subtitles, Politics and Spin: The Latest from Channel 4's Walter Presents Foreign Drama Strand". *Guardian*, 8 January. Accessed 18 May 2017 from www.theguardian.com/tv-and-radio/tvandradioblog/2016/jan/08/subtitles-politics-and-spin-the-latest-from-channel-4s-walter-presents-foreign-drama-strand.

LEGO TUBE. 2016. "Re: Walter Presents/Launches January/All 4". Accessed 6 November 2017 from www.youtube.com/watch?v=q3y_1n9UOuE&lc=Uggx6p6bNwkMNXgCoAEC.

McCausland, Sinead. 2017. "Interview: Walter Iuzzolino on Foreign TV Drama". *Quench: Cardiff Univerisity's Award-Winning Lifestyle Magazine*, April. Accessed 25 May 2017 from http://cardiffstudentmedia.co.uk/quench/film-tv/interview-walter/.

McKay, Alastair. 2016. "Blue Eyes, More4: Meet Alex Haridi, the Man Behind the Political Scandi-noir Thriller That's 'a More Violent House of Cards'". *Evening*

Standard, 24 March. Accessed 13 June 2017 from www.standard.co.uk/stayingin/tvfilm/blue-eyes-meet-the-creators-of-the-political-scandinoir-thriller-series-that-s-a-more-violent-house-a3211081.html.

Marispiper. 2017. "Subtitled Drama (typically European crime dramas on BBC4) [online forum comment #482]". 9 April. Accessed 6 November 2017 from https://forums.digitalspy.com/discussion/comment/86043559#Comment_86043559.

Mittell, Jason. 2015. *Complex TV: The Poetics of Contemporary Television Storytelling*. New York and London: New York University Press.

O'Donovan, Gerard. 2017. "Locked Up Crackles with Wit, Even with Subtitles, in Captivating Return: Series Two Episode One Review". *Telegraph*, 27 April. Accessed 1 November 2017 from www.telegraph.co.uk/tv/2017/04/27/locked-crackles-wit-even-subtitles-captivating-return-series/.

Oltermann, Philip. 2016. "Deutschland 83 has Wowed the World – Pity the Germans Don't Like It". *Guardian*, 17 February. Accessed 1 November 2017 from www.theguardian.com/commentisfree/2016/feb/17/deutschland-83-wowed-world-germans-dont-like-it.

Oxford Dictionaries [online]. 2017. *Curate*. Accessed 25 May 2017 from https://en.oxforddictionaries.com/definition/curate.

Radio Times. 2016. "Who is Walter? Meet the Foreign Drama Expert who Brought Deutschland 83 to Channel 4". *Radio Times*, 26 February. Accessed 1 November 2017 from www.radiotimes.com/news/2016-02-26/who-is-walter-meet-the-foreign-drama-expert-who-brought-deutschland-83-to-channel-4/.

Raeside, Julia. 2016. "The Passenger: A French Thriller that Outruns and Outguns True Detective". *Guardian*, December. Accessed 18 May 2017 from www.theguardian.com/tv-and-radio/2016/dec/01/the-passenger-french-thriller-outguns-true-detective-six-part-drama.

Razaq, Rashid. 2016. "Beauty and the Baker is Channel 4's First Hebrew Language TV Drama as Hit Israeli Show Arrives in the UK". *Evening Standard*, 23 August. Accessed 13 June 2017 from www.standard.co.uk/stayingin/tvfilm/beauty-and-the-baker-is-channel-4-s-first-hebrew-language-tv-drama-as-hit-israeli-show-arrives-in-a3327481.html.

Rockenberger, Annika. 2014. "Video Game Framings". In *Examining Paratextual Theory and its Applications in Digital Culture*, edited by Nadine Desrochers and Daniel Apollon, 252–86. IGI Global.

Schleiermacher, Friedrich. 2012. "On the Different Methods of Translating". In *The Translation Studies Reader*, edited by Lawrence Venuti. Translated by Susan Bernofsky, 43–63. London and New York: Routledge.

Sherwin, Adam. 2015. "Walter Presents: Channel 4 Launches New Digital Service Offering Best TV Shows from Around the World". *Independent*, 27 November. Accessed 25 May 2017 from www.independent.co.uk/arts-entertainment/tv/news/walter-presents-channel-4-launches-new-digital-service-offering-best-tv-shows-from-around-the-world-a6751791.html.

Simpson, Natalie. 2013. "YouTube Comments Explained: How they Work". *YouTube Help Forum*. Google. 16 December. Accessed 13 June 2017 from https://productforums.google.com/forum/#!topic/youtube/cMrA2Vv66xk.

Snyder, Ilana. 2015. "Discourses of 'Curation' in Digital Times". In *Discourse and Digital Practices: Doing Discourse Analysis in the Digital Age*, edited by Rodney H. Jones, Alice Chik and Christoph A. Hafner, 209–25. New York and London: Routledge.

Starkey, Jon. 2016. "Yes and thought it was just briliant". 18 May. Accessed 6 November 2017 from www.facebook.com/groups/899789073442944/permalink/1019320008156516/?comment_id=1019320408156476&comment_tracking=%7B%22tn%22%3A%22R7%22%7D.

tartan-belle. 2017. *"Subtitled Drama (typically European crime dramas on BBC4)* [online forum comment #477]". 9 April. Accessed 6 November 2017 from https://forums.digitalspy. com/discussion/comment/86041956#Comment_86041956.

Tate, Gabriel. 2016. "Deutschland 83: 'A Lot of People were Happy in East Germany'". *Guardian*, 3 January. Accessed 13 June 2017 from www.theguardian.com/tv-and-radio/2016/jan/03/channel-4-cold-war-drama-deutschland-83.

Thelwell, Mike, Pardeep Sud and Farida Vis. 2012. "Commenting on YouTube Videos: From Guatemalan Rock to El Big Bang". *Journal of the American Society for Information Science and Technology* 63 (3): 616–29.

Travis, Ben. 2016. "Locked up, Channel 4: Five Things you Need to Know About the Gripping Prison Drama". *Evening Standard*, 17 May. Accessed 13 June 2017 from www. standard.co.uk/stayingin/tvfilm/locked-up-channel-4-five-things-you-need-to-know-about-the-gripping-prison-drama-a3250436.html.

——. 2017. "Case, Channel 4: Five Things to Know About the Icelandic Crime Drama". *Evening Standard*, 24 January. Accessed 1 November 2017 from www.standard.co.uk/stayingin/tvfilm/case-channel-4-five-things-to-know-about-the-icelandic-crime-drama-a3448716.html.

Tryon, Chuck. 2013. *On-Demand Culture: Digital Delivery and the Future of Movies*. New Brunswick, NJ and London: Rutgers University Press.

TV Magazine. 2017. "ON DEMAND House of Cards Series 5, Bordertown, Poldark and Flaked are all at your fingertips this week". *Sun*, 27 May. Accessed 8 June 2017 from www.thesun.co.uk/tvandshowbiz/3659697/house-of-cards-series-5-bordertown-poldark-and-flaked-fingertips-this-week/.

Venuti, Lawrence. 1995. *The Translator's Invisibility: A History of Translation*. New York: Routledge.

Walter Presents: Deutschland 83 [video]. 2016. Accessed 16 December 2017 from www. channel4.com/programmes/deutschland-83/on-demand/.

Walter Presents: Heartless [video]. 2016. Accessed 5 November 2017 from www.youtube. com/watch?v=ofDrYIZCEBw.

Walter Presents: Spin [video]. 2016. Accessed 16 December 2017 from www.channel4.com/programmes/spin/on-demand/.

Walter Presents: Elite Squad [video]. 2017. Accessed 8 June 2017 from www.channel4.com/programmes/elite-squad/on-demand/.

Walter Presents: Valkyrien [video]. 2017. Accessed 8 June 2017 from www.channel4.com/programmes/walter-presents/videos/all/walter-presents-valkyrien/5358756559001.

WhoAteMeDinner. 2017. "Warning: another Walter Presents drama next week". 17 February. Accessed 6 November 2017 from https://forums.digitalspy.com/discussion/2206308/warning-another-walter-presents-drama-next-week.

Wichert, Tom. 2016. "Where is the second series of Locked Up?" 29 July. Accessed 6 November 2017 from www.facebook.com/groups/899789073442944/search/?query=Wichert.

Williams, Holly. 2015. "The Man Behind Foreign Drama Streaming Service 'Walter Presents' on TV's New International Hotspots". *Independent*, 28 December. Accessed 8 June 2017 from www.independent.co.uk/arts-entertainment/tv/the-man-behind-foreign-drama-streaming-service-walter-presents-on-tvs-new-international-hotspots-a6788201.html.

PART III

Towards a theory of paratextuality for translation

7

TRANSLATION AND PARATEXTS

Terminology and typologies

In this and the following chapter, I outline a framework for the study of paratexts in translation-related contexts, based on the insights gained in previous chapters. As noted in the Introduction, the framework is intended to be useful – and used – but does not claim to be definitive; like Genette's own framework, it invites further development, particularly in a context of ever-changing technologies and shifts in translation and publishing practices. In elaborating this framework, I have taken as my guiding principle the idea, neatly expressed by Annika Rockenberger (2014, 271) in relation to paratextual theory and videogames, that developing a theoretical framework is 'not a matter of truth and verification but a matter of practical adequacy'. In this chapter, I discuss terminological choices, distinguishing between various top-level terms and making a case for preferring certain terms over others. As part of these reflections, I propose a definition of the key term *paratext*, and explore ways in which the borderlines of the definition might be established in conjunction with research questions specific to any given research study. In the second part of the chapter, I expand the five key variables on which Genette's typology of paratexts is constructed, arguing in favour of an eclectic approach that is able to tailor itself to the specificities of any given research project.

Terminology

Paratext

One of the key questions that researchers face when adapting any theory to a new disciplinary context is whether to use the same terms or to prefer (or coin) alternative ones. Adopting the term *paratext* is by no means a given: as we saw in Chapter 2, a number of translation scholars have opted for alternative terms such as *bindings* (Harvey 2003), *extratextual* material (Susam-Sarajeva 2006), or *macro-structural* features

(Lambert and van Gorp 2014); in other disciplines, as we saw in Chapter 3, scholars have argued in favour of the alternative term *paracontent* (Bhaskar 2011), or of using *framings* as the wider umbrella term and limiting *paratext* to a smaller subset of material within that (Rockenberger 2014). In my view, the term *paratext* is to be preferred over other options, albeit in conjunction with a definition that departs from Genette's. My main reason for advocating use of the term *paratext* over other possibilities is pragmatic: *paratext* now has an established tradition of use across a range of disciplines with which translation studies intersects, as well as within translation studies itself, and by continuing to use it we are more explicitly able to engage with the theoretical developments that have taken place since Genette and to incorporate our own research into that tradition.

Setting out a definition of the term *paratext*, however, is more difficult than might be imagined, not least because Genette's own theory of the paratext itself refrains from offering an explicit definition of the term and carries a number of inherent contradictions, as shown in Chapter 1. While translation studies scholars have tended to respond to these difficulties by disposing of the authorial intention criterion and limiting the paratext effectively to Genette's peritext, this solution only works well up to a point. Although it offers a clear way of distinguishing between paratexts, text, and wider context whilst allowing for the inclusion of material authored by the translator, as soon as we extend translation research from literary texts to digital, web-based or audiovisual ones, a definition of paratext that depends on physical location swiftly becomes unworkable. For this reason, I propose a definition that is primarily functional, and which can be summarised as follows:

A paratext is a consciously crafted threshold for a text which has the potential to influence the way(s) in which the text is received.

In this definition, 'text' is understood as denoting any written or spoken words forming a connected piece of work. The type of text thus referred to might be a work of literature, a newspaper article, a television programme or film, a speech, and so on. Crucially, a text may be in its original language or it may be translated; in other words, in this model a translated text would be considered a text in its own right and with its own paratexts, as opposed to being viewed as a paratext to an original text, as in Genette's model. Another way in which this definition departs from Genette's is in its use of the indefinite article: Genette generally refers to 'the paratext' in the singular, and to 'paratextual elements'. The majority of scholars who have built on Genette, however, have tended instead to speak of 'a paratext' and of 'paratexts', and my definition thus ties in with current use rather than with Genette's original formulation.

The openness of this definition of paratext, which does not specify where a paratext needs to be placed relative to the text, or indeed when it needs to be accessed relative to the text, allows it to encompass the traditional elements through which a text is made into a book as well as the larger range of elements which function as thresholds to digital or audiovisual texts. It includes those thresholds which could be entry points to the text even part-way through someone's encounter with it, as in the case of a preface read during or after the reading of the text itself, or the recap of a TV series accessed between episodes. The definition does not specify who the paratext-creator needs to be, neither in absolute terms, nor in relation to the text-creator, and thus allows us to include paratexts produced by translators and other agents. As we will see in the next chapter, the openness of the definition also gives it potential to be used to discuss questions relevant to interpreting, whereby the interpreter is able to craft a threshold to the interpreted words using body language or other means which will have an influence on how the text is perceived.

The main constraining aspect built into this definition is the qualifier 'consciously crafted'. This qualifier places broader context as well as happenstance (for example, the individual circumstances through which a particular reader comes to a text) outside the scope of the paratext. This is, of course, not to ignore the fact that contextual and incidental factors can have a bearing on the way a text is received; such factors are sometimes of paramount importance, and in that sense may indeed function as thresholds in a manner similar to paratexts on occasion. Excluding them from the domain of the paratext, however, allows us to place a boundary between paratext and what Genette (1997, 407) terms the 'beyond-text', preventing what Rockenberger (2014, 267) describes as the 'paratext's collapse into the vastness of "the context"'. The broader context can and should be interrogated alongside paratexts where the research questions call for such analysis but, in this definition, would not be considered part of the paratext itself.

Another way in which the openness of this definition is of benefit is in terms of the way it evokes both a producer- and a receiver-based perspective. As argued in Chapter 1, Genette himself alternates between these two perspectives without explicitly acknowledging that he is doing so, and his failure to interrogate the implications of this difference in perspective lies at the heart of the contradictions inherent to his model. The definition of the paratext that I propose above does not rely on parameters which are the preserve of only one perspective, and aims to be adequate to research that takes a producer-based approach (research into translation processes, for example) as well as that which takes a receiver-based perspective (such as research into translation products). At the same time, in any given piece of research, the particular perspective adopted – and, more precisely, the particular research questions being posed – may require the researcher to supplement the above definition with further criteria for determining what is to be included or excluded from a paratextual corpus, as I shall explain in the next section.

Delineating a corpus of paratexts

To explore how such a process might work out in practice, let us consider three examples of what might be considered borderline cases of paratexts according to the above definition. For the first example, let us take the case of thresholds that are crafted but never made available to readers or viewers, such as a translator's preface that was written but never published. Such material does not fit comfortably with the definition proposed above: while consciously crafted as a threshold, it is unlikely to influence text reception. Whether or not to include such borderline material in a paratextual corpus would depend on the research perspective that is being adopted. If the focus is on reception, then it would be excluded. However, if the focus is on production (for example, a study of translators' interactions with authors and others involved in the production process), then it would form an important part of the paratextual corpus.

For the second example, let us take the case of thresholds created by fans – or even opponents – of the texts in question. Although this type of material fits more comfortably within the definition outlined above, once again it is the research questions that will determine whether or not such material should be included in a corpus of paratexts. If the goal is to understand how the text-producers seek to influence the reception of their text by manipulating paratextual material, then it would be irrelevant, even though it is 'consciously crafted'; if, on the other hand, we are interested in the way in which readers or viewers (or a particular sub-group thereof) understand a text, then those fan-created paratexts would be included. Of course, when we are addressing questions of reception, we also need to address questions of whether thresholds are actually used; how we are to do this, and indeed to what extent it can be done, will be discussed in the next chapter.

Finally, for our third example, let us consider the case of handwritten inscriptions on individual copies of books – a dedication, perhaps, from the author, editor or translator to the recipient, or a previous owner's name, handwritten on the inside title page. Such inscriptions occupy a borderline place according to the definition suggested above: some of them (such as the dedication) may be consciously crafted as thresholds, others (such as the name inscribed to show ownership) may not; in either scenario, they might influence how the text is received, but only for the reader of that particular copy rather than more broadly. Once again, whether or not to include such inscriptions in a corpus of paratexts depends on the research questions of the study concerned: if the goal is to understand how groups of people (say, the intellectual elite of a particular nation) received a particular text or author, then such material would be irrelevant (unless, perhaps, the inscription was in the copy of the book owned by a leading member of that group and thus could be shown to have influenced the group indirectly). If, however, we are interested in one particular individual's reading of a text and how they came to it, then all such material re-enters the domain of the paratextual – assuming that it can be unearthed.

In all of these hypothetical cases, while the definition of paratext allows for us to include in a paratextual corpus a wide range of material, it is the research questions linked to the specific study that determine and justify whether or not all of that material should actually be included in a paratextual corpus, particularly when it occupies a borderline position. Specific research questions thus work together with the broad definition to help us develop a systematic and consistent approach to designing a research project.

Framing and frames

The terms *frame* and *framing* are widely used across a range of disciplines including linguistics, sociology, and cognitive research, and as Werner Wolf (2006, 2) notes, have 'acquired a plethora of divergent and occasionally conflicting meanings'. In translation studies, scholars are perhaps most likely to be familiar with the set of meanings presented by Mona Baker in her research into translation and activism, within the context of a narrative theoretical framework. Baker defines narratives as 'the stories we tell ourselves and others about the world(s) in which we live' (Baker 2007, 151), and argues that 'people's behaviour is ultimately guided by the stories they come to believe about the events in which they are embedded' (Baker 2006, 3). In this model, framing is one of the processes through which narratives are constructed; with regard specifically to translation and interpreting, it encompasses a wide range of devices and strategies from translation selection to the linguistic choices made in the course of translating or interpreting or – crucially for our purposes – in the composition or translation of paratextual material. The definition of 'framing' put forward by Baker ties in with her use of narrative theory and foregrounds the dynamic nature of the process. Hence she defines framing as 'an active strategy that implies agency and by means of which we consciously participate in the construction of reality' (Baker 2006, 106), and explains that framing 'involves setting up structures of anticipation that guide others' interpretation of events, usually as a direct challenge to dominant interpretations of the same events in a given society' (Baker 2007, 156).

This process can be enacted through translation decisions as well as through translation paratexts, and paratexts are thus conceptualised in Baker's model as locations in which framing – an action – can happen. This view has much in common with Theo Hermans's (2007) emphasis on paratexts as places where translators can 'signal their agenda' (33) or their ideological sympathy or antipathy towards the author or text (53ff.), as outlined in Chapter 2.[1] A similar view of the interrelation between paratext and framing is evident in the key concept entry for 'paratexts' in *The Routledge Companion to Translation Studies* which reads: 'paratexts are material additions to a text which comment on, evaluate, or otherwise **frame** it' (Munday 2009, 214, my emphasis).

It is important to note that in all of these outlines, it is the verb *to frame* (or its participle, *framing*) that is used, rather than the related noun *a frame*. In other words, conceiving of paratexts as places where framing takes place is different from viewing paratexts as frames – or to put this another way, since the point under discussion here is terminology – suggesting that *paratexts* can be seen as sites in which *framing* takes place is not the same as replacing the term *paratext* with the term *frame*. Such a move is not uncommon in writing on paratexts and paratextual elements: Marie Maclean (1991, 273), for example, in a brief discussion of the importance of Genette's *Seuils*, argues that his book 'raises some extremely central questions about literature' and suggests that 'not the least of these is the relationship between a text and its frame'. Her elaboration of the frame shows that she is using the term as a synonym for *paratext*, even though Genette himself does not use the term *cadre* [frame] with this meaning at any point. A similar terminological merging is proposed by Ann Lewis (2007) in her introduction to a volume exploring the concept of the frame in relation to a range of French cultural artefacts. She argues that Genette's theory provides an 'indispensable reference point' (18) and states that 'although Genette does not invoke the frame explicitly, his understanding of the paratext as a "frange aux limites indécises qui entoure d'un halo pragmatique l'œuvre littéraire", is clearly analogous to our understanding of the frame, applied within a literary context' (18).[2] Another example of a shift towards labelling a *paratext* a *frame* can be found in Yra van Dijk's (2014) exploration of digital paratexts, in which she draws on Derrida's reflections on the *parergon* as well as on Genette's work. In her analysis, van Dijk compares the institutional framing that is enacted by digital search engine results to the institutional framing that happens when paintings are hung in a museum, and argues that the paratext is 'a "frame" that frames the work as such, and thus without it there would be no work' (van Dijk 2014, 26).[3]

While van Dijk's analysis suggests that there might be some intellectual benefits to seeing paratexts as frames, I would argue that using the term *frame* as a synonym for *paratext* would cause unnecessary confusion. This is principally because the term *frame*, as a noun, is already used to refer to a specific concept (or, more precisely, several interrelated concepts) in disciplines with which translation studies intersects. In cognitive science, the notion of the frame was first developed by Marvin Minsky (1974) and is defined as 'a data-structure for representing a stereotyped situation, like being in a certain kind of living room, or going to a child's birthday party' (1). In linguistics, frame semantics draws on the notion of the cognitive frame to account for 'how people perceive, remember, and reason about their experiences, how they form assumptions about the background and possible concomitants of those experiences, and even how one's own life experiences can or should be enacted' (Fillmore and Baker 2009, 314). In sociology, a frame similarly 'designates interpretive structures that render events and occurrences subjectively meaningful' (Snow 2011, 235) or in other words accounts not so much for how we understand language (as in frame semantics), but how we work out what is going on at any given moment in our social interactions. In the context of mass media communication, a frame is 'a central organizing idea for news content that supplies a context and suggests what the issue is through the use of selection, emphasis, exclusion, and elaboration' (Tankard et al., cited in Johnson-Cartee 2005, 24).[4] Researchers have shown that the choice of one particular frame over another can have a powerful influence on public opinion on a particular issue.[5]

In all of these disciplines, a frame is not a physical object, but an idea, a way of understanding and interpreting reality – and a powerful one at that. Frames, in these contexts, are thus closely linked to the verb *framing*, discussed above, such that framing can be understood as the process of presenting events within a given existing frame, or of setting up an alternative frame through which they are to be perceived.[6] By opting not to use the term *frame* as a synonym for *paratext*, we allow for the possibility that scholars analysing paratextual material may wish to draw on the concept of the frame as defined in cognitive, linguistic, or communicational terms, for the purposes of their analysis. This may be particularly relevant for translation scholars working on news translation, but would also be of importance to anyone looking to combine paratextual analysis with frame semantics, narrative theory or theories of cognition.

Extratext

While *frames* and *framing* have an extensive and complex history of use both in conjunction with research into paratexts and independently of it, the term *extratext* has a more limited history. In the context of translation studies research into paratexts, the term *extratext* has a certain level of prominence thanks to its use by Şehnaz Tahir-Gürçağlar (2002) in what is probably the most frequently cited article on paratexts in the discipline, as well as its inclusion in the title of one of only two existing edited volumes on paratexts in translation studies, *Text, Extratext, Metatext and Paratext in Translation* (Pellatt 2013a). In the case of the latter, the wording of the title suggests that the volume will adopt a framework in which a threefold distinction is made between the various types of text that intersect with the text. However, the term *extratext* is not actually used at all in any of the essays included in the volume, and in her introduction Pellatt offers a definition only of *paratext*, and does not refer to extratexts. Pellatt's (2013b, 1) definition of paratext is broad, and includes material that is 'external to the core text', such as reviews:

> In this volume we regard paratext as any material additional to, appended to or external to the core text which has the functions of explaining, defining, instructing, or supporting, adding background information, or the relevant opinions and attitudes of scholars, translators and reviewers . . . The range of paratext is vast, encompassing authorial comment and external comment and explanatory material.[7]

In light of the wide-ranging nature of this definition of paratext, it would seem most likely that Pellatt views *extratext* as a sub-category of *paratext*, but this point is not made explicitly and the structure of the title does not really support this assumption.

Tahir-Gürçağlar's (2002) article offers a much clearer indication of the distinctions between *paratext* and *extratext*, including an explanation of the differences between *epitext* and *extratext*, both of which denote material unattached to the text itself. In general terms, she explains that *extratexts* refers to 'the general meta-discourse on translation circulating independently of individual translated texts' (44), while *paratexts* refers to 'presentational materials accompanying translated texts and the text-specific meta-discourses formed directly around them' (44). With regard to the distinction between *epitexts* and *extratexts* more specifically, she further explains that the former are 'comments, reviews, criticisms or interviews dealing with specific works' (58) while the latter are 'general statements on translation, or . . . other socio-cultural phenomena that may have a bearing on how translations are produced and received' (58). The definition of extratexts as 'socio-cultural phenomena' indicates that extratexts need not necessarily be textual in nature, but can encompass anything that helps towards a 'contextualization of translational phenomena' (58).

In contrast with Tahir-Gürçağlar, Sharon Deane-Cox (2014) uses a narrower definition of both *paratext* and *extratext*. In her framework, paratextual material is that which is 'closely linked to the text having stemmed from the translator, author, publisher and/or authorized third party' (29), while extratextual material encompasses 'those articles and reviews that are related to the translations, the translators, the publishers and/or the source text authors' (29). Another contrasting use of the term *extratext* can be found in Szu-Wen Cindy Kung's (2010) study of Taiwanese literature in English: here, Kung draws on spatial rather than sender-based criteria to distinguish between *paratexts* and *extratexts*, taking *paratext* to refer to 'the surface fragments that cover all the textual material that introduces a text proper . . .; literally all the material that surrounds the text and forms a book' (165), and *extratext* to refer to 'material outside the book, such as letters, interviews, book reviews, which in all consist of the intertextuality of any text' (165). To a large extent, Kung is thus replacing Genette's term *epitext* with the term *extratext*, albeit without addressing the question of criteria for inclusion or exclusion from the category itself, other than its spatial distance from the text.[8] For Kung's and Deane-Cox's corpora, which are composed of literary print texts, making a terminological distinction between *paratext* and *extratext* either on a spatial basis or on a sender basis functions fairly well: in the case of Deane-Cox's framework in particular, the distinction allows her to stay close to Genette's original criterion of author intention (expanding it slightly to include translators) and prevents a radical enlarging of the domain of the paratext in line with Genette's warnings.[9]

The term *extratext* itself, however, is to some degree problematic, since in its more conventional usage as an adjective, *extratextual* refers to things that are non-textual. Thus, in a study of a genre such as autobiography, for example, scholars might contrast 'extratextual reality' with elements that form part of the fictional world, while in a study of reading practices scholars might track patterns of 'extra-textual utterances'.[10] Deane-Cox (2014) herself uses *extratextual* in this other sense at several places in the introduction to her study, talking, for example, of an 'extratextual perspective' (5) on retranslation, or of the 'textual and extratextual dynamics of retranslation' (7). By this she does not mean exploring the way in which extratexts such as articles and reviews play in to retranslation decisions, but other factors such as 'canonicity, ideology, economics, and the subjectivity of the translator' (13). The existence of this more common meaning of extratextual means that using *extratext* to denote a particular variety of text can give rise to ambiguities (such that 'extratextual material', for example, could refer to extratexts or to anything at all outside the core text). This in itself is not a reason to reject the term, since many terms denote concepts as well as having a broader set of meanings, and scholars are accustomed to clarifying term usage at the outset of a study.

However, a more significant reason for not incorporating the term *extratext* into my proposed framework is that the function-based definition of paratext that I put forward above renders it unnecessary.

Let us briefly explore this issue with respect to one of the main text types that Deane-Cox and Kung allocate to the category of extratextual material, namely reviews. While reviews of any kind of cultural product serve a variety of functions, ranging from something resembling a marketing function to something that is closer to taking part in the intellectual or artistic discussions that form part of the reviewed material itself, their function as a threshold to the cultural product in question is often paramount. If I want to work out whether or not to spend my evening watching a film, for example, I will generally do this by looking for a review of the film or for an overall approval rating based on aggregated reviews from a variety of sources. Or, to give an example from another domain of life, if I read in a newspaper review of an expensive upmarket restaurant that the onion starter is 'mostly black, like nightmares, and sticky, like the floor at a teenager's party' (Rayner 2017), there is no chance that I will be forking out £600 to eat there. These reviews clearly serve as thresholds: I pause there, consider the information and opinions presented, and decide either to enter (watch the film, go to the restaurant) or turn away. Reviews thus fit comfortably within the domain of the paratext in the definition that I proposed above and do not require a different term such as *extratext* because of their origin or their extraneity to the text.[11] Of course, in comparison with some of the peritexts of a printed edition of a text, there is less certainty that these thresholds will be used by readers, but the same could be said for many other paratexts, particularly in digital contexts, as already noted above. We will return to this issue in the next chapter.

Metatext

In *Introduction à l'architexte*, Genette (1979, 87) introduces his readers to the term *métatextualité* ['metatextuality' (Genette 1992, 82)], one of four different kinds of 'textual transcendence' (Genette 1992, 81). He explains that the term is modelled on the distinction between language and metalanguage (metalanguage being generally understood to be language that comments on language), and that it refers to 'the transtextual relationship that links a commentary to the text it comments on' (Genette 1992, 82). He states jokingly that 'all literary critics, for centuries, have been producing metatext without knowing it' (Genette 1992, 82). We should note that the label *metatext* functions only in relational terms: in other words, a text is a metatext in relation to the specific text on which it comments. Defined in this way, *metatext* can be seen to be complementary to the term *paratext*, as defined above. The essential distinction between them is as follows:

A paratext is a threshold to the text.

A metatext is a commentary on the text.

Before we discuss the overlap between these two terms, we should note that this use of *metatext* contrasts with the use of the term in early descriptive translation studies. In these research traditions, *metatext* carries a much broader meaning, encompassing not only commentary or literary criticism but any text which interprets or models the original text, including translations.[12] James Holmes (1988, 24) famously argued that verse translations should be termed 'metapoems' on the basis that they combine critical interpretation with being 'acts of poetry' in their own right, suggesting: 'this poetry is of a very special kind, referring not to Barthes's "objects and phenomena . . . external and anterior to language", but to another linguistic object: the original poem'. One of the most extended considerations of translations as metatexts was presented by Anton Popovič in *Problémy literárnej metakomunikácie: Teória metatextu* [*Problems of Literary Metacommunication: Theory of Metatext*] (1975), summarised in an English-language article that appeared the following year. In this model, metatext similarly refers to 'all types of processing (manipulation) of the original literary text, whether it is done by other authors, readers, critics, translators, etc.' (Popovič 1976, 226). Popovič (1976, 226) stresses that it is only texts that 'develop or modify in some way the semiotic, meaning-bearing, side of the original text' which are considered metatexts; those that simply reproduce the text without introducing any textual changes are not. While there is some similarity between this conceptualisation of translations as metatexts and Genette's suggestion that translations can be viewed as a form of paratext, the key difference is that, in Genette's conceptualisation, translations are paratexts to the extent that they convey something about the author's intention, whereas in Popovic's, translations are metatexts because they manipulate the meaning of the original text in some way. In other words, the translation-as-paratext concept in Genette's model is applicable only to the extent that the translation does not change the author's meaning as expressed in the original text, whereas translations are only considered metatexts in Popovič's model if they *do* enact some kind of transformation of the original text.

While the work of Holmes, Popovič and others was of crucial importance in establishing research approaches and methodologies in descriptive translation studies,[13] *metatext* is rarely used in translation studies today in the sense in which they developed the term. Instead, scholars tend to use *metatext* or its associated adjective, *metatextual*, in the narrower sense outlined by Genette and in keeping with its dictionary meaning,[14] namely to refer to texts (or aspects of texts) which comment on another text. Theo Hermans (2007), for example, when discussing the case of Laureen Nussbaum's 'extensively introduced and annotated' (29) excerpts from an existing translation, argues that her discussion 'has a metatextual aspect in that it constitutes a critical commentary on the previous translation' (32).

If we conform to this more general current usage and restrict our use of the term *metatext* to the sense in which Genette uses it – namely, to refer to text which comments on another text – we are forced to accept a certain amount of overlap between the two terms, since paratexts often comment on the text as a means of providing a threshold to it. This is a point which Genette (1997, 343) himself freely acknowledges, arguing that it is 'not at all paradoxical, and still less is it perplexing'.[15] Although the definition of paratext that I have proposed above is slightly different from Genette's, the same issues of slipperiness remain, particularly at the border between paratext and other kinds of text that comment on the core text in some way. Genette's solution to this conundrum is not to try and impose stricter borders around the paratext, but to argue in favour of a pragmatic approach to theoretical frameworks, establishing the precise borders between paratext and metatext on a case by case basis:

> 'The paratext,' properly speaking, does not *exist;* rather, one chooses to *account in these terms* for a certain number of practices or effects, for reasons of method and effectiveness or, if you will, of profitability. The question is therefore not whether the note does or does not 'belong' to the paratext but really whether considering it in such a light is or is not useful and relevant. The answer very clearly is, as it often is, that that depends on the case.
>
> *Genette 1997, 343, italics in original*

Following Genette's line of reasoning, we can summarise the complementarity of the terms *paratext* and *metatext* as follows:

- Some paratexts are metatextual, or in other words comment on the text.
- Some metatexts are paratextual, or in other words are consciously crafted thresholds to the text.
- In cases of significant overlap, deciding whether to label such material *paratext* or *metatext* will depend on the overall perspective of the study as defined by the research questions.

Before we leave this discussion of metatext, I would like to briefly explore the interplay between metatext and metadiscourse, since this is an area that potentially gives rise to terminological confusion. The term *metadiscourse*, which is widely used by scholars across a range of disciplines, has as its 'core conceptualisation' (Ädel and Mauranen 2010, 1) the idea of 'discourse about discourse' (Ädel and Mauranen 2010, 1). In translation studies, the term tends to be used to refer to discussions of translation that appeal to or contribute to more general discourse about translation (what translation is, how it should be carried out, etc.). Theo Hermans (2007, 33), for example, speaks of a 'metadiscursive domain in which translators observe their own translations and those of others', and stresses that metadiscourse can be a feature both of paratexts such as prefaces as well as being staged within translations themselves (see, for example, his discussion of Edward Harwood's 1768 English translation of the New Testament in Hermans (2007, 36)). Metadiscourse is thus to be distinguished from metatext on the basis that the former represents commentary on translation as a phenomenon, while the latter is commentary on a specific text. In practice, of course, when a metatext is commenting on a translated text, it also becomes metadiscourse as soon as it makes appeal, even implicitly, to broader debates about translation. Nevertheless, it is still helpful to hold these two terms apart from each other, since it is not necessarily the case that one entails the other: translation paratexts, for example, can be metadisursive without being metatextual, and vice versa.[16]

Paratranslation

The term *paratraducción* [paratranslation] was coined by researchers at the University of Vigo, Spain in 2004.[17] It has been developed intensively through the activities of the *Grupo Traducción & Paratraducción* [Translation & Paratranslation Research Group] at the same university since 2005, although its take-up by other academics based in other Spanish universities has been limited.[18] Within Anglophone translation studies, the term is rarely employed.[19] In one sense, the idea of paratranslation is simple: echoing Genette's (1997, 1) formulation that a paratext is 'what enables a text to become a book and to be offered as such to its readers', José Yuste Frías (2010, 291) explains that 'la paratraduction est ce par quoi une traduction se fait produit traduit, se proposant comme tel à ses lecteurs' [paratranslation is what enables a translation to become a translated product and to be offered as such to its readers]. The study of paratranslation is in this basic sense the study of the translation of paratextual elements. The need for a new concept to encompass this angle of study is argued on the basis that translation decisions pertaining to paratextual elements can often only be explained by taking into account ideological considerations and historical perspectives (see Garrido Vilariño 2011, 65–6), and in order to account for the translation of multisemiotic texts (see Yuste Frías 2010). The concept is also, however, given added complexity: Yuste Frías (2012, 119) suggests that 'paratranslation aims at becoming a symbolic reference to the physical or virtual space occupied by all the professional translators within the real, everyday market', while Garrido Vilariño (2011, 65) states even more ambitiously that 'the concept of *paratranslation* aims to become the centre of knowledge of the human being, of the languages and cultures in our modernity'.

Whilst perhaps helpful as a means of calling attention to the involvement of multiple agents in the process of publishing translations and the complexity of the translation process,[20] the need for a new term and concept to emphasise these aspects is not at all clear. Over the last thirty or more years in translation studies in many regional and national traditions considerable attention has been paid to the cultural and ideological factors that play into the translation process, without adoption of a new term in place of *translation*. More recently, the surge of interest in Bourdieusian and actor–network theoretical frameworks has provided translation studies researchers with a vocabulary and a basis from which to investigate questions of agency and to take into account the social and institutional contexts in which translations are produced, once again without the need for recourse to a new term to replace *translation*. Similarly, research into translation in multimodal environments, and applications of multimodal theory to translation studies, have helped towards reconceptualisation of translation processes and products that emphasise their composite nature whilst not changing the basic terms – *translation/translating* – used to denote them (for a summary of multimodal translation research, see Pérez-González 2014). In all of these developments, researchers have effectively taken the approach of expanding the conceptualisation of *translation* and of what the study of translation might mean, moving on from a linguistic and text-based focus to one that can account for ideology, historical context, cultural dynamics, social structures and interactions, and interplay between verbal and non-verbal elements.

Another disadvantage of the term *paratranslation* is that it subsumes a range of different creative and commercial activities under a term that contains the word *translation* and thus risks implying that the objects under study involve some kind of interlingual transfer. Of course, with a careful delineation of the meaning of the new term, this faulty assumption can be countered. However, if we simply retain existing terminology – stating, for example, that we are studying the 'paratexts of translations' (rather than 'paratranslations') – this problem disappears: the paratexts could be verbal and non-verbal material of any variety, translated, adapted or originally created. Since, in many cases, paratexts are 'not translated per se but reimagined or completely transformed' (Watts 2005, 161), adopting terminology that allows for as much openness as possible with regard to the type of activities that are involved is clearly desirable. For these reasons, even while acknowledging the importance of many of the issues highlighted by paratranslation group scholars, I would not advocate adoption of the term *paratranslation* itself.

Typology

In Chapter 1, I summarised the five features that lie at the heart of Genette's paratextual typology – namely the paratext's spatial, temporal, substantial, pragmatic and functional characteristics. The survey of adaptations of Genette's theory to translation studies, digital culture and media in Chapters 2 and 3 has already given us a sense of how some of the variables used by Genette have been altered to suit contexts other than print literature in its original language of composition. In this section, I suggest key ways in which each of Genette's parameters needs to be expanded for his typology to be made adequate to contemporary translation studies and to the definition of paratext outlined above.

Space

Genette's primary spatial distinction is between peritext and epitext, as explained in Chapter 1. As we saw in Chapter 3, this distinction is inadequate for digital and audiovisual texts, and scholars working in these domains have developed their own sets of variables for describing where a paratext appears, or the movements through space with which it is associated. These include Stewart's (2010) distinction between off-site, on-site and in-file paratexts, and McCracken's (2013) dynamic model of centrifugal versus centripetal paratexts. Another set of variables not discussed in Chapter 3, but equally worthy of consideration, is presented by Daniel

Dunne (2016, 282) in an application of Genette's framework to videogames: he suggests that videogame paratexts can be categorised spatially as 'in-game', 'in-system' or 'in-world'. Other scholars working in digital and media domains do not attempt to categorise paratextual elements on the basis of spatial features at all, preferring instead to categorise them according to other features, notably temporality and function.[21]

Given that translation scholars might be working in any of these research domains, including with traditional literary texts, it does not make sense to argue *a priori* in favour of one set of distinctions over another. In some research contexts, adopting Genette's distinction between *peritext* and *epitext* will be perfectly adequate; in others, the nature of the material under study will mean that an alternative set of variables is preferable. Overall, with respect to the variables that are established for this and for any other paratextual feature, I would encourage translation scholars to adopt terms already in use in paratextual research in the relevant interconnecting disciplines. By providing in-depth exploration of Genette's original framework and its many adaptations across disciplines in this book, it is my hope that I may have simplified the task of assessing the merits of particular terms already in use and adopting or adapting them appropriately.

Substance

Genette's focus on print literature leads him to prioritise paratexts whose mode of existence he labels 'textual' (Genette 1997, 7) and, to a certain extent and in his own words, to 'elud[e]' the question of a paratextual element's substantial status (Genette 1997, 7). The other categories briefly sketched by Genette (1997, 7) are 'iconic (illustrations)' and 'material (for example, everything that originates in the sometimes very significant typographical choices that go with the making of a book)'. Less explicitly, but no less significantly, in the course of a discussion of the 'mediated paratext' (Genette 1997, 357) – such as interviews with the author that appear in print or in audiovisual form – Genette suggests that non-verbal phenomena such as facial expressions can be seen to convey commentary on what the author is saying. Although Genette does not coin a term for this mode of paratextual expression, or even explicitly label it as a form of paratext as such, we can see here the foundations for consideration of what has subsequently been called the 'corporeal paratext' (Knape 2013, 265). This paratextual mode has particular importance for interpreting, and will be explored in that context in further detail in the next chapter.

When Genette's framework is applied to digital and audiovisual domains, it quickly becomes clear that Genette's terms for describing the substantial status of paratexts need further refining. In particular, it becomes important to note that the paratext itself is considered to have its own mode and medium of expression as well as actually *being* the medium of expression of the text itself. In Genette's (1997) model, the paratext includes 'the materialization of a text for public use' (17): it is the manuscript (3), the way in which the book is folded or bound (17), the typesetting and choice of paper (34), and so on. Following Genette's logic, digital studies scholars have argued that anything which plays a part in converting binary code into a readable or viewable text should be considered paratextual, as we saw in Chapter 3. This includes features of materialisation such as source code, metadata and algorithms, features through which texts can be accessed such as e-reading devices and computer interfaces, as well as features through which texts are made discoverable, such as search engines, websites and online archives. In light of the complexity of the material and materialising qualities of paratexts in digital contexts, and for greater clarity overall, I propose the following basic categories for describing a paratext's substantial status. I have provided examples of sub-categories under each one for the purposes of further clarification, rather than with the goal of providing an exhaustive taxonomy. Depending on the type of material under study, scholars may opt to use and further refine some of these categories and sub-categories and disregard others.

- the mode of expression of the paratextual element, e.g. words vs images, writing vs speaking vs body language,[22] static vs dynamic
- the medium of expression of the paratextual element, e.g. digital vs print; manuscript vs printed book; web-based vs stand-alone
- the medium through which a text is materialised, e.g. digital or print book format, other formats such as posters, videos, etc.; typesetting and other presentational features
- the medium through which a text is accessed, e.g. e-reading devices, computers, apps, books, magazines, websites
- the medium through which a text is discovered, e.g. search engine, websites and hyperlinks, catalogues and databases.

The above list covers the four kinds of substantial status envisaged by Genette with the exception of what he terms the 'factual' (Genette 1997, 7) paratext. This omission is not accidental: if we accept the definition of paratext presented earlier in this chapter, then factual information, not being consciously crafted, would not be considered part of the paratext. Of course, if factual information is made explicit by any consciously crafted threshold, then it becomes part of the paratext; in these cases, however, the substantial status of the factual information is not purely factual but has been made physically manifest in some way. In other words, if we accept the definition above, there is no immaterial paratext; for something to be a consciously crafted threshold, it must find some kind of manifestation or alternatively be the medium through which the text itself is made manifest, as per the last three categories listed above. The wording that I have used for those categories indicates that it may be more intuitive to categorise these types of paratexts not so much in terms of what they *are*, but what they *do*. In other words, when studying certain types of texts with their paratexts, it may be more practical to use a functional typology rather than one based on the spatial and substantial status of paratextual elements.

Time

While the changes discussed in the previous sections are motivated primarily by the desire to adapt Genette's framework to digital and audiovisual contexts and to the internet era, the reconsideration of Genette's temporal and pragmatic variables that follows is motivated by a desire to adapt it more specifically to translation-related contexts. Genette's framework is based on the premise that a text is published in its complete form at a particular moment in time (in other words, print texts will have a date of publication). As outlined in Chapter 1, Genette's typology of temporal variables is calculated relative to the appearance of the text in its original language or relative to the life of the author. Thus, in his model, a translation preface that appears at the same time as a translated version of that text would be classed as a 'later' or 'delayed' preface, i.e. appearing some time after its text (understood to be the original) (see Genette 1997, 6). In our model, however, as argued above, the translated version is considered a text in its own right, and a translation preface or any paratextual material that appears at the same time as the translated version would be classed as *original* rather than *later* if we retain Genette's terms. The issue of whether or not to retain Genette's terms for temporal variables is a tricky one: on the one hand, as a general rule, retaining Genette's terminology (which has been widely adopted in literary studies) simplifies the task of talking across disciplines; on the other, in some cases the terms already stand for something else within the adopting discipline and cannot be used without giving rise to some ambiguity or confusion. This is the case for Genette's use of the term *original* to denote paratextual material that appears at the same moment as the text, since in translation contexts (and in lay writing about translation), *original* is frequently used as a synonym for *source text* (or *prototext*, in other terminology). To avoid such confusion, and to adapt Genette's variables to a context in which the translated texts are generally the point of focus, I would argue for a reformulation of Genette's termporal variables along the lines outlined below. In these formulations, 'ST' stands for *source text* and 'TT' stands for *target text* in accordance with standard usage in translation studies.

- pre-ST
- with ST
- post-ST
- pre-TT
- with-TT
- post-TT.

In each case, the temporal label also specifies the text for which the paratextual material is the consciously crafted threshold. Thus a pre-ST paratext is one that is consciously crafted for the ST; although it also pre-dates the TT, it is not crafted as a threshold to the TT itself and thus would not normally be labelled 'pre-TT'. Similarly, while many if not most of the paratexts that are created for the TT will appear after the ST, they would not generally be labelled 'post-ST' but rather 'pre-TT', 'with TT' or 'post-TT', depending on which of these labels applies. Of course, as my hedging language above implies ('not normally', 'not generally'), there might be exceptions to this general approach. For example, scholars studying cases where bilingual or multilingual readers or viewers use ST paratexts as thresholds to their own reading or viewing of the TT may find it more appropriate to consider all of the ST paratexts as belonging to the pre-TT category. In other cases, scholars may need to make distinctions between different editions of the source text or its translations, and expand the list of variables accordingly. Furthermore, the positing of six discrete variables does not rule out interaction between them. As in Genette's model, there is fluidity around when paratexts appear, disappear and reappear: a 'with-TT' or 'post-TT' paratextual element, for example, may become a 'pre-ST' paratext in a case where a text which has gone out of print in the source language draws on the success of the text in the target culture to create promotional material for a new edition of the ST. Furthermore, in cases in which products are released simultaneously in a range of languages, it will not be possible – nor desirable – to distinguish between pre-ST and pre-TT paratexts, since in such cases there is arguably no 'ST–TT' distinction to be made at all. Scholars working in domains in which this type of scenario is common will almost certainly find it preferable to adopt a simpler set of variables or alternatively to specify the language of publication of the text(s) instead of using the labels 'ST' and 'TT'. Once again, it is important to stress that the framework that I am proposing here, while more suited to translation-related contexts than Genette's, will require further development in some situations.

Senders and addressees

As we saw in Chapter 1, Genette's pragmatic typology allows for a wide range of situations of communication, but does not offer a way of distinguishing specifically between translators and other senders; neither does it offer a means of distinguishing between source culture addressees and target culture addressees. As we saw in Chapter 2, some translation studies scholars have argued in favour of disentangling translators from Genette's general category of allographic senders and allotting them their own distinct category in a paratextual typology. This undoubtedly makes sense. As I am aiming to develop a paratextual framework that will be adequate to many different kinds of translation situation, however, it is necessary to expand the typology of senders still further. Thus, building on theoretical reflections by Gray (2010) and others, it will be useful to have some way of distinguishing between those senders who are authorised by the text-producers to produce paratexts for the text in question (along the lines of Gray's (2010, 143) 'industry-created' paratexts), and those who produce paratexts independently (along the lines of Gray's (2010, 143) 'viewer-' or 'audience-created' paratexts). For the latter category, we can also usefully distinguish between paratexts produced by fans (or, indeed, viewers or readers who have negative views about the text) and those that are produced by professionals, such as journalists or critics writing for review publications. With regard to addressees, in many studies of translation paratexts – particularly those which adopt a comparative approach between source text and target text paratexts – we will also need to distinguish between source and target culture addressees in addition to Genette's distinctions between general public, readers, critics and others.

While these additions allow us to expand Genette's typology to take explicit account of translation, they represent a simplification of what is in fact a more complex – or composite – pragmatic situation. To illustrate this problem, let us take the case of the author's preface that appears in translation as one of the paratexts of a translated version of the author's text. When categorising such a preface, we might decide that the sender of this paratextual message is the author, and in one sense this is correct. However, the translator has also played a part in creating it, so in another sense it would be better to describe the sender as being both author and translator, or perhaps the author via the translator's mediation. The same issues of duplication can be seen to arise for texts as well as for paratexts, and have been discussed by Cees Koster (2008), amongst others. Koster suggests distinguishing between extratextual and intratextual levels, and replacing the term *sender* with the more abstract *sender-function* to denote the complex and composite nature of the pragmatic relationship that obtains on the intratextual level:

> On the extratextual level there is no problem in distinguishing between translator and author as empirical subjects with their distinct psychologi-cal, social and cultural circumstances, but on the intratextual level we have to posit that a text has one sender; that is to say, one sender-function: this sender-function may be fragmented, decentred, impersonal or what you will. From the single, independent text perspective the sender has to be considered an amalgamation between translator and author.
>
> *Koster 2008, 32*

In one sense, it could be argued that the contrast between extratextual reality and intratextual situation can be overcome in the same manner in which Genette deals with prefaces that have in fact been written by another individual but which are attributed to the author: in such cases, in Genette's framework, the author would be classed as the sender. In the case of a translated authorial preface, so a reason-ing along these lines might go, the author is the one who has signed the preface, so remains the sender, even if the actual words come from the translator. Yet the case of a translated authorial preface is slightly different, in the sense that both the author *and* the translator have signed it: while the author's name may be the one that features at the end of the preface, as part of the translated work the preface is also attributed to the translator – if not within the preface itself, then in that part of the paratext in which the translator's name appears. We are thus left with a complex situation in which the sender of a paratext for a translated text may be the author (in the case of an untranslated preface, copied without alteration to the paratext of the translated text), the translator (in the case of a translator's preface written for the translated work) or an amalgamation of author-translator (in the case of a preface written by the author for the original work and translated for inclusion in the paratext of the translated version). Similar difficulties apply to other senders, such as publishers or editors: as we have seen, singular labels such as these often conceal composite extratextual realities, and studies that focus on questions of agency will need to develop a complex matrix, allowing for multiple different scenarios of interaction between the key senders.

This point also has relevance for the addressee: while making a distinction between source culture addressees and target culture addressees may be adequate in some situations, in others a more complex category may be needed. On a basic level, the distinction between 'source' and 'target' culture readers ignores the fact that many cultural products in circulation in the source or target culture will have readers and viewers from multiple cultures, particularly when the language used in the cultural product is a global one.[23] Furthermore, the composite nature of trans-lated products means that the intended addressees are also composite: in the case of the translated authorial preface, for example, we can presume that the author wrote it with source culture addressees in mind, yet through the mediation of the transla-tor, the translated version of that preface addresses itself also to some degree to the target culture audience. Other variables to take into account on the addressee side relate to the size of the intended audience: as in Genette's model, it may be helpful to distinguish between paratexts that target all potential readers (e.g. a film trailer, an advert), those which target more specific groups of potential readers, and those which speak to actual readers. Debates over how to define and describe intended, implied, model or empirical readers have shown any straightforward idea of the 'reader' of a text to be deeply problematic;[24] furthermore, opting to use the label *reader* at all – as opposed to *viewer* or *consumer* – may not be appropriate to many research contexts. This sketch of pragmatic variables will therefore need adapting to the material at hand, and the frameworks thus devised will need to strike a bal-ance between a sufficient level of simplicity (to allow paratexts to be categorised) and consideration of the complexities hidden within each label.

Function

As noted in Chapter 1, Genette does not set out a typology of functional variables in the same way as he does for the other aspects of the paratext, arguing instead that, while it is possible to identify the basic illocutionary force of paratextual elements, the detailed functions need to be worked out inductively from empirical data. In addi-tion, unlike the regimes of place, time, substance and pragmatics, 'functional choices are not of an 'either–or' (Genette 1997, 12) nature; in other words, they cannot be said to compose a typology as such.[25] While not disputing this overall approach, Dorothee Birke and Birte Christ (2013, 67–8) criticise Genette's 'rather vague' account of paratext function and suggest that the overall function of paratexts can be described in more differentiated terms 'as an interplay of three different aspects':

'interpretive', 'commercial' and 'navigational'. Other scholars have developed lists of functions specific to particular types of text. Amy Nottingham-Martin (2014, 296–7), for example, identifies six functions of transmedia storytelling paratextual elements: navigational, commercial, didactic, world-building, community-building and text-activating. In a translation context, Urpo Kovala (1996, 134) identifies nine 'micro-functions' of paratexts to literary translations: 'identification, metatextual function, placing, giving background information, illustration, reference to reader, advertising, and the artistic and legal/bibliographic'.

Working in the context of videogames, but also in part working deductively using reflections on Genette's own model, Rockenberger (2014, 262) outlines a more extensive list, which she suggests may be relevant to all media. In my view, Rockenberger's list has great potential for use in translation studies, not least because it draws on a vocabulary with which translation scholars are likely to be familiar thanks to the popularity of functionalist translation theories. I therefore present it with minor alterations below:[26]

1) *Referential*: identifying the work, establishing its legal and discursive fingerprint
2) *Self-referential*: drawing attention to the paratext or its elements
3) *Ornamental*: decorating and 'looking nice'
4) *Generic*: categorising the work, indicating genre, establishing a 'generic pact' concerning the appropriate attitude of reception; includes categorisation as a translation
5) *Meta-communicative*: explicitly reflecting on the conditions and constraints of mediated communication in general and the work's placing in particular; includes reflections on translation and/or the difficulties of the translation process
6) *Informative*: mediating true empirical data, clarifying internal and external relations and properties of the work, explicitly revealing intentions, removing epistemic obstacles to the reader's understanding, including, in translation contexts, clarifying culture-specific references for a new audience; referring to other helpful information or services
7) *Hermeneutical*: offering certain cognitive framings, directing attention, exposing certain aspects or qualities, mediating relevant contexts, instructing the understanding or interpretation – i.e. the explanation of the text's characteristics as a result of authorial decisions and actions – and thus widening or restricting interpretative options
8) *Ideological*: promoting a certain viewpoint; taking distance from the ideological stance of the text or, particularly in translation situations, of the author or source culture
9) *Evaluative*: claiming or demanding value and cultural significance
10) *Commercial*: advertising, praising, selling; attracting and directing buyer's attention; cultivating needs; referring to and recommending other products
11) *Legal*: (a) informative (informing about legal entitlements), (b) illocutionary (symbolically establishing legal rights and obligations, formal or informal contracts and guarantees)

12) *Pedagogical*: establishing standards for behaviour
13) *Instructive, operational*: facilitating and guiding reception and use of the product, offering orientation, suggesting, organising and structuring possible approaches to the product, recommending actions; includes navigational paratexts
14) *Personalisation*: only for *interactive* paratext elements – temporarily adjusting elements to personal needs

adapted from Rockenberger 2014, 262–3

It should be stressed that many paratextual elements serve more than one function simultaneously: a preface, for example, may be informative, hermeneutical, ideological and evaluative, while a title page may be referential, generic, ornamental, and even instructive.[27]

As in Genette's model, it may prove useful to complement lists of function with lists of themes, outlining for example the typical themes that might be addressed in translation prefaces. Background research carried out for Chapter 4, for example, suggests that the themes addressed in translators' prefaces to philosophical texts published in the UK and the US over the last 150 years show a remarkable degree of constancy, with almost all prefaces outlining the importance of the author or work, the need for the translation, the high quality of the translation, the difficulty of translation in general terms, as well as offering an interpretation of the work for the reader. This suggests that translators' prefaces to this type of text and in this cultural context are above all evaluative (and through this, indirectly, commercial) but also serve important meta-communicative and hermeneutic functions. Identifying thematic patterns of this kind for the key paratextual elements specific to translations and matching them to the functions identified above carries a number of benefits for translation research: it deepens our appreciation of what paratexts do; it allows us to note changes in patterns of theme and function over time, or across cultures; and, at a basic level, it helps us not to treat as extraordinary or noteworthy something which actually represents common practice in a given culture or era.

Concluding remarks

While this chapter has demonstrated some of the complexities involved in developing typologies adequate to the exploration of translation paratexts, it also reveals the potential that inheres in this kind of research. For example, by developing classificatory tools and adopting systematic approaches to the study of paratextual elements, we are reminded to pay attention to all aspects of translation thresholds, not just those which seem intuitively more important or which form a more obvious grouping. Rather than limiting our research to a sender-based category such as translators' prefaces or translators' notes, for example, we might opt to study a less salient set of elements such as those fulfilling legal functions, gaining important new insights in the process.[28] Another benefit of working with typologies is that it makes us alert not only to how paratextual elements are translated but how they are not: in Chiara Bucaria's (2014, 308) words, we are more likely to note 'paratexts that stand out for their absence', something which can be of considerable importance to studies contrasting paratextual framing across cultures.

Notes

1 We should note, however, that Hermans's use of the term *framing* is more restricted than Baker's: whereas Baker sees framing as encompassing a wide range of discursive practices that can occur not only within paratextual material but also within translations or oral interpreting events, Hermans (2007, 60) conceives of framing as 'one device for signalling the dissociation from alien and the affirmation of indigenous values'. The example that he provides of another device for doing the same thing is the non-translation of specific passages in a text. This implies, even if it does not explicitly state, that framing is conceptualised as something which takes place only through material placed around the translation rather than through techniques used in the translation itself. See Hermans (2007, 52–65) for further details.

2 An English translation of Genette's words cited here is provided in Macksey (1997, xvii): 'fringe at the unsettled limits that enclose with a pragmatic halo the literary work'. For a more detailed reflection on the intersection between notions of framing and Genette's paratext, see Berlatsky (2009).

3 Van Dijk is drawing here on Jonathan Culler's reading of Derrida's exploration of the *parergon*. See Culler (2007 [1982], 193–9) for further details.

4 The bibliographical details for the paper which Johnson-Cartee is citing are as follows: J.W. Tankard, L. Hendrickson, J. Silberman, K. Bliss and S. Ghanem (1991) 'Media Frames: Approaches to Conceptualization and Measurement', paper presented at the Association for Education in Journalism and Mass Communication Convention, Boston. While this paper is widely cited in studies of news media, the paper itself would appear to be available in only one library worldwide, in the form of a fourteen-page photocopy, according to worldcat.org. I have therefore provided an indirect reference for the citation.

5 See, notably, Nelson, Clawson and Oxley's (1997) study of perceptions of a Ku Klux Klan rally.

6 We should note that Baker's (2006, 106) definition of *frames* differs slightly from those proposed by scholars in communication theory, since she assigns it a more dynamic meaning: 'frames are defined as . . . strategic moves that are consciously initiated in order to present a movement or a particular position within a certain perspective'.

7 In the paragraph that follows, however, Pellatt (2013b, 2) appears to limit *paratext* to Genette's *peritext*, and opposes it to *epitext*: 'In this volume we are mainly concerned with paratext, attached to or inserted in the core text, and epitext, comment which is external to the published volume.'

8 Kung's appeal to the notion of intertextuality indicates the need for some degree of connection between the extratexts and the text itself, but the nature of that connection is not made explicit, and the decision to label such material *extratexts* rather than *intertexts* is not discussed.

9 Indeed, Deane-Cox (2014, 29) presents the motivation for her proposed terminology as being in part a desire to heed Genette's warning that the zone of the paratext should not be enlarged.

10 For an example of the first type of study, see Shen and Xu (2007); for the second, see Hammett, van Kleeck and Huberty (2003).

11 Regarding reviews as paratexts concords with the approach proposed by Jonathan Gray (2011, 114), who argues that press reviews of television are 'an often-overlooked paratext'.

12 Indeed, writing in 1978, Marcel Janssens (1978, 5, italics in original) calls translation 'metatext *par excellence*'.

13 Other important reflections on the term and the related notion of translation as metaliterature can be found in Lefevere (1978) and van Gorp (1978).

14 The Oxford English Living Dictionaries (2017) define *meta-text* as 'A text lying outside another text, especially one describing or elucidating another.'

15 See, for example, his discussions of allographic prefaces (Genette 1997, 270) and allographic notes (Genette 1997, 343).

16 To give an example of how these terminological distinctions can be maintained, I would argue that the translation prefaces discussed by Rodica Dimitriu (2009), which analyse 'translations *as translations*, highlighting translation problems and describing strategies for dealing with them' (Dimitriu 2009, 194, italics in original) would best be described as paratexts containing metadiscourse, rather than as metatexts.

17 Yuste Frías (2010, 291n3) states that he created the term in the final stages of the supervision of Garrido Vilariño's thesis, motivated by the need to find an umbrella term for the paratextual elements of various translations of Primo Levi's *Se questa è un uomo*. According to Garrido Vilariño (2011, 76n2), the group was initiated by Alexis Nouss. The largest number of publications are by Yuste Frías, although Garrido Vilariño and others have also made important contributions, and the group promotes the concept through its own webpages, the university's online TV channel and various blogs.

18 The Spanish database of articles in indexed journals, Dialnet, finds just tweleve hits for the term 'paratraducción', most of which are for articles by academics linked to Vigo University.

19 At the time of writing, I could find only one researcher working within the Anglo-American translation studies tradition who incorporates the term into her discussions (see Pellatt 2013c, 2018).

20 In his outline of the way in which the 'Translation and Paratranslation' research group at the University of Vigo took shape, Garrido Vilariño (2011, 76) identifies one of the main motivations of the group as being 'to absolve translators of all responsibility for the manipulations that have traditionally been attributed to them'.

21 A similar point is made by Dunne (2016, 279), who notes that 'paratext in Gray's analysis has been significantly remodelled to suit film's temporal qualities, rather than Genette's spatial focus'.

22 If we think of the distinction between writing, speaking and gesturing as differences in the way in which the message is materialised (i.e. typed or handwritten marks vs human voice or body movements), then we could equally well consider each one to be a medium rather than a mode of expression. While writing and speech stand somewhat in opposition to each other (a message is rarely spoken and written at the same time), gesture often accompanies speech. It is also possible to envisage situations in which gesture functions as a paratext to the text of a speech, as we will see in the discussion of corporeal paratexts in the following chapter.

23 Kate Sturge (2007, 11) refers to this as 'the fallacy of source–target dichotomies' and observes that Western translation studies is yet to take full account of this issue.

24 For a brief summary of such debates, see Koster (2008).

25 By definition, typologies aim to identify types, or classes, which are 'both exhaustive and mutually exclusive' (Bailey 1994, 3).

26 The original list can be viewed in Rockenberger (2014, 262–3). I have added illustrations of how the categories are relevant to translation contexts, and have reduced the categories from sixteen to fourteen, eliminating 'pragmatic: controlling and managing the work's overall public reception' and 'staging: image cultivation or self-display, biased depiction of the author and/or his work, thereby promoting certain expectations of pro-attitudes'. In my view, the label 'pragmatic' is likely to result in confusion, given that the term *pragmatic variables* is being used above in Genette's sense of referring to sender and receiver of the paratextual message; furthermore, the function to which Rockenberger's category refers is very broad and in this sense serves as an umbrella term encompassing many of the other functions. 'Staging' has been eliminated primarily for reasons of overlap, notably with 'ideological' and 'hermeneutical'.

27 I am thinking, for example, of the subtitle added to the American paperback version of Frantz Fanon's (1968) *Les Damnés de la terre*, 'A Handbook for the Black Revolution that is Changing the Shape of the World', where the word *handbook* can be seen to be instructing the reader on how to use the text. For an analysis of the role this and other paratexts played in the reception of Fanon's work, see Batchelor (2017).

28 As I have shown in a study of translations of the West African Mande epic *Sunjata* (see Batchelor 2018 in press), incorporating discussion of copyright assignation into reflections on the authorship of ethnographic literature is of crucial importance to understanding the way in which such texts circulate globally.

References

Ädel, Annelie, and Anna Mauranen. 2010. "Metadiscourse: Diverse and Divided Perspectives". *Nordic Journal of English Studies* 9 (2): 1–11.

Bailey, Kenneth D. 1994. *Typologies and Taxonomies. An Introduction to Classification Techniques*. Thousand Oaks, London and New Delhi: Sage Publications.

Baker, Mona. 2006. *Translation and Conflict: A Narrative Account*. London and New York: Routledge.

——. 2007. "Reframing Conflict in Translation". *Social Semiotics* 17 (2): 151–69.

Batchelor, Kathryn. 2017. "The Translation of *Les Damnés de la terre* into English: Exploring Irish Connections". In *Translating Frantz Fanon across Continents and Languages*, edited by Kathryn Batchelor and Sue-Ann Harding, 40–75. London and New York: Routledge.

——. 2018 in press. "Sunjata in English: Paratexts, Authorship, and the Postcolonial Exotic". In *The Palgrave Handbook of Literary Translation*, edited by Jean Boase-Beier, Lina Fisher and Hiroko Furukawa. Palgrave Macmillan.

Berlatsky, Eric. 2009. "Lost in the Gutter: Within and Between Frames in Narrative and Narrative Theory". *Narrative* 17 (2): 162–87.

Bhaskar, M. 2011. "Towards Paracontent: Marketing, Publishing and Cultural Form in a Digital Environment". *Logos* 22 (1): 25–36.

Birke, Dorothee, and Birte Christ. 2013. "Paratext and Digitized Narrative: Mapping the Field". *Narrative* 21 (1): 65–87.

Bucaria, Chiara. 2014. "Trailers and Promos and Teasers, Oh My! Adapting Television Paratexts across Cultures". In *Media and Translation: An Interdisciplinary Approach*, edited by Dror Abend-David, 293–313. New York, London, New Delhi and Sydney: Bloomsbury Academic Publishing.

Culler, Jonathan. 2007 [1982]. *On Deconstruction: Theory and Criticism after Structuralism*, 25th anniversary edition. New York: Cornell University Press.

Deane-Cox, Sharon. 2014. *Retranslation: Translation, Literature and Reinterpretation*. London: Bloomsbury.

Dimitriu, Rodica. 2009. "Translators' Prefaces as Documentary Sources for Translation Studies". *Perspectives* 17 (3): 193–206.

Dunne, Daniel. 2016. "Paratext: The In-Between of Structure and Play". In *Contemporary Research on Intertextuality in Video Games*, edited by Christophe Duret and Christian-Marie Pons, 274–96. IGI Global.

Fanon, Frantz. 1968. *The Wretched of the Earth*. Translated by Constance Farrington. New York: Grove Press.

Fillmore, Charles J., and Collin Baker. 2009. "A Frames Approach to Semantic Analysis". In *The Oxford Handbook of Linguistic Analysis*, edited by Bernd Heine and Heiko Narrog, 313–39. Oxford: Oxford University Press.

Garrido Vilariño, Xoán Manuel. 2011. "The Paratranslation of the Works of Primo Levi". In *Translating Dialects and Languages of Minorities*, edited by Federico M. Federici, 65–88. Bern: Peter Lang.

Genette, Gérard. 1979. *Introduction à l'architexte*. Paris: Editions du Seuil.

——. 1992. *The Architext: An Introduction*. Translated by Jane E. Lewin. Berkeley, Los Angeles and Oxford: University of California Press.

——. 1997. *Paratexts: Thresholds of Interpretation*. Translated by Jane E. Lewin. Cambridge: Cambridge University Press.

Gray, Jonathan. 2010. *Show Sold Separately: Promos, Spoilers, and other Media Paratexts.* New York and London: New York University Press.

———. 2011. "The Reviews are In: TV Critics and the (Pre)creation of Meaning". In *Flow TV: Television in an Age of Media Convergence*, edited by Michael Kackman, Marnie Binfield, Matthew Thomas Payne, Allision Perlman and Bryan Sebok, 114–27. New York and Abingdon: Routledge.

Hammett, Lisa A., Anne van Kleeck and Carl J. Huberty. 2003. "Patterns of Parents' Extratextual Interactions during Book Sharing with Preschool Children: A Cluster Analysis Study". *Reading Research Quarterly* 38 (4): 442–68.

Harvey, Keith. 2003. "'Events' and 'horizons' – Reading Ideology in the 'Bindings' of Translations". In *Apropos of Ideology*, edited by María Calzada Pérez, 43–69. Manchester: St Jerome Publishing.

Hermans, Theo. 2007. *The Conference of the Tongues.* Manchester: St Jerome Publishing.

Holmes, James S. 1988. *Translated! Papers on Literary Translation and Translation Studies.* Amsterdam: Rodopi.

Janssens, Marcel. 1978. "The Medial Mode: By Way of Introduction". In *Literature and Translation: New Perspectives in Literary Studies*, edited by James S. Holmes, José Lambert and Raymond van den Broeck, 1–6. Leuven: acco.

Johnson-Cartee, Karen S. 2005. *News Narratives and News Framing: Constructing Political Reality.* Lanham and Oxford: Rowman & Littlefield.

Knape, Joachim. 2013. *Modern Rhetoric in Culture, Arts, and Media.* Berlin and Boston: De Gruyter.

Koster, Cees. 2008. "The Translator in Between Texts: On the Textual Presence of the Translator as an Issue in the Methodology of Comparative Translation Description". In *Translation Studies: Perspectives on an Emerging Discipline*, edited by Alessandra Riccardi, 24–37. Cambridge: Cambridge University Press.

Kovala, Urpo. 1996. "Translations, Paratextual Mediation, and Ideological Closure". *Target* 8 (1): 119–47.

Kung, Szu-Wen Cindy. 2010. "Network & Cooperation in Translating Taiwanese Literature into English". In *Translation: Theory and Practice in Dialogue*, edited by Antoinette Fawcett, Karla L. Guadarrama García and Rebeccca Hyde Parker, 164–80. London and New York: Contiuum International Publishing Group.

Lambert, José, and Hendrik van Gorp. 2014. "On Describing Translations". In *The Manipulation of Literature: Studies in Literary Translation*, edited by Theo Hermans, 42–53. Abingdon and New York: Routledge.

Lefevere, André. 1978. "Translation: The Focus of the Growth of Literary Knowledge". In *Literature and Translation: New Perspectives in Literary Studies*, edited by James S. Holmes, José Lambert and Raymond van den Broeck, 7–28. Leuven: acco.

Lewis, Ann. 2007. "Introduction: Reading and Writing the Frame". In *Framed! Essays in French Studies*, edited by Lucy Bolton, Gerri Kimber, Ann Lewis and Michael Seabrook, 11–31. Peter Lang.

McCracken, Ellen. 2013. "Expanding Genette's Epitext/Peritext Model for Transitional Electronic Literature: Centrifugal and Centripetal Vectors on Kindles and iPads". *Narrative* 21 (1): 105–24.

Macksey, Richard. 1997. "Foreword". In *Paratexts: Thresholds of Interpretation*, by Gérard Genette, xi–xxii. Cambridge: Cambridge University Press.

Maclean, Marie. 1991. "Pretexts and Paratexts: The Art of the Peripheral". *New Literary History* 22 (2): 273–9.

Minsky, Marvin. 1974. "A Framework for Representing Knowledge". *AI Memos (1959–2004)*, Artificial Intelligence Lab Publications, MIT, DSpace@MIT. Accessed 9 October 2017 from http://hdl.handle.net/1721.1/6089.

Munday, Jeremy. 2009. "Paratext". In *The Routledge Companion to Translation Studies*, edited by Jeremy Munday, 214–15. London and New York: Routledge.

Nelson, Thomas E.,Rosalee A. Clawson and Zoe M. Oxley. 1997. "Media Framing of Civil Liberties Conflict and its Effects on Tolerance". *American Political Science Review* 91 (3): 567–83.

Nottingham-Martin, Amy. 2014. "Thresholds of Transmedia Storytelling: Applying Gérard Genette's Paratextual Theory to *The 39 Clues* Series for Young Readers". In *Examining Paratextual Theory and its Applications in Digital Culture*, edited by Nadine Desrochers and Daniel Apollon, 287–307. IGI Global.

Oxford English Living Dictionaries. 2017. *meta-text*. Oxford: Oxford University Press. Accessed 10 October 2017 from https://en.oxforddictionaries.com/definition/meta-text.

Pellatt, Valerie, ed. 2013a. *Text, Extratext, Metatext and Paratext in Translation*. Newcastle upon Tyne: Cambridge Scholars Publishing.

——. 2013b. "Introduction". In *Text, Extratext, Metatext and Paratext in Translation*, edited by Valerie Pellatt, 1–6. Newcastle upon Tyne: Cambridge Scholars Publishing.

——. 2013c. "Packaging the Product: A Case Study of Verbal and Non-verbal Paratext in Chinese-English Translation". *Journal of Specialised Translation* 20: 86–106.

——. 2018. "Translation and Chinese Paratext and Paratext of Chinese Translation". In *Routledge Handbook of Chinese Translation*, edited by Chris Shei and Zhao-Ming Gao, 164–85. London and New York: Routledge.

Pérez-González, Luis. 2014. "Multimodality in Translation and Interpreting Studies: Theoretical and Methodological Perspectives". In *A Companion to Translation Studies*, edited by Sandra Bermann and Catherine Porter, 119–31. Chichester, UK: John Wiley & Sons.

Popovič, Anton. 1975. *Problémy literárnej metakomunikácie: Teória metatextu*. Nitra: KLKEM.

——. 1976. "Aspects of Metatext". *Canadian Review of Comparative Literature* Autumn: 225–35.

Rayner, Jay. 2017. "Le Cinq, Paris: Restaurant Review". *Guardian*, 9 April. Accessed 21 September 2017 from www.theguardian.com/lifeandstyle/2017/apr/09/le-cinq-paris-restaurant-review-jay-rayner.

Rockenberger, Annika. 2014. "Video Game Framings". In *Examining Paratextual Theory and its Applications in Digital Culture*, edited by Nadine Desrochers and Daniel Apollon, 252–86. IGI Global.

Shen, Dan, and Dejin Xu. 2007. "Intratextuality, Extratextuality, Intertextuality: Unreliability in Autobiography versus Fiction". *Poetics Today* 28 (1): 43–87.

Snow, David A. 2011. "Frame". In *The Concise Encyclopedia of Sociology*, edited by George Ritzer and J. Michael Ryan, 235–6. Chichester, UK: Wiley-Blackwell.

Stewart, Gavin. 2010. "The Paratexts of Inanimate Alice: Thresholds, Genre Expectations and Status". *Convergence* 16 (1): 57–74.

Sturge, Kate. 2007. *Representing Others: Translation, Ethnography and the Museum*. Manchester: St Jerome Publishing.

Susam-Sarajeva, Şebnem. 2006. *Theories on the Move: Translation's Role in the Travels of Literary Theories*. Amsterdam and New York: Rodopi.

Tahir-Gürçağlar, Şehnaz. 2002. "What Texts Don't Tell: The Uses of Paratexts in Translation Research". In *Crosscultural Transgressions: Research Models in Translation Studies 2: Historical and Ideological Issues*, edited by Theo Hermans, 44–60. Manchester: St Jerome Publishing.

van Dijk, Yra. 2014. "The Margins of Bookishness: Paratexts in Digital Literature". In *Examining Paratextual Theory and its Applications in Digital Culture*, edited by Nadine Desrochers and Daniel Apollon, 24–45. IGI Global.

van Gorp, H. 1978. "La Traduction littéraire parmi les autres métatextes". In *Literature and Translation: New Perspectives in Literary Studies*, edited by James S. Holmes, José Lambert and Raymond van den Broeck, 101–16. Leueven: acco.

Watts, Richard. 2005. *Packaging Post/Coloniality: The Manufacture of Literary Identity in the Francophone World*. Lanham, Boulder, New York, Toronto and Oxford: Lexington Books.

Wolf, Werner. 2006. "Introduction. Frames, Framings and Framing Borders in Literature and Other Media". In *Framing Borders in Literature and Other Media*, edited by Werner Wolf and Walter Bernhart, 1–40. Amsterdam and New York: Rodopi.

Yuste Frías, José. 2010. "Au seuil de la traduction: la paratraduction". In *Event or Incident/ Evénement ou Incident: On the Role of Translation in the Dynamics of Cultural Exchange/Du Rôle des traductions dans les processus d'échanges culturels*, 287–316. Bern: Peter Lang.

———. 2012. "Paratextual Elements in Translation: Paratranslating Titles in Children's Literature". In *Translation Peripheries: Paratextual Elements in Translation*, edited by Anna Gil-Bardají, Pilar Orero and Sara Rovira-Esteva, 117–34. Bern: Peter Lang.

8

TRANSLATION AND PARATEXTS

Research topics and methodologies

Almost all of the research discussed in the earlier chapters of this book takes translation products as its point of focus, and the book as a whole thus gives a rich sense of the paratext's relevance to product-oriented research. For this reason, this chapter summarises the research topics and methodologies associated with such studies only briefly, dwelling primarily on questions of methodology that have received limited attention, such as approaches to image-based paratexts. The remainder of the chapter seeks to initiate a discussion of the potential of paratextual research for domains of study to which it has yet to be applied with any intensity, namely process-oriented research, interpreting studies and translation as literary criticism.

Product-oriented research

Research that focuses on paratexts as products falls broadly into two different categories. The first looks at paratexts as ends in themselves, and attempts to map the paratextual practices that are associated with translated texts. This is usually done in relation to a particular period of time or cultural context, and is often restricted by text genre or paratextual element. The second type of study investigates paratexts as the means to some other end: paratexts are thus viewed as documents or artefacts that are of interest *because of what they tell us about something else*. Very broadly, that 'something else' falls into one of three overlapping categories: the translated text, the past and the present. While it is useful to distinguish between paratexts studied as ends in themselves and paratexts studied as means to another end in this way, we should bear in mind that the two types of study feed into one another: understanding paratextual practices is crucial for interpreting specific paratexts, while the paratexts that are studied from the second angle can be added to the sum of data on which researchers draw to map paratextual conventions.

The study of paratextual conventions

The motivations for studying paratextual conventions in connection with translation are twofold. First, identifying the conventions associated with specific times, places, text types and genres allows us to make informed observations about changes to paratextual elements as texts are translated. For example, if a book is published in the source culture with a striking image on the front cover, and the same book appears in the target culture with a plain cover, any commentary on the meaning of that shift will depend on an understanding of conventions governing the use of cover images. In some times and places, a plain cover might be associated with the underground press (see, for example, Farzaneh Farahzad's (2017) discussion of *jeld-sefid* in 1970s Iran); in others, a plain cover might be the norm for literary fiction (as is the case in France). This type of research examines paratextual conventions governing both non-translated and translated products in source and target cultures with the goal of making valid observations when comparing products across cultures. The second type of research is interested in mapping paratextual practices specifically in relation to translations, with the overall goal of understanding the position of translation within a given culture over a particular period of time. Such studies might address the status of translation (e.g. by looking at where and how the translator and fact of translation are acknowledged in paratexts), or examine prevailing or competing views about translation, as expressed in a range of types of paratextual elements.

The methodological challenges associated with such research primarily concern the delineation of the corpus: researchers will need to address the question of how large the corpus needs to be in order to make generalisations that can be considered to hold water; if researching translations, they will need to develop a process for working out whether a given text is a translation or not, where this information is either not provided or not considered to be reliable within the paratexts themselves; they will also need to formulate a procedure for assessing whether borderline cases should be included or excluded from the corpus. Another challenge concerns the writing up of such research: while it may be tempting to simply catalogue the features of paratextual elements, or in other words to produce research that is purely descriptive, some level of contextualisation and critical analysis of the findings is needed if such research is to achieve its real value. If we consider Genette's own study, which maps the paratextual conventions governing canonical French literature, we see that Genette does not just catalogue, but also analyses, pointing out the implications of doing things one way rather than another, addressing the subtleties of meaning that can be found in apparently small decisions, nuancing generalisations by discussing exceptions, and incorporating analysis of the functions that the paratextual elements serve.

Paratexts as documents for analysing the translated text

Analysis of translated texts serves primarily to answer 'what' and 'how' questions, such as: 'What was the overall approach taken by the translator?', 'How did the translator deal with a particular feature of the source text?', 'How is the translator's discursive presence manifest in this text?' and so on. While the analysis of paratexts can contribute to answering questions of this sort,[1] paratextual analysis is above all helpful when trying to answer 'who' and 'why' questions, such as: 'Who is responsible for the translation decisions that we see in the translated text?', 'Why was this translation produced?', 'Why was this key term translated in this way?' As with any document, the statements or implied statements found within paratexts need to be critically assessed with regard to their reliability, a point that I shall explore in greater detail below.

Paratexts as documents for understanding the past

At a very basic level, paratexts can be useful for finding raw data for historical studies. The information recorded in a translation's paratexts, for example, can be crucial for tracking the publication history of a particular text, building up a database of translations published by a particular publishing house or in a particular country, or providing the bare bones of translator biographies. In many cases, identifying the information present in paratexts is straightforward, but in some cases, it may require expertise in a relevant domain such as book history (see, for example, Guyda Armstrong's (2013) study of medieval paratexts, discussed in Chapter 2). The ease with which such information can be found varies, as does the reliability of the information itself; for a discussion of the difficulties associated with historical research into Arabic editions of Frantz Fanon's *Les Damnés de la terre* (*The Wretched of the Earth*), for example, see Harding (2017, 108–9).

At a deeper level, paratexts can be used to understand the past in two ways: first, as documents which tell us about the past by virtue of having been shaped by the past; and, second, as documents which may themselves have influenced the past. A study such as Gaby Thomson-Wohlgemuth's (2009), discussed in Chapter 2, falls into the first category, drawing on paratextual material to deepen understanding of the way in which GDR society functioned, while a study such as Şebnem Susam-Sarajeva's (2006), also discussed in Chapter 2, explores the influence of introductions, prefaces and back-cover information on the reception of French theory in particular receiving cultures.[2] Studies often cut both ways: the paratexts can be seen to have been shaped by the context, but in turn contribute to shaping the context, strengthening or challenging prevailing discourses. Assessing the balance in direction is not always straightforward. Determining the actual (as opposed to potential) influence of a paratext is also very difficult; this point will be discussed further below.

Paratexts as documents for understanding the present

In parallel with research which draws on paratexts as documents for understanding the past, research into present-day contexts takes one of two broad approaches: in the first, paratexts are viewed as documents that are influenced by the broader context and as such can tell us things about the society in which they are produced; in the second, paratexts are seen as factors which themselves exert an influence over society, or some aspect thereof. Like research into the past,[3] this kind of research falls into the broad category of 'context-oriented' research according to Gabriela Saldanha and Sharon O'Brien's (2014) division, and often draws on conceptual frameworks developed in disciplines such as cultural studies, postcolonial studies and sociology. Examples of context-oriented studies discussed in Chapter 2 include those by Cecilia Alvstad (2012), Mona Baker (2006) and Richard Watts (2005), but there are many others. The primary methodological challenges associated with this kind of research are similar to those facing studies that use paratexts to understand the past, and will be discussed below. As we shall see, the main difference is that there are a number of additional solutions open to researchers for addressing some of these challenges.

Questions of methodology

The basics of good research practice are as applicable to studies of paratexts as they are to any other kind of research. Readers looking for general guidelines on methodology and research project design are advised to consult appropriate sources, such as Susam-Sarajeva (2009), Pym (2014), Saldanha and O'Brien (2014) or Williams and Chesterman (2014). In this section, I shall discuss some of the issues that, while not unique to paratexts, often emerge as particularly pressing in paratextual research.

The nature and reliability of paratexts as documents

The basic principles for analysing sources apply to paratexts as to any other documents. These include assessing the authenticity of the source, reading it in context, interrogating author bias, and compensating for these issues by weighing sources against each other.[4] Given the varied functions of paratextual elements, and the fact that reading them for what they reveal about the broader context is often to read them against their original purpose, it is particularly important to analyse their content in light of the motives and constraints governing their use. This involves asking such questions as:

- Who is the target audience of this paratext (e.g. a board of censors, a potential purchaser of the translated product, a rival academic school of thought, etc.)?
- What is this paratextual element intended to achieve (and how does its function or functions affect what the paratext producer is likely to say with regard to the translation)?
- What are the conventions governing the content and tone of this paratextual element in the relevant culture? Or, to use Alexandra Lopes's (2012, 129) words, highlighted in Chapter 2, how is this paratextual element 'constrained by the accepted discursive practices applicable to the format'?

Even when we are dealing with paratextual elements that appear to speak directly to the questions that we are seeking to answer, the multiple functions of many paratextual elements need to be borne in mind. In the case of a translation preface, for example, we might imagine that the translator's comments on his or her translation strategy are intended to convey information about that strategy – but that is not necessarily the case. Instead, the translator's comments may be crafted to stress the reliability of the translation or to increase the likelihood of it being well received: for example, if a literal approach is the most acceptable or in vogue approach at the time of writing, translators may assert that they have followed such an approach even if this is not really the best reflection of what they have done. Alternatively, translators' comments on their strategy may be designed primarily to take up a particular position with regard to academic debates or schools of thought, or to highlight some particular aspect of the author's thinking, and so on.

How do we know if people actually came to the text through a given paratext?

One of the basic premises of paratextual theory is that paratexts serve as thresholds through which people come to a text, and therefore exert an influence on the ways in which that text is received. Yet, in many cases, we cannot be sure that people did come to the text through a particular paratext: the reader of a book may not bother looking at the preface, the viewer of a film may not have seen the poster at the bus stop, and so on. The issue becomes particularly pressing in the digital era, with its associated proliferation of industry- and audience-created thresholds, as we saw in Chapter 3. There are two kinds of solution to this problem: first, we can try to find out whether the text was indeed accessed through the threshold in question; second, we can word our reflections and conclusions in a manner appropriate to the degree of uncertainty affecting this part of our research. Solutions of the first type are generally more available for researchers looking at relatively recently created paratexts, and some of them were discussed briefly in Chapter 3. They include:

- Looking for evidence that the threshold was used (or potentially used) by a significant number of receivers of the text. This might, for example, involve obtaining circulation figures for newspapers in which paratexts appeared, assessing the relative prominence of the paratext (e.g. placement of an advert), or obtaining statistics on visitors to a website (or, even more pertinently, click-throughs from a web-based paratext to its text).
- Looking for evidence that the threshold was used by the particular receivers of the text in whom we are interested. In historical research, this might be limited to searching for references to a paratextual source in other documents, while in contemporary research it could extend to researching discussion forums and other platforms on which viewers or readers post opinions about texts, and to carrying out interviews or surveys with the text-receivers.

In many if not most cases, it will not be possible to gain a complete and reliable picture of the extent to which a threshold was actually used, and we will therefore need to complement these efforts with the second kind of solution, building an appropriate amount of qualifying language into our discussion of our research findings. Rather than stating categorically that the paratext means that the text would have been perceived in a particular way, for example, we can stress that the findings only hold insofar as the paratext was read, in the spirit of the 'what if' model proposed by Amy Nottingham-Martin (2014, 293) and as discussed in Chapter 3.

How do we know if people were actually influenced in the way in which the paratext-creator envisaged?

This question is related to the previous one, in the sense that they both boil down to knowing whether or not a paratext actually functioned in the way(s) envisaged by the one who created it. Once again, there are two kinds of solutions in parallel with the solutions to the previous question: we can try and find out how people were actually influenced by the paratext, or we can adjust our writing style to take account of our uncertainty. The evidence that might be obtained to show that a text was accessed through a particular threshold can also sometimes be used to explore the nature of the paratext's influence on receivers: with regard to discussion forums and other web-based sites, for example, we saw in Chapter 3 that these can be considered as 'pre-constituted audience research, providing evidence of how viewers make sense of texts' (Gray 2010, 146). In practice, however, unless our research is focused on a small group of text receivers whose views we can investigate at length and in depth, we are likely to need to adopt the second kind of solution as well. Urpo Kovala's (1996, 141) caution that we should be wary of assuming a passive recipient of paratextual messages is certainly worth heeding. Jonathan Gray echoes this point, drawing on Michel de Certeau's metaphor of walking in the city to illustrate the agency which receivers have with regard to paratexts:

> [de Certeau] likens textual structure to urban structure and design, but notes that we can walk through a city in many different ways. Urban planners, traffic flow experts, and owners of private property have their preferred notions of how they want you to get from one place to another, and they cut down all sorts of options or try to make other options more enticing. But in the end we have agency, and we do not have to follow their paths entirely. This is what paratext creators are doing – they are some of the key would-be urban planners and land developers of the textual world.
>
> *Brookey and Gray 2017, 107*

The degree to which text receivers are likely to follow the paths laid out by paratext creators depends to some extent on the type of paratext: whereas receivers of a promotional paratext are likely to receive it with a certain amount of scepticism thanks to their understanding of how advertising functions, receivers of what might appear to be factual information – such as the information that a text is an 'authorised translation', as discussed in Chapter 4 – might be more likely to do so passively. These kinds of considerations need to be built into discussion of research findings.

Analysing images and multimodal texts

It is probably fair to say that the academic background of the majority of translation studies scholars is not in art history or visual culture, or in other words in disciplines which provide training in reading images.[5] Furthermore, translation studies has historically 'favoured the study of written and spoken discourse' (Pérez-González 2014b, 119) rather than non-verbal elements. Many paratexts, however, such as book covers, trailers, websites, transmedia stories and video prefaces, are image-based or combine linguistic and visual elements. If we are to take full account of these images and of the interplay between words and images, we need to have some level of competence in methodologies used in image-based disciplines. As with methodologies for textual analysis, existing frameworks are particularly useful for helping us move from asserting what is shown to analysing what is meant, and for knowing which factors to consider when asking *how* things are shown.

In this section I summarise key elements of what Gunther Kress and Theo van Leeuwen (1996) term the 'grammar of visual design' (1), a methodology that pays attention to the way in which 'depicted people, places and things are combined into a meaningful whole' (1). This contrasts with visual lexis, which concerns the denotative and connotative meanings (iconographic, symbolic, etc.) of the individual things, people or places depicted. In Christian traditions, for example, a peacock symbolises eternal life and resurrection, while in art that draws on Roman mythology it evokes Juno, goddess of marriage. In Islamic art and in Eastern traditions, it has still other meanings. Visual lexis is thus typically deeply rooted in particular cultural, religious or artistic traditions, and it is not practical to attempt any kind of summary of how to read such images here. In contrast, while the grammar of visual design also needs to be examined with a keen eye on differences in cultural traditions as well as the researcher's own positionality,[6] the basic tenets of analysis and terminology can be applied to static and dynamic images of all kinds. Furthermore, Kress and van Leeuwen's framework of visual grammar underlies recent efforts to develop frameworks for exploring multimodality in translation studies, particularly in relation to subtitling.[7] Choosing it over other possible frameworks thus also carries the advantage of strengthening current expansions of methodologies in translation studies rather than introducing another set of terms and ideas. Following Kress and van Leeuwen (1996), then, I outline below a sample of questions relevant to the analysis of three different factors pertaining to the images that might be encountered in paratexts: representation and interaction (between viewer and image), modality (the relationship between the image and reality) and composition (interaction between depicted elements). Readers are encouraged to consult Kress and van Leeuwen (1996) for examples and a full elaboration of their methodology.

Representation and interaction

Factors of representation and interaction are largely concerned with ascertaining the degree to which the image is an offer or a demand. In the case of the former, the image '"offers" the represented participants to the viewer as items of information, objects of contemplation' (Kress and van Leeuwen 1996, 124), whereas in the case of the latter, the image 'demands something from the viewer, demands that the viewer enter into some kind of imaginary relation with him or her' (122).[8] The following questions might be asked:

- Is the viewer of the image positioned as an object of the gaze of the represented participant, or is the represented participant the object of the viewer's gaze?
- If the former, what is the participant's expression and what sort of relationship does the represented participant seek to establish with the viewer (e.g. one of superiority, disdain, seduction, etc.)?
- What is the size of frame (close-up, medium shot, long shot)? Is the imaginary relationship between viewer and participant one of friendship (associated with close-ups) or is it impersonal (long shots)? With which kind of messages is the size of frame conventionally associated? For example, in news reporting, the close-up is used for 'subjects who are revealing their feelings' (133), whereas the 'breast-pocket shot' (133) is commonly used for experts and interviewers. This point reminds us of the importance of analysing images with a full awareness of cultural and historical conventions, since it is in part these conventions that help determine what is meant by depicting an image in a certain way.
- In images depicting people, is the horizontal angle frontal (conveying involvement) or oblique (conveying detachment)? Is the vertical angle high (conveying superiority or power of the viewer over the represented participant), low (conveying the superiority of the represented participant over the viewer), or eye-level (conveying equality)?
- In the case of scientific or technical images, is the angle frontal ('the angle of "this is how it works"' (149)) or top-down ('the angle of maximum power . . . contemplating the world "from a god-like point of view"' (149))?"
- How is point of view narrativised through the sequencing of images (in films) or other means (e.g. by including the hands of the imaginary viewer in an advertisement)?

Modality

Modality is concerned with the relationship between the image and reality. Images that have a high modality are those which depict things, people or places as though they were real, whereas those with a low modality present them as 'imaginings, fantasies, caricatures, etc.' (161). The following questions might be asked:

- What are the levels of colour saturation, differentiation and modulation? The closer the use of colour to the way in which colour appears in the real world, the more the image will be taken to represent things as though they are real. For example, when colours have low saturation, we are likely to judge the image as 'ethereal' (163).
- What is the level of contextualisation? An absence of background lowers modality, with represented participants being depicted as generic rather than as individuals.
- What are the levels of abstraction, depth, illumination and brightness? Once again, the closer the levels to the way things appear in real life, the higher the degree of modality.

Composition

Composition explores the ways in which the depicted elements are related to each other and interact with each other. These questions can be asked of composite and multimodal texts as well as of single images, and thus apply 'not only to pictures, but also . . . to layouts' (184). The following aspects might be considered:

- How are the elements placed relative to each other and to the viewer? Specific informational values are connected with the various zones of the image. In general, the left-hand side of images is used for information that is already known, whereas elements presented on the right-hand side are presented as new information (187). The top of an image is usually connected with the ideal, or with elements that make an emotive appeal, whereas the bottom of an image is more typically used for the 'real', or for practical informa- tion (193). Layouts that use a centre and margin structure (more common in Eastern than in Western designs) present the nucleus of information in the centre and subservient elements in the margins (206).
- Which elements are salient? The degree to which the viewer's attention is drawn to any particular element depends on such things as foreground and background placement, whether an element overlaps or is overlapped by another, relative size, contrasts in tonal value, differences in sharpness, etc. (122–3).
- How are elements connected to each other or separated from each other through framing devices? These devices might include elements that create dividing lines (e.g. doorframes in the background of a photograph or picture), continuities or discontinuities of colour or shape, or empty spaces between elements (214–18). Another way of emphasising connectedness is through vectors, i.e. elements which 'lead the eye from one element to another' (216), such as roads, buildings or abstract graphic elements.

Process-oriented research

As noted above, most translation-related research into paratexts to date has focused on translation as products. The key exceptions to this are the studies by Anna

Matamala (2011), Nathalie Mälzer (2013) and Siri Nergaard (2013), discussed in Chapter 2, which enquire into the roles played by different agents in the production of paratexts for translated products, and which might thus be classed as 'participant-oriented' research in Saldanha and O'Brien's (2014) model. Studies of this kind are of great importance for deepening our understanding of the cultural and sociological factors affecting translation processes, and enable us to move away from the still-present tendency to talk about 'the translator' when analysing translation products. In this section, however, I would like to discuss the potential importance of paratextual theory to the third type of 'translator studies', outlined by Andrew Chesterman (2009), namely cognitive translation process research.

Using paratexts in cognitive studies of translation process

In the burgeoning research area of translation and cognition, attention has tended to focus on micro-level decision-making and behaviour, with experiments usually based around short texts and extracts rather than complete texts in their published format.[9] Although some theorists do incorporate consideration of paratextual features into their analytical models, they tend to subsume such features under broader headings. Lucas Nunes Vieira (2016, 91–2), for example, identifies a category called 'translation context/world knowledge' and explains that this involves 'aspects such as readership, genre-specific issues, source- and target-culture specific issues, real-world use of the text, knowledge of the subject matter, intertextuality, etc.'. It is likely that translators would derive some of this knowledge from paratextual elements, or at the very least look for confirmation of assumptions there: a book's cover, for example, is likely to convey something about readership and genre, as well as intended if not actual uses of the text in the real world. Other aspects of this knowledge (for example, of the subject matter) would be derived from non-paratextual sources. By treating both types of knowledge together, models such as this one do not encourage interrogation of cognitive processing of paratextual elements or of the interconnections between text- and paratext-reading processes.

To my knowledge, the only theorist who draws on the term *paratext* to denote a particular translation process or subprocess is Hans P. Krings (2001), but he uses the term in a different sense to the sense in which it is used by Genette, and indeed in this book. In his study – which limits itself to the post-editing of machine-translated instruction manuals (245) – paratexts are 'pictorial information of all kinds (photographs, charts, line drawings, etc.)' (246). In our conceptualisation of the paratext, in contrast, such elements would be considered to be part of the text. Closer to our category of the paratext would be those elements which Krings refers to as 'features of the text surface, such as titles and subtitles, optical emphasis of key concepts, explicit statements of the topic, summaries, and paragraphs in certain positions' (246), but overall Krings pays little attention to them.

Although paratextual elements have thus received only marginal consideration in research into translation processes, their potential to bring deeper understanding to this domain of enquiry is considerable. In particular, research into paratexts could open up greater insights into the impact of source text paratextual elements on overall translation approach and micro-level decision-making, as well as on translators' emotional stances towards the material they are translating. Such studies could also help us understand which paratextual elements are treated as part of the source text, and which are treated as external resources;[10] they could also offer insight into the cognitive processes that underlie the creation of new paratextual elements for the target text.

Since the term *paratext* encompasses an extremely wide range of textual and non-textual material and a plethora of functions (beyond the overarching and defining function of serving as a threshold), any research into the role played by paratexts in translation processes would need to narrow down its focus to specific paratextual elements, rather than interrogating the role played by paratexts in any general sense. Key questions that would need to be addressed would be as follows:

To which paratextual elements belonging to the original text do translators actually have access when translating?

While translators may sometimes work from source texts that are in the form of published works, or in other words which are complete with their paratexts, on many occasions they are likely to work with texts in a format separate from (some of) their paratexts. Literary translators, for example, may be sent manuscript versions of a source text that is yet to be published in its original language, while translators of other kinds of material are likely to receive it electronically in one of many different file formats. While the above question cannot be answered in general terms, some observations on practices typical to particular sections of the translation industry can undoubtedly be made and will be of great importance to any findings on how translators draw on paratexts when translating. Most interesting, perhaps, will be the implications of such findings for conceptualisations of the translation process that depend on conceiving of translators as readers of the source text. If it is shown that a common or even default scenario is for translators to translate without access to the source text paratexts, then their experiences as readers will be markedly different from those of other source text readers.

Which research methods are most suited to exploring the role of paratexts in translation processes?

As with the previous question, addressing this question will depend in large part on the particular kind of paratextual element being analysed. For researchers investigating the influence of such elements as book cover or title on a translator's overall approach or attitude to the translation, then 'postactional' (Krings 2005, 348) methods such as retrospective commentary or interviews are most likely to be of use, though it may also be possible to employ 'periactional' (Krings 2005, 348) approaches such as think-aloud protocols. For example, think-aloud experiments could be set up in which translators were asked to think aloud their very first reactions to the text as guided by the paratexts. Alternatively, existing think-aloud data could be scanned for any data that indicate thinking derived from considerations of paratextual material. For researchers examining paratextual elements which occupy a spatial position close to the text (such as the footnotes that accompany scholarly editions of some texts), it may be possible to employ technology-supported observation methods including eye-tracking and key-logging, or in other words to incorporate paratexts into what has become known as Translation Process Research (TPR).[11] Such methods might, for example, allow researchers to answer questions about how much time (if any) the translator spends looking at notes and how the translation solutions change after the notes have been consulted.

What are the specific methodological challenges associated with this kind of research?

In addition to the general challenges facing translation process researchers,[12] one of the aspects to which particular thought would have to be given in paratexts research is how to reduce or eliminate bias that is likely to result when subjects know that what is being investigated are the paratexts. If subjects are aware that researchers are interested in how they use paratexts, this automatically creates bias in the sense that it suggests to the subject that they should consider paratexts, when they might otherwise not have done so. For example, knowing that the experiment concerns the use of paratexts, they might read a source text preface in the experiment when their more standard practice would be not to. This problem can be avoided by setting up blind experiments, or in other words experiments in which the subject does not know what is being investigated. However, for some types of research this might result in completely impractical levels of time wastage: a blind study of the influence of the back-cover blurb of a book on the translation process, for example, would require subjects to do the translation experiment even if they did not consult the back-cover blurb at all, meaning that hours' worth of data might be collected only perhaps to reveal that the blurb was not used.

Interpreting studies

As we have seen, the notion of the paratext has been applied above all to written and audiovisual texts, rather than to spoken texts. Hong Jiang's (2013) article, noted in Chapter 2, represents a rare effort to explore the relevance of the notion of the paratext to interpreting, and the overall thrust of her argument is that paratextual devices 'are not really available to the interpreter' (211). Thus, whereas translators can use prefaces to indicate their disapproval of a text, Jiang (211) argues that interpreters do not have the possibility of signalling their disagreement with the speaker using a 'word of introduction' or similar; and whereas a translator can insert footnotes and other devices 'to help guide, to inform, or to define positions, the interpreter can hardly step out of the oral text he produces and put in an oral paratext as if an observer' (212). Nevertheless, Jiang shows that interpreters do employ a range of framing devices in order to make their ethical positions clear. In his overview of multimodality in interpreting and translation, Luis Pérez-González (2014b) similarly keeps devices used in dialogue interpreting separate from the notion of the paratext, examining the former under the rubric of 'semiotics of the human body' (122) and limiting paratexts to the domain of written texts.

Jiang's and Pérez-González's approaches may owe themselves in part to the narrow definition of paratext that they adopt, limiting it effectively to Genette's peritext in line with many other translation scholars. If we take the broader definition of paratext proposed in the previous chapter, however, then the potential for considering paratexts in conjunction with interpreting increases. If paratexts are the thresholds through which receivers come to a text, then in a very basic sense the interpreter him- or herself is the threshold through which listeners obtain access to the interpreted text. If we accept this premise, then we can start to explore the ways in which the thresholds provided by interpreters may be consciously crafted and how they might shape the listener's understanding of the text, be this a speech (in monologic interpreting) or a conversational turn (in dialogue interpreting). Where these two criteria are met, then our definition of paratext would allow for the threshold provided by the interpreter to be considered a paratext to the words that are being interpreted. Whether or not it is useful to consider things in this way is another question, and I hope that the brief sketch provided below will invite further discussion of the potential for linking paratexts and interpreting studies in this manner.

According to professional codes of conduct, which demand accuracy and impartiality,[13] interpreters are not supposed to shape the original message in any way at all. This human threshold, in other words, should *not* function as a paratext: it should have no influence over the way a text is received even if it is the means through which the text is accessed. In reality, as numerous research studies have shown,[14] interpreters do shape and influence the text in a wide range of ways, sometimes involuntarily (owing to the intrinsic difficulties of the task or the interpreting situation, or simply to their very presence), and sometimes deliberately (to smooth the cultural interaction or to convey their own ethical position). In the spirit of Genette's substantial variables, discussed in the previous chapter, we could provisionally identify three types of paratextual device open to exploitation by interpreters, bearing in mind that on many occasions they are used in a manner that makes them inseparable from each other.

Prosodic

One of the means by which interpreters may alter the threshold to the text that they are interpreting is by inflecting their tone. An angry or disdainful tone used by a speaker, for example, might be turned into a more neutral tone in an effort to ease the interaction between interlocutors. On the other hand, an interpreter might take his or her own distance from something a speaker says by using a tone that is exaggeratedly neutral (conveying, through the near-robotic voice, the message that 'I, on a personal level, have nothing whatsoever to do with this'). Whilst indicating disagreement using other kinds of prosodic variation such as sarcasm or a tone of open disbelief would run counter to interpreting codes of practice,[15] crafting a more neutral threshold through prosodic means appears to be widely acceptable. Although there is general agreement that 'full accuracy ought to properly include transmission of voice tone' (Edwards 1995, 81), it is generally conceded that interpreters would not be expected to reproduce more extreme prosodic variations such as yelling (Edwards 1995, 81), crying whilst speaking (Parker 2015, 198), or singing (Parker 2015, 198).[16] In court room settings at least, reproducing prosodic elements in full is seen as unnecessary because the original speaker's distress or mirth will be 'sufficiently evident visually' (Parker 2015, 198). The presence of the original speaker in dialogue-interpreting settings raises questions about the nature of the threshold provided by interpreters, and will be addressed below.

Linguistic

Interpreters have a variety of linguistic means at their disposal for crafting thresholds to interpreted texts. These include adding their own clarifications or interjections, interrupting or intervening in discussions, or using more subtle means such as switching from direct to indirect speech. These devices may be employed for a variety of purposes that include serving the client's best interests, facilitating conversational interaction and taking a personal distance from what is said. Once again, the ideal model of the neutral, invisible interpreter that is affirmed in professional codes of practice and training programmes would preclude the use of many of these devices, but they would appear to be widely present in interpreting practice, particularly in community interpreting and other kinds of dialogue interpreting (see, for example, Angelelli 2000; Mason and Stewart 2001). Even in monologic interpreting, however, they may not be entirely absent, as Ivana Čeňková's (1998) study of professional Czech conference interpreters suggests.[17] Furthermore, if booth colleagues are considered to be one of the audiences of interpreted text, then comments made by interpreters to their colleagues during or after conference interpreting might also be considered to be a form of linguistic paratext.[18]

Corporeal

The third type of paratext is corporeal, to return to a category proposed by Joachim Knape (2013) in the context of studies of rhetoric, briefly noted in Chapter 7. Knape's (2013, 265) outline of the threefold purpose served by the human body in spoken performance offers a useful indication of how the notion of a corporeal paratext might be transferred to situations involving interpreting:

> The [human] body simultaneously represents the instance of text production, the medium of the text, and at a higher level, occasionally constitutes a type [of] paratextuality created by body language . . . The declamatory element of a text designed to praise someone, for instance, can be counteracted by extra-communicative elements created by the body as a medium, such as the use of an ironic gesture.

While it is unlikely that an interpreter operating within professional codes of conduct would draw on any of the devices that Knape (2013, 265n52) provides as examples of corporeal paratext (pointing a thumb downwards, laughing), it is nevertheless possible to envisage situations in which interpreters demonstrate their stance towards interlocutors or their words by adopting particular body postures or facial expressions. Ian Mason and Wen Ren (2014, 130), for example, discuss a video of an asylum hearing in which the interpreter 'direct[s] her gaze away from the speaker and thus partly toward the interviewer, also frowns, narrows her eyes, and draws her lips sideways', arguing that 'in doing so, she clearly signals her negative evaluation of and distancing from what is being said'. An alternative type of corporeal paratext might involve neutralising the body language of the speaker in a manner similar to the toning down of prosodic variations discussed above: in a series of recommendations for practising interpreters, for example, Besson, Graf, Hartung, Kropfhäusser and Voisard (2005) suggest that, when faced with an angry speaker who is banging on the table, the interpreter should 'express the message with less violent body gestures, but with a severe tone of voice'.

In dialogue interpreting, in a more general sense, it is widely acknowledged by researchers that the interpreter is a third participant, 'and will inevitably bring to the interaction his or her own person' (Hale 2007, 12; see also Mason and Stewart 2001). This means that, even if the interpreter is striving to observe impartiality, factors connected with the interpreter's physical presence will influence the way in which the interpreted messages are received, the interlocutors' assumptions about the interpreter's own stance,[19] and even the way in which the conversation between the primary parties progresses. These factors might include such things as the interpreter's gender, his or her overall manner or mood, his or her positioning in the room, eyecontact, gaze direction, the dynamic that develops directly between the interpreter and one or both of the primary parties, and so on.[20] While some of these would be consciously crafted and thus eligible to be considered paratexts, others would fall into the broader category of context. It is possible that other people involved in the interpreting exchange may be the ones doing – or attempting to do – the crafting of corporeal paratexts: Cecilia Wadensjö (2001, 72, 83) reports, for example, on instances in which therapists take charge of the physical positioning of the interpreter or give instructions on the way in which interpreters are to hold their gaze and limit their physical movements.

Discussion

The brief outline of prosodic, linguistic and corporeal thresholds provided above indicates that there may be some potential in applying the notion of the paratext to interpreting studies research. While the outline has focused on the means available to interpreters for consciously crafting paratexts to the texts that they are interpreting, other angles of study might address the ways in which interpreters deal with the paratexts provided by speakers, or the ways in which speakers change their own paratexts in light of the fact that their words are being mediated through an interpreter. While further research would be needed to gain a clear picture of the potential benefits of linking paratexts and interpreting, we might reasonably expect such a move to result in researchers paying (more) attention to hitherto overlooked and apparently inconsequential phenomena, in parallel with what many scholars see as the principal achievement of paratext research in other disciplines. This might further interpreting research in the following ways.

First, since the conscious crafting of paratexts may be more relevant to situations in which interpreters are less likely to attempt to observe (or be aware of) professional codes of conduct, paratextual studies may encourage greater focus on interpreting practices in non-professional and ad hoc settings. While recent years have seen an increase in such research,[21] Pérez-González and Susam-Saraeva's (2012, 149–50) observation that translation and interpreting studies have 'so far focused overwhelmingly on professional instances of linguistic and cultural mediation' still holds true. It is worth reminding ourselves that the vast majority of interpreting activity in the world takes place on a non-formalised basis by people who would not label themselves 'interpreters' as such, and those who live in societies in which interpreting is a fact of everyday life can probably point to many instances in which the threshold set up by the ad hoc interpreter has been particularly stark.

Second, examining the different kinds of paratexts used in interpreting and their frequency of use in various settings is likely to highlight differences in the nature of interpreting as an activity across those settings. The broad label 'interpreting' encompasses a vast range of communicative events, from the relatively well-paid and well-regarded activity of monologic conference interpreting through dialogue interpreting in various institutional contexts and across a range of power differentials, to unremunerated interpreting by non-professional interpreters and ad hoc interpreting by family members or community peers. As Claudia Angelelli (2000, 590) suggests with regard to conference and community interpreting, 'a single standard of interpretation is insufficient since the great difference in the situations, considered as communicative events, require different performances by the interpreter'. As sites of interpreter agency, the paratextual elements that are connected with interpreting performances are likely to yield valuable insights into these differences and stand to offer a strong empirical basis for revisiting theories of interpreting.

Third, and in connection with the above, a focus on interpreting paratexts serves to further problematise the model of the interpreter as invisible, neutral machine, a model which has been shown to correspond poorly with the realities of the workplace, yet which still underlies interpreter training programmes and codes of practice.[22]

If the study of such threshold elements can thus be argued to hold potential benefits for interpreting research, it does not necessarily follow that the notion of the paratext represents the most appropriate framework for analysing them. As a counter to the three potential benefits outlined above, let me now present three possible objections to a marriage between paratextual theory and interpreting research.

First, whereas the concept of the paratext has intuitive appeal in disciplines that focus on texts, it is less intuitive to speak of paratexts when we are concerned with dialogue and conversational interaction. The definition of paratext put forward in the previous chapter is dependent on there being a text to which the paratext can be the threshold, and a text is taken to denote any written or spoken words forming a connected piece of work. While a speech would thus be considered to be a text, it is unlikely that a conversation, interrogation, consultation or other form of dialogic exchange would be.[23] In some contexts, the purpose of the exchange itself may not be informational at all: the exchange may be phatic in nature, or in other words designed to initiate or maintain social interaction, and the body language that is used on such occasions (smiling, shaking hands, adopting a welcoming posture, etc.) is as much a part of the message as the words themselves.

Second, even if we do stretch the definition of text in order to allow for the thresholds that are crafted for dialogic interactions to be considered under the rubric of the paratext, the notion of the threshold also reveals itself as problematic. In many interpreting contexts, the speaker whose words are being interpreted is present: listeners can usually hear the speaker's voice and can often see him or her as well. In face-to-face interpreting, the interlocutors can form direct impressions of each other (based on physical appearance, demeanour, etc.) and can communicate directly on some level (through non-verbal communication or through limited comprehension of the other's verbal language). A key feature of the paratext, in Genette's analysis, is that it gives access to the text, making it present in the world; there can be no text without paratext (Genette 1997, 3). In interpreting, however, while the interpreter is in some senses the threshold through which the listener receives the spoken text, as suggested above, in many cases the interpreter is not the only – and perhaps not even the primary – means through which the speaker's words and intentions are made present. Furthermore, the notion of the threshold may well be too blunt an instrument for trying to capture the variety of functions of the interpreter's various interventions, which include 'help[ing] parties understand concepts and terms, bridg[ing] linguistic and cultural gaps, communicat[ing] affect as well as language, facilitat[ing] mutual respect, control[ling] the flow of communication traffic, or even align[ing] with one of the parties resulting in gatekeeping or the channeling of opportunities' (Angelelli 2004, 50). While some of these activities fit reasonably well with the notion of paratexts as threshold, others represent a far less intuitive match.

Third, and in connection with the previous points, it may well be more helpful to analyse dialogic interpreting activities using theories and frameworks from disciplines that are primarily concerned with social interaction, rather than adapting a concept that has been developed in literary studies, as is the case for the paratext. Interpreting studies scholars have profitably engaged with ideas developed in sociology and linguistics, including ethnography of communication (e.g. Angelelli 2000; Berk-Seligson 2002), social systems theory and conversation analysis (Baraldi and Gavioli 2012) and theories of face and politeness (e.g. Mason and Stewart 2001; Hale 2007). Other theoretical frameworks that have been applied to interpreting include concepts of power developed by Foucault and Wenger (Mason and Ren 2014), the demand–control model developed in the field of occupational health (e.g. Dean and Pollard 2001) and theories developed in disciplines relevant to the specific interpreting setting, such as trauma theory (Wadnesjö 2001). While there is a general consensus that more can be done to benefit from theoretical frameworks developed in other disciplines,[24] it seems likely that the concept of the paratext will prove productive primarily for monologic forms of interpreting rather than dialogic ones.

Literary criticism: translation as paratext

In Chapter 2, we saw that the few translation studies scholars who have explicitly addressed Genette's notion of translation as paratext have found it to be of limited use. My own enquiry into the phenomenon of translation authorisation in Chapter 4 suggests that assuming any kind of privileged paratextual relevance for translations that are labelled 'authorised' is deeply problematic. Yet, before we dismiss the potential for this perspective to offer a fruitful avenue for research, it will be useful to consider the ways in which it overlaps with research perspectives that are based on the premise that translation is a mode of intense or critical reading. This is an idea that is evoked by Maïca Sanconie (2007) in her discussion of translation as paratext, mentioned in Chapter 2. Sanconie appeals to the premise in order to justify her own decision to write a translator's preface:

> J'ai en quelque sorte outrepassé ma fonction pour produire un commentaire essentiellement critique . . . Rédigée à la suite d'un 'acte de lecture le plus complet qui soit', cette évaluation critique . . . manifeste . . . toute l'ambiguïté du commentaire péritextuel, en rupture avec ce que Paul Bensimon . . . appelle la 'pratique silencieuse de traduire' mais, en même temps, dans la continuité de la pratique d'une lecture privilégiée du texte.
> [In a sense I stepped out of my role by producing a critical commentary . . . Written after the 'most comprehensive act of reading that exists', this critical evaluation . . . has all the ambiguity of peritextual commentary, contrary to what Paul Bensimon . . . calls the 'silent practice of translation' but, at the same time, in keeping with the practice of a privileged reading of the text.]
>
> *2007, 178*

In Sanconie's analysis, the deep level of insight into the source text that the translator gains through the translation process justifies the translator's decision to move out of the shadows and take up a commenting, critiquing role. The words that she cites as part of this justification – 'acte de lecture le plus complet qui soit' – are taken from a piece by Michel Morel (2006), 'Eloge de la traduction comme acte de lecture' [In praise of translation as an act of reading]. Morel (25) argues that translation is 'l'acte de lecture . . . le plus complet possible dans la mesure où pour réussir, . . . le traducteur est de nécessité contraint d'observer de la façon la plus ajustée et la plus fidèle possible le texte en jeu dans toutes les finesses de son fonctionnement [the most comprehensive act of reading possible, in the sense that in order to succeed, the translator is inevitably compelled to take account of all of the subtleties of the text in the most faithful and tailored way possible]. This process means that the translator is 'plus proche du critique qu'on ne l'imagine' [closer to the critic than is generally assumed] (25).

The possibility for translators' readings to serve to deepen understanding of source texts in a manner similar to those provided by critics is affirmed in a tribute to the literary translator Michael Hamburger published in *Modern Poetry in Translation*. With regard to two poetry anthologies published as dual-language editions, Charlie Louth (2004) argues that 'the translations [function] above all, and very modestly, as aids to understanding, as paths'. He subsequently explains that the translations fulfil this role in conjunction with the introductory essays, also provided by Hamburger:

> Each edition is an introduction: in the mode and manner of the translations, in that the original poems are printed alongside, and because an essay provides the reader with exactly what he or she needs to know for a full understanding of the context of the particular poet's work. Hamburger is a great writer of the introductory essay . . . His critical prose has the same virtues as his translations – it is in service of that of which it speaks, concerned to elucidate, illuminate, connect, explore, but without pushing a particular interpretation: it aerates, opens up, releases possibilities, without ever leaving the ground of its subject, founded as it is in the close knowledge translation gives.

Many of the points that Louth makes are similar to Morel's: Louth speaks of the 'close knowledge translation gives' and indirectly affirms Morel's suggestion that translators are like critics by showing that in Hamburger's case, both roles are combined in a single person. The critical value of a translator's reading of a source text, then, can be argued both deductively (by considering the translation reading process in the abstract) and inductively (by providing case studies of particular translators).

However, both Louth's and Morel's analyses show that assuming that this means that a translation can function as commentary, in the sense suggested by Genette, is problematic and contingent upon at least two things. First, while a commentary directly expounds the critic's reading of the source text, a translation is a composite of the translator's reading of the source text and of his or her judgement of 'ce qui, dans le milieu langagier d'arrivée, peut y répondre directement ou indirectement' [what corresponds to it directly or indirectly in the target language context], to cite once more from Morel (2006, 25). This means that reading a translation as commentary is contingent on an ability to find the translator's critical reading of the source text in the midst of the 'infinitely complex commerce the act of translation represents' (Louth 2004). The extent to which it is possible to distil the translator's commentary from the translation in this way is questionable: in the case of

Hamburger's poetry translations, Louth's praise of the introductory essays provided by Hamburger in conjunction with the translations suggests that such a reading is greatly helped – and perhaps only made possible – if the translator provides direct commentary as well. This returns us to Sanconie's (2007, 178) suggestion, outlined in Chapter 2, that the commentary function of a translation may need to be 'channelled' through a preface for it to receive its full value.

The other condition on which the function of translations as commentaries would appear to be dependent is the translator's approach to his or her task. In the case of Hamburger, Louth (2004) suggests that he 'seeks to remain invisible as a translator, discreet and selfeffacing, in the service of the poems he is transposing. His translations . . . put themselves at the service of the originals, and of the reader, tending to explain and clarify rather than adding their own difficulties'. Hamburger's approach, in other words, is hermeneutic, seeking to arrive at an informed understanding of the source text and to convey that understanding to the target text readers.[25] Yet not all translators approach their task in this way.

An alternative model for transforming the translator's intimate reading of the source text into a target language text is provided by Clive Scott (2012). Like Morel, Scott (2012) reaches for a superlative to describe the relationship of translation to reading, foregrounding through the back-cover blurb to his book the premise that 'the act of translation is perhaps the ultimate performance of reading'. However, rejecting a hermeneutical mode of reading,[26] he advocates instead a mode of reading that is 'phenomenological' (1), 'constructivist' (21) and 'radial' (21), resulting in translations that are 'intimately part of an autobiography of reading and associating' (22). Indeed, when we read Scott's translations, which play intensely not only with punctuation and space, but also with typography and doodling, what we are reading are Scott's own 'sensations and memories' (30) or, in other words, *his* experience of reading the original text. Scott's use of the term 'autobiography' in the citation above is apposite, for in Scott's translations we read about Scott's life – his history of reading, his intertextuality, his ways of thinking and being within and between languages, his 'individual reading metabolism' (30). The translations thus tell us, above all, about the translator; more generally, they also 'model a translational practice in which all readers of literature are exhorted to indulge' (10). Both of these goals are a long way from Genette's idea of translation as paratext, which would have us read the translation in order to understand more of the original author's intentions.

Another angle from which to explore the potential of translation to open up insights into source texts is provided by Marilyn Gaddis Rose (1997). Invoking through the title of her volume the idea that translation can be a type of literary analysis, Gaddis Rose argues that translation offers an 'enhancement of literary experience' (1). Drawing on a term coined by Joanne Englebert, she suggests that this enhancement is achieved through a 'stereoscopic' (54) mode of reading, or in other words 'a reading that moves back and forth among source texts and one or more target texts' (54). Through this back-and-forth between original and translation(s), the reader gains access to what Gaddis Rose calls the 'interliminal text' (7), the 'infinitely expanding and contracting circumference' (7) that is 'part of the work's potential' (7). The reader is thus able to 'examin[e] literature from the inside, . . . feel it from within' (13). Deeper understanding may be achieved through conflict, in cases where readers disagree with the translator's choices and are thus forced to articulate their own readings (7), or through complementarity, when readers find that the translations open up 'new spaces for thinking' (14). In this model, although reading translations influences perceptions of the original text, in line with Genette's view of translations as paratexts, both the goal of the process and the conceptualisation of the reader are fundamentally different. In Genette's framework, the reader is someone on whom the author seeks to exert an influence, and translations are read in order to understand the author's intentions more fully; in Gaddis Rose's model, in contrast, the reader is seen as working in 'collaboration with the author' (73) to explore meanings that are 'loosely enclose[d]' (73) by both texts and translations, rather than being contained within the original text alone.

In summary, then, the notion that translations can serve as paratexts in the sense of providing commentary on original works is open to problematisation and exploration from a number of angles. Nevertheless, the enquiries into the intersection between translation, reading and literary criticism discussed above indicate that placing translations alongside originals rather than in place of originals has considerable value for deepening our appreciation of the work in question. In academic environments in which few scholars outside languages departments are proficient in languages other than English, as is the case in the UK, emphasising the benefits of juxtaposing originals and translations – or, at the very least, multiple translations of the same text – is certainly not without importance.[27]

Notes

1 As noted in Chapter 2, however, researchers need to be wary of assuming that what translators say about these matters in paratexts actually holds true in the translations themselves.
2 As noted in Chapter 2, Susam-Sarajeva (2006, 15 *passim*) uses the term *extratextual material* rather than *paratext* to denote such elements.
3 Whether or not a research project describes itself as historical or contemporary depends on the research perspective and subject matter, rather than on the dates of paratext production. While the paratexts of literary fiction published in 2000, for example, might be considered as part of a present-day study of literary systems, fan-created paratexts published in the same year (i.e. prior to Web 2.0) would be more likely to form part of a historical study.
4 For an overview of analysing historical sources, see Tosh (2015, 98–121). Although Tosh's outline concerns historical research, many of the principles also apply to the analysis of contemporary documents.
5 We should note that art history and visual culture are separate disciplines with rather different foci of study and associated methodologies. For the sake of simplicity, I shall not discuss these differences here, but see Elkins (2003) for further detail.
6 For an example of how this might play out in practice, see Kratz (1994).
7 See, notably, Taylor (2003) and Pérez-González (2014a).
8 All page numbers in this section refer to Kress and van Leeuwen (1996).

9 For recent overviews of translation process research, see Brems, Meylaerts and van Doorslaer (2014) or Ferreira and Schwieter (2017).

10 In Krings's (2005, 345) outline of the groups of factors relevant to the translation process, this would come down to working out which paratextual elements might be classed as task-related factors (which includes such things as text type), and which might come under the heading of environment-related factors (which includes reference resources and technological aids).

11 For an overview of TPR, see Jakobsen (2014) or Alves (2015).

12 See Krings (2005) for a cogent discussion of these.

13 See, for example, Corsellis (2008, 43), though see also Taylor-Bouladon's (2001, 147–9) discussion of interpreter loyalty in diplomatic contexts.

14 See, for example, Angelelli (2004, 2–3): 'There exists a discrepancy between the role that is prescribed for interpreters (through codes and rules …) and that which unfolds in practice, where interpreters bring the self to the interaction.'

15 This would not preclude its use in real-life situations, as noted above.

16 See also the informal discussion of this issue on interpreting.info, which suggests: 'you certainly do not want to be laughing, let alone start yelling into the mic. But put a smile on your lips and your listeners will immediately connect and inherit the mirth. Make your voice sound deeper and the delivery faster, take the smile off your face and you will sound angry' (Buck 2012). Angelelli's (2004) study of the interpreter's role also indicates that significant numbers of interpreters see their role as being to establish trust and facilitate mutual respect, something which may involve 'ton[ing] down' (54) disrespectful comments.

17 Responses to the question of what is irritating about other interpreters included 'the habit of interspersing the interpreted speech with one's own comments and remarks' (Čeňková 1998, 167).

18 As part of her practical advice to trainee interpreters, Taylor-Bouladon (2001) warns them to use the cough button if they want to 'make a brief sarcastic comment about what the speaker has just said' (97), and to turn the microphone off once the speaker has finished, since 'delegates do not want to hear your comments … nor do they want to hear the comments of your highly-strung colleague who erupts into your booth to let off steam about the stupidity of the delegate she has just interpreted' (98). Although these comments are made with humour, they are also undoubtedly intended to reflect the realities of human responses to real-life working situations.

19 Jiang (2013, 212) argues, for example, that 'it is almost impossible … for interpreters who work for the Americans in Afghanistan to assert neutrality between the invasion power and their own people. Their physically being with the Americans is seen as taking the position of allying with them'. See also Palmer's (2007) study of interpreting in Iraq post-2003.

20 For studies that include analysis of such features, see Wadensjö (2001) and Davitti (2012).

21 See, for example, Antonini and Bucaria (2016), Evrin and Meyer (2016) and Antonini, Cirillo, Rossato and Torresi (2017).

22 See Angelelli (2004, 20–22) for further discussion, and Salaets and Balogh (2017) for an overview of recent scholarship on this topic.

23 This tallies with Wadensjö's (1998, 38–44) distinction between monological and dialogical views of language and associated conceptualisations of interpreting.

24 On issues of face, for example, Pöllabauer (2015, 212) states that these 'have received scant attention in interpreting studies to date', while body language is described as an 'under-researched area' (Merlini 2015, 154) in the *Routledge Encyclopedia of Interpreting*.

25 To the extent that such an approach assumes an invariant core of meaning rather than conceiving of the meaning of the source text as variable, it could alternatively be categorised as 'instrumental' (Venuti 2010, 5–6). I will not attempt to assess Hamburger's approach or to examine the boundary between these two designations here, since my aim is to oppose such meaning-focused approaches with Scott's very different phenomenological one.

26 There are occasional suggestions that the translations that result might bring deeper understanding of the original texts, along the lines of the benefits outlined by Louth (2004). For example, in the introduction, Scott (2012, 10) concedes that 'the translations which appear in this book do indeed claim to cast new light on their STs', and in his *éloge* of Malcolm Bowie, he talks of 'gifted readers like Bowie' (187), a reference which implies that the readings of some readers may be more worth reading than those of others.

27 For a cogent reflection on the use of translated texts in academia, see Wright (2016, 98–108).

References

Alves, Fabio. 2015. "Translation Process Research at the Interface. Paradigmatic, Theoretical, and Methodological Issues in Dialogue with Cognitive Science, Expertise Studies, and Psycholinguistics". In *Psycholinguistic and Cognitive Inquiries into Translation and Interpreting*, edited by Aline Ferreira and John W. Schwieter, 17–40. Amsterdam and Philadelphia: John Benjamins.

Alvstad, Cecilia. 2012. "The Strategic Moves of Paratexts: World Literature through Swedish Eyes". *Translation Studies* 5 (1): 78–94.

Angelelli, Claudia. 2000. "Interpretation as a Communicative Event: A Look through Hymes' Lenses". *Meta* 45 (4): 580–92.

——. 2004. *Revisiting the Interpreter's Role*. Amsterdam and Philadelphia: John Benjamins.

Antonini, Rachele, and Chiara Bucaria, eds. 2016. *Non-professional Interpreting and Translation in the Media*. Bern: Peter Lang.

Antonini, Rachele, Letizia Cirillo, Linda Rossato and Ira Torresi, eds. 2017. *Non-professional Interpreting and Translation: State of the Art and Future of an Emerging Field of Research*. Amsterdam and Philadelphia: John Benjamins.

Armstrong, Guyda. 2013. *The English Boccaccio: A History in Books*. Toronto: University of Toronto Press.

Baker, Mona. 2006. *Translation and Conflict: A Narrative Account*. London and New York: Routledge.

Baraldi, Claudio, and Laura Gavioli. 2012. *Coordinating Participation in Dialogue Interpreting*. Amsterdam: John Benjamins.

Berk-Seligson, Susan. 2002. *The Bilingual Courtroom: Court Interpreters in the Judicial Press*. Chicago: University of Chicago Press.

Besson, Chantal, Daria Graf, Insa Hartung, Barbara Kropfhäusser and Séverine Voisard. 2005. "The Importance of Non-verbal Communication in Professional Interpretation". *AIIC Webzine*. Accessed 23 November 2017 from https://aiic.net/page/1662/the-importance-of-non-verbal-communication-in-professio/lang/1.

Brems, Elke, Reine Meylaerts and Luc van Doorslaer. 2014. "Translation Studies Looking Back and Looking Forward: A Discipline's Meta-reflection". In *Known Unknowns of Translation Studies*, edited by Elke Brems, Reine Meylaerts and Luc van Doorslaer, 1–16. Amsterdam and Philadelphia: John Benjamins.

Brookey, Robert, and Jonathan Gray. 2017. "'Not Merely Para': Continuing Steps in Paratextual Research". *Critical Studies in Media Communication* 34 (2): 101–10.

Buck, Vincent. 2012. "It's a good question, and it's likely to attract personal, subjective answers". 23 March. Accessed 23 November 2017 from http://interpreting.info/questions/760/using-a-tone-of-voice.

Čeňková, Ivana. 1998. "Quality of Interpreting – A Binding or a Liberating Factor". In *Translators' Strategies and Creativity: Selected Papers from the 9th International Conference on Translation and Interpreting, Prague, September 1995*, edited by Ann Beylard-Ozeroff, Jana Králová and Barbara Moser-Mercer, 163–70. Amsterdam and Philadelphia: John Benjamins.

Chesterman, Andrew. 2009. "The Name and Nature of Translator Studies". *Hermes – Journal of Language and Communication Studies* 42: 13–22.

Corsellis, Ann. 2008. *Public Service Interpreting: The First Steps*. Basingstoke: Palgrave Macmillan.

Davitti, Elena. 2012. "Dialogue Interpreting as Intercultural Mediation. Integrating Talk and Gaze in the Analysis of Mediated Parent–Teacher Meetings". PhD Thesis, Manchester University. Accessed 23 November 2017 from www.escholar.manchester.ac.uk/uk-ac-man-scw:162289.

Dean, Robyn K., and Robert Q. Pollard Jr. 2001. "Application of Demand–Control Theory to Sign Language Interpreting: Implications for Stress and Interpreter Training". *Journal of Deaf Studies and Deaf Education* 6 (1): 1–14.

Edwards, Alicia B. 1995. *The Practice of Court Interpreting*. Amsterdam: John Benjamins.

Elkins, James. 2003. *Visual Studies. A Skeptical Introduction*. London and New York: Routledge.

Evrin, Feyza, and Bernd Meyer, eds. 2016. *Non-professional Interpreting and Translation: Translational Cultures in Focus*. Special Issue of *European Journal of Applied Linguistics* 4 (1). Berlin: De Gruyter.

Farahzad, Farzaneh. 2017. "Voice and Visibility. Fanon in the Persian Context". In *Translating Frantz Fanon across Continents and Languages*, edited by Kathryn Batchelor and Sue-Ann Harding, 129–50. London and New York: Routledge.

Ferreira, Aline, and John W. Schwieter. 2017. "Translation and Cognition: An Overview". In *The Handbook of Translation and Cognition*, edited by Aline Ferreira and John W. Schwieter, 3–18. Hoboken, NJ: Wiley Blackwell.

Gaddis Rose, Marilyn. 1997. *Translation and Literary Criticism: Translation as Analysis*. Manchester: St Jerome Publishing.

Genette, Gérard. 1997. *Paratexts: Thresholds of Interpretation*. Translated by Jane E. Lewin. Cambridge: Cambridge University Press.

Gray, Jonathan. 2010. *Show Sold Separately: Promos, Spoilers, and other Media Paratexts*. New York and London: New York University Press.

Hale, Sandra Beatriz. 2007. *Community Interpreting*. Basingstoke: Palgrave Macmillan.

Harding, Sue-Ann. 2017. "Fanon in Arabic: Tracks and Traces". In *Translating Frantz Fanon across Continents and Languages*, edited by Kathryn Batchelor and Sue-Ann Harding, 98–128. London and New York: Routledge.

Jakobsen, Arnt Lykke. 2014. "The Development and Current State of Translation Process Research". In *Known Unknowns of Translation Studies*, edited by Elke Brems, Reine Meylaerts and Luc van Doorslaer, 65–88. Amsterdam: John Benjamins.

Jiang, Hong. 2013. "The Ethical Positioning of the Interpreter". *Babel* 59 (2): 209–23.

Knape, Joachim. 2013. *Modern Rhetoric in Culture, Arts, and Media*. Berlin and Boston: De Gruyter.

Kovala, Urpo. 1996. "Translations, Paratextual Mediation, and Ideological Closure". *Target* 8 (1): 119–47.

Kratz, Corinne A. 1994. "On Telling/Selling a Book by its Cover". *Cultural Anthropology* 9 (2): 179–200.

Kress, Gunther, and Theo van Leeuwen. 1996. *Reading Images: The Grammar of Visual Design*. London and New York: Routledge.

Krings, Hans P. 2001. *Repairing Texts: Empirical Investigations of Machine Translation Post-Editing Processes*, edited by Geoffrey S. Koby. Translated by Geoffrey S. Koby, Gregory M. Shreve, Katja Mischerikow and Sarah Litzer. Kent, OH: Kent State University Press.

——. 2005. "Wege ins Labyrinth – Fragestellungen und Methoden des Übersetzungsprozess forschung im Überblick". *Meta* 50 (2): 342–58.

Lopes, Alexandra. 2012. "Under the Sign of Janus: Reflections on Authorship as Liminality in Translated Literature". *Revista Anglo Saxonica* 3: 129–55.

Louth, Charlie. 2004. "The Traveller – A Tribute to Michael Hamburger". *Modern Poetry in Translation* 3 (1). Accessed 10 November 2017 from www.poetrymagazines.org.uk/magazine/record.asp?id=16756.

Mälzer, Nathalie. 2013. "Head or Legs? Shifts in Texts and Paratexts brought about by Agents of the Publishing Industry". In *Authorial and Editorial Voices in Translation 2. Editorial and Publishing Practices*, edited by Hanne Jansen and Anna Wegener, 153–76. Quebec: Editions québécoises de l'oeuvre.

Mason, Ian, and Miranda Stewart. 2001. "Interactional Pragmatics, Face and the Dialogue Interpreter". In *Triadic Exchanges. Studies in Dialogue Interpreting*, edited by Ian Mason, 51–70. Manchester: St Jerome Publishing.

Mason, Ian, and Wen Ren. 2014. "Power in Face-to-Face Interpreting Events". In *The Sociological Turn in Translation and Interpreting Studies*, edited by Claudia V. Angelelli, 115–33. Amsterdam: John Benjamins.

Matamala, Anna. 2011. "Dealing with Paratextual Elements in Dubbing: A Pioneering Perspective from Catalonia". *Meta* 56 (4): 915–27.

Merlini, Raffaela. 2015. "Dialogue Interpreting". In *Routledge Encyclopedia of Interpreting*, edited by Franz Pöchhacker, 149–55. London and New York: Routledge.

Morel, Michel. 2006. "Eloge de la traduction comme acte de lecture". *Palimpsestes* Special Issue: 25–36.

Nergaard, Siri. 2013. "The (In)visible Publisher in Translations: The Publisher's Multiple Translational Voices". In *Authorial and Editorial Voices in Translation 2 – Editorial and Publishing Practices*, edited by Hanne Jansen and Anna Wegener, 177–208. Quebec: Editions québécoises de l'oeuvre.

Nottingham-Martin, Amy. 2014. "Thresholds of Transmedia Storytelling: Applying Gérard Genette's Paratextual Theory to *The 39 Clues* Series for Young Readers". In *Examining Paratextual Theory and its Applications in Digital Culture*, edited by Nadine Desrochers and Daniel Apollon, 287–307. IGI Global.

Nunes Vieira, Lucas. 2016. "Cognitive Effort in Post-editing of Machine Translation: Evidence from Eye Movements, Subjective Ratings, and Think-aloud Protocols". PhD Thesis, Newcastle University. Available from http://hdl.handle.net/10443/3130.

Palmer, Jerry. 2007. "Interpreting and Translation for Western Media in Iraq". In *Translating and Interpreting Conflict*, edited by Myriam Salama-Carr. Amsterdam and New York: Rodopi.

Parker, James E.K. 2015. *Acoustic Jurisprudence: Listening to the Trial of Simon Bikindi*. Oxford: Oxford University Press.

Pérez-González, Luis. 2014a. *Audiovisual Translation: Theories, Methods and Issues*. Abingdon and New York: Routledge.

——. 2014b. "Multimodality in Translation and Interpreting Studies: Theoretical and Methodological Perspectives". In *A Companion to Translation Studies*, edited by Sandra Bermann and Catherine Porter, 119–31. Chichester, UK: John Wiley & Sons.

Pérez-González, Luis, and Şebnem Susam-Saraeva. 2012. "Non-professional Translating and Interpreting". *The Translator* 18 (2): 149–65.

Pöllabauer, Sonja. 2015. "Face". In *Routledge Encyclopedia of Interpreting Studies*, edited by Franz Pöchhacker, 212–13. London and New York: Routledge.

Pym, Anthony. 2014. *Method in Translation History*. Abingdon and New York: Routledge.

Salaets, Heidi, and Katalin Balogh. 2017. "Participants' and Interpreters' Perception of the Interpreter's Role in Interpreter-Mediated Investigative Interviews of Minors: Belgium and Italy as a Case". In *Ideology, Ethics and Policy Development in Public Service Interpreting and Translation*, edited by Carmen Valero-Garcés and Rebecca Tipton. Bristol: Multilingual Matters.

Saldanha, Gabriela, and Sharon O'Brien. 2014. *Research Methodologies in Translation Studies.* Abingdon and New York: Routledge.

Sanconie, Maïca. 2007. "Préface, postface, ou deux états du commentaire par des traducteurs". *Palimpsestes* 20: 177–200.

Scott, Clive. 2012. *Literary Translation and the Rediscovery of Reading.* Cambridge: Cambridge University Press.

Susam-Sarajeva, Şebnem. 2006. *Theories on the Move: Translation's Role in the Travels of Literary Theories.* Amsterdam and New York: Rodopi.

———. 2009. "The Case Study Research Method in Translation Studies". *The Interpreter and Translator Trainer* 3 (1): 37–56.

Taylor, Christopher. 2003. "Multimodal Transcription in the Analysis, Translation and Subtitling of Italian Films". *The Translator* 9 (2): 191–205.

Taylor-Bouladon, Valerie. 2001. *Conference Interpreting – Principles and Practice.* Adelaide: Crawford House.

Thomson-Wohlgemuth, Gaby. 2009. *Translation under State Control: Books for Young People in the German Democratic Republic.* New York and London: Routledge.

Tosh, John. 2015. *The Pursuit of History: Aims, Methods and New Directions in the Study of History*, 6th edition. London and New York: Routledge.

Venuti, Lawrence. 2010. "Genealogies of Translation Theory: Jerome". *boundary* 2 37 (3): 5–28. doi:10.1215/01903659-2010-014

Wadensjö, Cecilia. 1998. *Interpreting as Interaction.* London and New York: Longman.

———. 2001. "Interpreting in Crisis: The Interpreter's Position in Therapeutic Encounters". In *Triadic Exchanges: Studies in Dialogue Interpreting*, edited by Ian Mason, 71–85. Manchester: St Jerome Publishing.

Watts, Richard. 2005. *Packaging Post/Coloniality. The Manufacture of Literary Identity in the Francophone World.* Lanham, Boulder, New York, Toronto and Oxford: Lexington Books.

Williams, Jenny, and Andrew Chesterman. 2014. *The Map: A Beginner's Guide to Doing Research in Translation Studies.* Abingdon and New York: Routledge.

Wright, Chantal. 2016. *Literary Translation.* London and New York: Routledge.

CONCLUSION

My final prayer:

O my body, make of me always a man who questions!

Frantz Fanon, Black Skin White Masks *(1986, 181)*

In the Introduction, I cited Genette's comparison of paratextuality to a treasure trove of questions. Like Genette's *Seuils*, this book has used the concept of the paratext to ask questions about small and peripheral elements that might not always seem worthy of study, yet which have the power to yield considerable insights. In so doing, the book has tried to answer another question, formulating a response to how Genette's theory of paratextuality can be adapted to translation studies. I have stressed that the answers provided to that question are open-ended, designed to provide a basis for a useful framework, whilst simultaneously showing themselves malleable to the times and places of study and the material at hand.

The study is open-ended in another sense too, its unfinished nature encapsulated by the further chapters that I would have liked to have included in this volume but for which I ran out of time and space. These include, most notably, more extended studies of the notion of translation-as-paratext, and of the applications of paratexts to interpreting, as well as a chapter exploring the benefits of using the concept of the paratext to study online news websites. I hope to pick up some of these discussions in subsequent publications, but for now they remain in the treasure trove, or at best only partly dug up.

One of the questions that has arisen in the course of this book is whether there is a need for a new metaphor to encapsulate the paratext and its concerns. So far I have answered this question only indirectly, by incorporating Genette's original metaphor of the threshold into my own revised definition of the paratext, rather than the metaphors of universe or ecosystem proposed by scholars in digital and media studies. While these new metaphors no doubt carry advantages, the fact that they are drawn from the domain of the natural, rather than the man-made, world makes them to my mind less intuitive. Paratexts, like the texts to which they give access, are created by people, and to examine them is to examine the activities of people: how people try and persuade, educate, share opinions for reasons of self-interest or benevolence, sell products, demonstrate allegiance, and so on. The metaphors of the universe and ecosystem also conjure a less clear picture of where humans are situated in relation to these man-made paratexts: whereas the threshold metaphor encourages us to imagine what humans do with the man-made entry point ('a threshold exists to be crossed', in Genette's (1997, 410) words), it is harder to imagine how humans navigate these paratextual constellations. Humans cannot, after all, travel around a universe but are constrained within a small planet belonging to a specific solar system, and their position within the ecosystem is similarly fixed. If the universe metaphor is helpful, it is perhaps primarily in the sense of the artificial universes of videogames like *No Man's Sky*, where gamers can travel at will throughout virtual space.

The threshold metaphor, then, seems to work better than these, even if it is not perfect for all the reasons that have been discussed previously. The ideas that it evokes – of travelling, entering, crossing from outside to inside – are also familiar to scholars in translation studies, where metaphors of travel and border-crossing have stood the test of time. But could this familiarity also be a disadvantage, as suggested by Emily Apter (2013, 100)? There are, as we know, many places where humans do not construct thresholds, but barriers: fences, barbed wire, walls; taller walls, bigger fences, razor wire; heat sensors, cameras, patrols; procedures, laws, fees; detention, forced repatriation; blank looks, the avoided gaze. Unlike paratexts to translated texts, which, even while shaping and constraining our encounter with the foreign, ultimately enable communication and interaction, the elaborate systems and borders designed to control crossing points and access for people are often constructed in such a way as to repel and prevent entry. More than this: inequality is often built into their design, such that they distinguish between those whom they repel or accept on the basis of nationality and wealth.

This brings me to the epigraph to this conclusion, themselves the closing words to Frantz Fanon's reflections on his lived experience of racism, and a different kind of questioning to that encouraged by Genette. While Genette's treasure trove opens up questions about acts of communication in the form of texts, Fanon's questioning revolves around non-communication, a mode of non-interaction that derives from fear of the other and the inability to see the human in the other. Before this closing prayer, Fanon (1986, 180–81) famously writes: 'The Negro is not. Nor is the white man . . . Superiority? Inferiority? Why not the quite simple attempt to touch the other, to feel the other, to explain the other to myself?' Fanon's questions are a call to us to supplement Genette's (1997, 410) caution, 'watch out for the paratext!' with another kind of warning: watch out for the places where there is no paratext, because there is no translation, no entering, no crossing of thresholds – or, at least, only for some.

References

Apter, Emily. 2013. *Against World Literature: On the Politics of Untranslatability*. London and New York: Verso.

Fanon, Frantz. 1986. *Black Skin White Masks*. Translated by Charles Lam Markmann. London: Pluto Press.

Genette, Gérard. 1997. *Paratexts: Thresholds of Interpretation*. Translated by Jane E. Lewin. Cambridge: Cambridge University Press.

INDEX

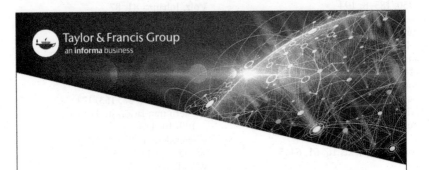